Generation

To Emma

Towards a free Palestine

Rich Wiles

Generation Palestine

Voices from the Boycott, Divestment and Sanctions Movement

Edited by Rich Wiles

PlutoPress
www.plutobooks.com

First published 2013 by Pluto Press
345 Archway Road, London N6 5AA

www.plutobooks.com

Distributed in the United States of America exclusively by
Palgrave Macmillan, a division of St. Martin's Press LLC,
175 Fifth Avenue, New York, NY 10010

British Library Cataloguing in Publication Data
A catalogue record for this book is available from the British Library

ISBN   978 0 7453 3244 4   Hardback
ISBN   978 0 7453 3243 7   Paperback
ISBN   978 1 8496 4779 3   PDF eBook
ISBN   978 1 8496 4781 6   Kindle eBook
ISBN   978 1 8496 4780 9   EPUB eBook

Library of Congress Cataloging in Publication Data applied for

10   9   8   7   6   5   4   3   2   1

Designed and produced for Pluto Press by Chase Publishing Services Ltd
Typeset from disk by Stanford DTP Services, Northampton, England
Simultaneously printed digitally by CPI Antony Rowe, Chippenham, UK and
Edwards Bros in the United States of America

For our children ...

Contents

Acknowledgements

This book is not only *about* the Palestinian BDS campaign, but its creation, as much as its format, is modelled on the movement. This is a book built on collaboration across borders, and collective work and vision. Many people have played their role in the creation of this book, and the available space here is not enough to pay due thanks to all. For this reason, I will attempt to concentrate on those without whom this book would not have become a reality.

At Pluto Press, my sincere thanks must go to Roger van Zwanenberg, who believed in this project wholeheartedly from the first moment we discussed it together. Also, the commissioning editor, David Shulman, has been of great assistance with his regular contact and advice as has the managing editor, Robert Webb. Jeanne Brady did an excellent job working through the copy-editing process. Many others within the Pluto team have also chipped in with valuable assistance which has been of great support throughout the production and editing process.

It goes without saying that all contributors in this volume have played significant roles and I would like to send my thanks to all for their contributions but, more importantly, my solidarity for their collective work for freedom and justice. Moreover, some contributors, such as Mick Napier and Omar Barghouti, have assisted in suggesting, and initiating contact with, other possible writers.

Some of the people featured within these pages I have known for several years, with others I sought help in establishing contact with them. In this regard, sincere thanks must first go to my friend Frank Barat, whose wealth of information, ideas and contacts were simply invaluable. Similarly, Will Parry put in endless hours of work for which I am hugely grateful. I would like to thank Ann Catrall at Sixteen Films for her assistance with Ken Loach, Rebecca O'Brien and Paul Laverty. Many others also helped out in similar veins, and special thanks should go to Ben White, the Scottish Palestine Solidarity Campaign (SPSC), and the US Campaign to End the Occupation.

In Palestine, integral support for this project has come from various individuals and collectives within the grass roots, civil society and academia. It is in this area that I feel particularly restricted by the available space within this short text, but thanks go to you all. The strength and guidance of friends and family in Aida must also be mentioned, amongst whom special thanks must go to Abu Miras who as so often was the first person that I discussed this project with, and who after his initial encouragement shared many ideas and hours of discussion.

On a personal note, to my mum, who stays with me every day, I send eternal love; to my dad Ken – your support and love is special always – and also to my brother Andy. To all in ''ull', I send my respect – we don't see enough of each other these days but no one is forgotten. To my new family in Ramallah and Beit Jala, I send my love and thanks for accepting me into the fold so generously.

I end these acknowledgements with thoughts to Cyrine, who has put up with my endless hours behind a computer screen and my frustrations, and without whose strength and support this book, and so much more in my life, could not have happened. You always stand beside me with such love, light and laughter, making all that we share special. 'Thank you' doesn't even come close.

Abridged versions of the chapters by Ronnie Kasrils and Ilan Pappe appeared in *The Case for Sanctions Against Israel* (New York and London: Verso, 2012).

Foreword
BDS

Archbishop Desmond Tutu

There was a time when the apartheid rulers strutted the political stage as monarchs of all they surveyed. Many western countries accepted the Cold War propaganda that apartheid South Africa was the last bastion of western civilisation against Soviet communist expansionism in Africa. Thus, there was hardly any condemnation of its vicious racist policies, in fact quite the contrary was true. After being awarded the Nobel Peace Prize in 1984, I was at last able to meet President Ronald Reagan and his Cabinet in the White House. I tried on that occasion to plead for sanctions. I failed dismally to persuade him. Instead, he extolled the virtues of his so-called 'constructive engagement' policy – dangling a carrot to urge South Africa to change gradually. That policy had disastrous consequences for us black South Africans. I later met the British Prime Minister, Mrs Margaret Thatcher (as she was then in 10 Downing Street) in 1987 to argue for the imposition of sanctions against the apartheid government. We had a friendly discussion but she was firmly opposed to such sanctions. In fact, she was later famously to describe Nelson Mandela as a terrorist. (In the US, it was not until 2008, 18 years after his release from prison, that Mandela was finally removed from the US Terrorism Watch List.)

Most western governments shared much the same views. Mercifully for us, civil society in most of these countries supported the efforts of the Anti-Apartheid Movement which eventually saw the US Congress pass its anti-apartheid legislation with a Presidential veto override. The people believed us when we condemned apartheid as evil, vicious and unjust in the extreme and they supported our efforts to end it non-violently. Had it all been left to the democratic governments of the West, we might still be languishing under the heavy burden of an oppressive regime. Whenever we advocated sanctions, the apartheid government and its sympathisers dubbed us communists and that was supposed to be the end of the debate. They never bothered to answer our strictures rationally. Actually it was a criminal offence to advocate sanctions – I myself was accused of economic sabotage, although I was never tried in a court of law.

I have described our experience at some length because it bears such remarkable parallels with the struggle of the Palestinian people for their freedom from the oppression and injustice imposed on them by successive Israeli governments. As soon as anyone has the temerity to criticise these Israeli policies *vis-à-vis* the Palestinians, then almost like a Pavlovian conditioned response, the critic is labelled anti-Semitic which is meant to discredit them in the same manner as the communist label was used against us in the anti-apartheid struggle. And almost all western governments, especially the US, are acquiescent in this process. Even on the rare occasions when they do finally condemn some Israeli outrage, they do nothing in practical political terms to show that they mean what they say. The Israeli government, just like the apartheid South African government before them, know they can get away with virtually anything.

It is breathtaking how the Israeli government can thumb their noses at the international community with impunity. This is another aspect that mirrors what happened with apartheid South Africa. The International Court of Justice gave an advisory opinion declaring South Africa's continued control of South West Africa illegitimate. Decades later, this same court gave another advisory opinion declaring Israel's so-called Apartheid Wall illegal. So what? Everyone knows that it contravenes international law for Israel to build settlements in the Occupied Territory. Yes – and so? The South African Apartheid regime continued its illegal administration of SWA without incurring any penalties. Israel has gone ahead constructing the Wall and building more settlements and ... nothing, no penalties, nothing.

It was so with us, until it became clear that despite all appearances to the contrary, this is in fact a moral universe. Right and wrong matter. God is a God who is notoriously biased in favour of the downtrodden, the despised, the weak. This is after all the God of the Exodus, who sided with a rabble of slaves against their oppressive overlord. Ultimately right will prevail, justice will triumph.

But humanity must play its role in this struggle. Much as with our case in South Africa, if Palestinians were to sit and wait for the democratic leaders of the western world to right their wrongs they may have to wait forever. It is in this context that Palestinians called for, and launched their Boycott, Divestment and Sanctions (BDS) campaign. When good people around the world supported our struggle by joining the Anti-Apartheid Movement there came eventually a tipping-point, through which the movement was able to apply enough pressure on governments to support change. The internal struggle and its international support network were truly complementary. It is now well past the time for us to do the same again. It happened in South Africa. It will happen any and everywhere. The BDS movement is as essential component of Palestine's struggle, and humanity's struggle for justice and true human liberation – it must be supported by us all.

Part I

BDS: The Historical Context

1
Palestine's Global Battle that Must be Won

Ramzy Baroud

INTRODUCTION: BEIT SAHOUR SHOWS THE WAY

On 19 September 1989, a serene Palestinian town on the outskirts of Bethlehem became grounds for what seemed like a one-sided battle. Hundreds of armoured Israeli military vehicles, and thousands of soldiers stormed the small town of Beit Sahour. Several military helicopters observed the fear-provoking scene from above, helping the numerous military men below coordinate their movement. On the other side, in this once restful, largely Christian-Palestinian town, residents remained home. No fighters in military fatigues awaited the arrival of the tanks at street corners. No guns. Not a semblance of armed resistance. But in Beit Sahour, true popular resistance was afoot. Indeed, Beit Sahour in 1989 was a focal point of collective action and boycott. It was a war without guns, like most of the activities carried out by rebelling Palestinians during the First Palestinian Intifada, the uprising that began in 1987. But Beit Sahour took the strategy of civil disobedience – refusing to pay taxes, boycotting the Israeli occupation and all of its institutions – to a whole new level, reminiscent of the legendary Palestinian strike of 1936. The Israeli mission in Beit Sahour on that day was aimed at forcing Palestinians to pay taxes, as hundreds of tax collectors were part of the military raid. Not only was there taxation with no representation, but the money exacted from occupied Palestinians financed the very military apparatus that tightened the noose around the neck of a beleaguered and oppressed population.

The Israeli government's response to this seemingly intolerable act was 'the biggest taxation raid in recent history'.[1]

The story of Beit Sahour, of course, didn't start on 19 September, but was a culmination of two overlapping histories, one concerning the First Intifada, and the other falls within a wider context of a well-rooted history of popular resistance that spans several generations. Yitzhak Rabin, Israel's defence minister at the time, wanted to teach the Beit Sahourians a lesson, thus the exaggerated military crackdown and awesome show of force. Obviously, the message was meant to reverberate beyond Beit Sahour to reach every town, refugee camp and village throughout the Occupied Territory, which were all engaged in various forms of boycott and civil disobedience. Indeed, the events that took place in Beit Sahour were a microcosm of a much larger political milieu. Both parties – the Israeli military and the Palestinians – behaved in ways that also corresponded to the same historical imperatives:

> The military and tax officers started exploring the possibilities for raiding Beit Sahour. The first waves started during June. They arrested groups of old people, six, seven or ten at a time, keeping them at detention centers, trying to figure out what the reaction of Beit Sahour would be, and also trying to make a penetration through these groups. On the other side, a perfect system of support was created in Beit Sahour, by which masses were visiting and comforting and showing solidarity to families of all those who were detained. At the same time, all those who were released were also visited and supported. Popular and neighborhood committees were in charge of all the arrangements. It was twenty-four-hour continuous work under severe conditions imposed by the military, for anyone who was identified as being active was risking administrative detention or even imprisonment of up to ten years (as Yitzhak Rabin declared).[2]

When all else failed, the military was summoned, occupation forces moved in en masse, and tax collectors worked their magic, confiscating all that they could seize. Many families were left with nothing, literally. Most of the confiscated furniture and other personal belongings were sold at auctions inside Israel. The small town fell under a 45 day military curfew, starting on the night of 21 September. Hundreds of Beit Sahour's residents were taken to military camps and many remained in prison under various pretexts.[3] The Israeli military may have thought it had won a decisive battle, but on that day a star near Bethlehem shone in the night sky of Palestine, connecting past and present, inspiring hope that people, despite the many years of military occupation, still had much power, enough for the steadfast residents of a small town to vex the leaders of Israel's political and military establishments.

The events in Beit Sahour, and the non-violent civil-disobedience campaign that defined the Intifada as a whole was not a historical anomaly, but consistent with a reality that seemed to be the most common thread in Palestinian revolts – first against British colonialism and ever-growing Zionist immigration prior to the establishment of Israel in 1948, and the successive popular revolts that followed. Within both the First Intifada (1987), and the First Revolution (1936), strategies of boycott in various guises figured prominently amongst myriad forms of resistance. Today's Palestinian-led movement for Boycott, Divestment and Sanctions (BDS) against Israel is often said to be modelled on the Anti-Apartheid Movement boycott campaigns, and in the international context that is certainly a valid reference, but the use of the boycott strategy also has indigenous roots within Palestine's history of resistance against oppression.

THE FIRST REVOLUTION

Jewish immigration to Palestine began gathering pace in the late nineteenth century, and what was initially perceived to be innocent immigration – whether prompted by religious callings or induced by the continued persecution of Jewish communities in Eastern Europe or the pogroms of Russia – had morphed into a multifaceted colonial scheme, with intense diplomacy and fervent military build-up. Much had changed since the first wave of Zionist immigrants arrived in 1882, to populate, among other communities, the first Zionist colony established five years earlier. Palestinians, based mostly in urban centres, were beginning to warn that the Jewish immigrants of the late nineteenth and early twentieth centuries were not the typical seekers of religious salvation and escapees of oppression. They were part of a Zionist programme to conquer Palestine, all of it, and displace its people.

In 1896, Theodor Herzl, a Hungarian Jew, inspired a wider following for the Zionist colonial programme with his book *Der Judenstaat* (plausibly translated to 'The Jewish State'). The book didn't merely sketch ideas concerning the founding of a Zionist homeland, but it also represented a blueprint for implementing them. A year later, the First Zionist Congress was convened at the behest of Herzl, in Basel, Switzerland, forming the World Zionist Organization (WZO). The WZO took on the task of incessant diplomacy and quickly branched off to establish other units, funds and institutions, one of which was the Jewish National Fund. Established in 1901, the London-based fund was entrusted with acquiring Palestinian lands for Jewish-only use, to be tended by Jewish-only labour. Between 1880 and 1914, thirty Zionist colonies were established in Palestine, and the Jewish population there numbered about eighty thousand, mostly European nationals.[4] This decidedly colonial project was framed within a greater imperialist project involving world powers. The secret treaty of May 1916, known as the Sykes-Picot Agreement, between Britain, France and Russia determined the fate of Palestine as a largely internationalised territory.[5] Worse, the secret formal letter of November 1917 that laid out British foreign policy by Foreign Secretary Arthur James Balfour, to a leading British Zionist, Baron Lionel Walter Rothschild promised Palestine as a national home for the Jews.[6] What was to be the future of the Palestinians, who were increasingly referred to as the 'non-Jewish' residents of Palestine?

The shared anxiety caused by Balfour's letter – known as the Balfour Declaration – and a growing awareness of the colonial project that was underway began inspiring the collective resistance of Palestinians, whose non-violent civil disobedience campaign at the time was most progressive in its design and outreach, even by today's standards. The Arab response to the letter was highly political and well structured. The political aspect of that popular resistance was channelled through the Palestine Arab congresses in the years 1919–23.[7] In conjunction with heightened political organisation, peaceful mass protests were held to underscore the unity between the political elite and Palestinian society. Notable amongst these early marches were the political rallies of 27 February and 8 March 1920 and various acts of civil disobedience on 11 March, which included 'holding unsanctioned public protests in Jerusalem, Jaffa, and Haifa, in addition to closing their shops and submitting petitions to British authorities'.[8]

Despite the eruption of violence on several occasions, including the bloody 1 May 1920 clash which resulted in the killing of 48 Arabs and 47 Jews,[9] the overall resistance campaign remained inclusive, popular, non-violent and politically coordinated with representatives from Palestinian communities throughout the country:

> Palestinians directed their resistance towards the British through the simplest and most basic non-violent methods of protest and persuasion: formal statements, declarations, petitions, manifestos, assemblies, delegations, processions, marches and motorcades. Arabs held street demonstrations, organized local strikes, sent delegations to London, organized support from Muslims in Mecca, and passed resolutions rejecting a Jewish homeland, opposing Jewish immigration and calling for the establishment of their representatives in the government. In addition to these protest and persuasions techniques, Palestinians utilized methods of noncooperation, including withdrawal from political systems and elections, general strikes, boycotts, tax withholdings and civil disobedience.[10]

Soon, Palestinian leaders began realising the nature of the daunting struggle ahead. Violent Zionist provocations and harsh British reprisals to Palestinian resistance seemed designed to demoralise the public. This called for a dual campaign, which defined the early 1930s. Regional and international efforts were now combined by an inward strategy aimed at political organisation and awareness campaigns that would engage Palestinians everywhere, even in the smallest of villages. But the growth of a collective Palestinian consciousness was met with intensifying Zionist immigration and military development. In 1933, 30,000 Jewish immigrants flocked to Palestine, a number that would reach 42,000 in 1934 and 61,000 in 1935. These were also the years of the rise of Nazi power in Germany, which no doubt played a role in convincing even greater numbers of Jews to follow the Zionist directive.

Now that British designs were no longer a subject for debate, and politicisation and organisation of Palestinian society had reached the point of saturation, Palestine was to experience its first open and collective rebellion against the Zionist colonial drive and the British role in espousing it and labouring to ensure its success. In April 1936, all five Palestinian political parties collaborated under the umbrella of the Arab Higher Committee (AHC), led by Haj Amin al-Husseini.[11] One of the AHC's first decisions was the hurried assembly of National Committees throughout Palestine. In May, al-Husseini summoned the first conference of the National Committees in Jerusalem, which collectively declared a general strike on 8 May 1936. Employing means of civil disobedience – as exemplified in its cry of 'No Taxation without Representation' – the 1936 uprising aimed to send a stern message to the British government that Palestinians were nationally unified and capable of acting as an assertive, self-assured society in ways that could indeed disturb the matrix of British mandatory rule over the country.

The first six months of the uprising, which lasted under different manifestations and phases for three years, was characterised at the outset by a widely observed general strike that was essentially a boycott of working within and supporting the structures and mechanisms of British mandatory rule. The strike lasted from May until October 1936. Palestine was simply shut down in response to the call of the National Committees and al-Husseini, a type of action that irked the British who saw the 'non-Jewish residents of Palestine' as deplorable, troublesome peasants with an untamed leadership that was, unlike the Jewish leadership, incapable of articulating a national programme, and most certainly incompetent of acting upon one, if such a programme were ever devised. Within a few years, Palestinians managed to challenge the conventional wisdom of the British, whose narrow Orientalist grasp on the Arabs as lesser beings with lesser or no rights – a model to be borrowed and amply applied by the Zionists, and official Israeli policies later on – left them unqualified to ponder any other response to a legitimate uprising but coercive measures.

Starting in the 1920s and extending to the late 1940s, Palestinians and their leaders resorted to various forms of resistance, beginning with political mobilisation, and ending with mostly ineffective (although with some notable exceptions) military attempts at defending Palestinian towns and villages as they fell before the Zionist military machine, backed or facilitated by colonial Britain. But within that period, Palestinian society was made to discover its own inner strength as a collective, employing strategies that predicated on the boycott of British and Zionist institutions.

LEGACY OF REVOLUTION

Combined British military might, and Zionist military and political advantage were enough to conquer Palestine during the events that lead to and included *al-Nakba*, or 'the Catastrophe' of 1948. Historic Palestine was depopulated of most of its non-Jewish inhabitants, who were expelled to many destinations. But the legacy of the collective struggle of the 1920s and '30s was to manifest itself repeatedly throughout the years and decades that followed.

The First Palestinian Intifada of 1987 is often juxtaposed with the popular and collective boycott and civil disobedience that defined the 1930s in general, and the 1936 revolt in particular. The Intifada was a collective retort to the 1967 Israeli occupation of East Jerusalem, the West Bank and the Gaza Strip. For two decades, the Occupied Territory was placed under the iron-fist governance of the so-called Israeli Civilian Administration, that is, the military. Palestinians in the Occupied Territory attempted to organise boycotts of the military administration, with varied degrees of success, throughout this period. General strikes were held, and strikers were routinely punished through imprisonments and fines. The Intifada, however, was a call for a collective popular response to the occupation which finally inspired and thus involved the whole Palestinian community.

When on 8 December 1987, thousands took to the streets of Jabaliya refugee camp, the Gaza Strip's largest and poorest camp, the timing and the location of their uprising was most fitting, most rational and necessary. It soon spread to include virtually all Palestinian areas and communities. It was as if Palestinians had lost every trace of fear. Collectively, they became most daring at a time when Israel expected them to be most pacified and subservient. And when they rebelled, as has always been the case, they took everyone by surprise.

A PEOPLE'S INTIFADA

The First Intifada may have been spontaneous – similar to the socio-economic, cultural and political processes that culminated in the 1936–39 revolt – but it required a form of organisation, sufficient enough to give it an articulate political voice, but nominal enough to avoid the traps of political centralisation which often mar popular revolts. As is the case in most popular grass-roots movements, widespread despair was translated into hope and direct action:

> As a news correspondent in those days it was astonishing to see young and old women coming out of the houses to join the men in street protests or supporting them in one way or another. On one occasion, from inside the Shifa hospital in Gaza City, I watched a crowd of young men who were pelting an Israeli army unit with stones. The soldiers were trying to get inside and arrest some of the Palestinians who had been injured in clashes earlier in the morning. Girls and women had formed a human chain to keep the shabab at the front line – the faces of the young men masked by kuffiyas – supplied with small rocks and pieces of jagged masonry. As tear-gas fired into the hospital, older women provided raw onion to help ease the stringing pain.[12]

In common with earlier phases of the Palestinian revolution, the First Intifada featured a wide range of resistance strategies which were predominantly unarmed. Amongst these, boycotts of various guises again figured prominently, such as that of the story of Beit Sahour. Similar ideas were employed across the country to varying levels and degrees of success.

Israel responded violently, much as colonial Britain had done decades earlier. Estimates vary on the number of Palestinians killed during the years of the Intifada, which is largely determined as the years between 1987 and 1993, the year when the Oslo Accords was signed between PLO leader Yasser Arafat and Israel. According to the United Nations Relief and Works Agency (UNRWA) statistics, 500 people were killed and 50,000 injured in the Gaza Strip alone during the years of the Intifada.[13] Gaza's Ahli Arab Hospital treated 13,000 cases during the same period. One-third of those treated were children under the age of 15.[14]

The Intifada represented a unity of purpose and courage, the sheer rage and resentment at the occupation, the sense of community, and the resolve and resilience of the refugees. But the Intifada's uncomplicated, yet poignant message was to be co-opted and corrupted by those who wished to use its achievements for personal and factional gains. It was once again the utilisation of popular action for often misguided political strategies of the leadership that proved most harmful. A secret peace accord that was signed between Arafat and the Israel leadership was promoted as a victory for the Intifada. Far from it: the Oslo Accords further confused Palestinian objectives as a small clique of political leaders who were mostly detached from struggling Palestinians on the ground hijacked the Palestinians' decision-making power.

However, a similar message to that of the 1936–39 revolt was effectively articulated, of collective values and action, that reasserted the role of the Palestinian people as creative, resilient and resourceful. It also imposed the Palestinian struggle on regional and global agendas, extenuating that the Palestinian people were the most relevant party in settling the conflict. Furthermore, the Intifada communicated a clear and resounding call for solidarity from the Palestinian people to the rest of the world. The central tenets of the First Intifada – civil disobedience and boycott, grass-roots Palestinian-led mobilisation, education, collective and inclusive resistance strategies, and internationalisation of the struggle – are principles that would, in later years, go on to help shape the Palestinian-led international campaign for Boycott, Divestment and Sanctions against Israel.

LESSONS LEARNED: THE DEVELOPMENT OF BDS

The fruits of Oslo, if any, were bitter. Confiscation of Palestinian land and settlement construction actually increased in the post-Oslo period, and the possibility of a territorially contiguous and politically independent Palestine looked extremely bleak, if not impossible. The nature of the new challenge compelled Palestinian civil society to organise differently. From the Israeli massacres and violence of the Second Intifada, which erupted in September 2000, a younger generation of Palestinian leaders, product of an ever-active civil society, academic institutions and non-factionalised segments of society, began shifting focus elsewhere. Learning from the mistakes of the past, the new efforts seemed coordinated but not centralised, articulated into political demands but not politically manipulated; equally important, while uniquely Palestinian in its leadership, the new movement was universal in its values, and both global and inclusive in its approach.

Many Palestinians knew well that a first step towards true freedom was reversing the process of isolation – by breaking away from the localised version of the struggle imposed by their leadership, and by leading an international campaign of Boycott, Divestment and Sanctions, so that Israel would realise that colonisation, oppression and military occupation should be costly.

Once more, ordinary Palestinians led the way. Following protracted sieges and subsequent military incursions that killed and wounded hundreds of Palestinians in the Jenin refugee camp and the Old City of Nablus in 2002, residents, although desperate for food and water supplies, rejected shipments of food, blankets and other handouts by the United States Agency for International Development (USAID).[15]

The rejection of aid by starving refugees in these areas was not the only example that empowered Palestinian society to think outside current parameters of struggle, but it was repeatedly highlighted by Palestinian intellectuals as a greatly inspiring model. Moreover, refusing aid supplied by the same government that provided Israel with 'gunships, bulldozers, and M16s ... used by Israel to raze'[16] these very communities, was a principled thing to do. To this day, many principled grass-roots Palestinian civil society organisations continue to boycott USAID, and repeated calls have been made by the Palestinian NGO Network (PNGO) for full and inclusive participation in this boycott.

The growing numbers of international solidarity activists who went to Palestine during the Second Intifada, along with the development of grass-roots Palestinian independent media projects on the ground, began building bridges between Palestinian communities and the rest of the world. The aspirations of the Palestinian people were being regularly communicated globally – despite the persisting information blockade caused by inherent mainstream bias within the mass media – but also experiences of other nations that directed popular revolts against colonial oppression were again being channelled back to the new generations of Palestinians, as they had been via the intra-Palestinian grass-roots education system within Occupation prisons during the First Intifada. The revolution was now becoming more inclusive and refreshingly multifaceted. Unlike the revolt of 1936 and the uprising of 1987, no military machine is now strong enough, and no self-seeking politicians are calculating enough to truly silence or overpower Palestinian society.

The new strategy was accompanied by upbeat organisation, at home and abroad, which reflected itself in terms of civil society initiatives, starting in Palestine, but echoing elsewhere, and a decided campaign began taking shape. On 6 July 2004, Palestinian academics and intellectuals – who later launched the Palestinian Campaign for the Academic and Cultural Boycott of Israel (PACBI) – made an open call to their colleagues in the international community:

... to comprehensively and consistently boycott all Israeli academic and cultural institutions as a contribution to the struggle to end Israel's occupation, colonization and system of apartheid, by applying the following: Refrain from participation in any form of academic and cultural cooperation, collaboration or joint projects with Israeli institutions; Advocate a comprehensive boycott of Israeli institutions at the national and international levels, including suspension of all forms of funding and subsidies to these institutions; Promote divestment and disinvestment from Israel by international academic institutions ... Support Palestinian academic and cultural institutions directly without requiring them to partner with Israeli counterparts as an explicit or implicit condition for such support.[17]

Progressively, the call was answered positively by academic institutions around the world, notably in South Africa, whose moral centrality to the Palestinian struggle was becoming more visible than ever before.[18]

The call made by academics articulated an intellectual basis for the boycott movement, and ignited a debate in many academic institutions across the world, most visibly in Britain. But the official launch of the Boycott, Divestment and Sanctions (BDS) campaign didn't begin until 9 July 2005, when a statement representing 171 civil society organisations throughout Palestine called on international civil society to stand in solidarity with the Palestinian people, by action, not words. The call intentionally coincided with the one-year anniversary of the 'historic Advisory Opinion of the International Court of Justice (ICJ) which found Israel's Wall built on occupied Palestinian territory to be illegal':[19]

Inspired by the struggle of South Africans against apartheid and in the spirit of international solidarity, moral consistency and resistance to injustice and oppression ... We, representatives of Palestinian civil society, call upon international civil society organizations and people of conscience all over the world to impose broad boycotts and implement divestment initiatives against Israel similar to those applied to South Africa in the apartheid era. We appeal to you to pressure your respective states to impose embargoes and sanctions against Israel. We also invite conscientious Israelis to support this Call, for the sake of justice and genuine peace.[20]

The Palestinian message was clear and decisive. Its universally rooted values and grounding within civil society deprived the arguments often used by Israeli apologists from any substance. Supporters of human rights and justice throughout the world finally had a platform from which they could advocate for Palestinian rights whilst practicing strategic direct action and practical solidarity. Since these initial calls were made, and despite incessant Israeli efforts aimed at thwarting the Palestinian international campaign, the BDS movement continues to grow and within it new victories are regularly being won. The sense of despair that for long years overshadowed the Palestine solidarity movement is now motivated by new ideas, and a forward-thinking strategy. Israel, which is now struggling to repair its image against what Israeli leaders describe as attempts at 'delegitimising' their country, are unable to resort to the same traditional methods of suppression to overwhelm the global uprising underway. Even if BDS efforts are not always successful, they have always succeeded in highlighting a debate that was once missing from most western academic and civil society institutions.

In April 2010, the student senate at the University of California, Berkeley debated the issue of divestment from US companies that were 'materially or militarily profiting' from the Israeli occupation of Palestinian territories. A divestment bill was put to a vote. Notable individuals, including Noam Chomsky, Archbishop Desmond Tutu, Naomi Klein and Alice Walker, issued statements in support of the bill. Nobel laureates Shirin Ebadi, Mairead Maguire, Rigoberta Menchu Tum and Jody Williams signed a letter echoing the outpouring of support:

We stand united in our belief that divesting from companies that provide significant support for the Israeli military provides moral and strategic stewardship of tuition and taxpayer-funded public education money. We are all peace makers, and we believe that no amount of dialogue without economic pressure can motivate Israel to change its policy of using overwhelming force against Palestinian civilians.[21]

The bill may have failed to garner the needed votes but it inspired further debates, and similar initiatives triumphed elsewhere. Most importantly, campuses and academic and civil society institutions around the world are becoming cornerstones in the Israel/Palestine debate, and a self-propelling momentum is generated with every announcement that another BDS victory has been won.

The Palestinian revolution, including the popular revolt of 1936–39 and the uprisings of 1987 and 2000, has finally managed to break away from the traditional formula of old, that of remote rebellions overwhelmed by violent coercion. The historical strategy of boycott has been developed, and given a high-profile inclusive international platform, learning also from the lessons of India's freedom struggle, the US Civil Rights Movement and, most significantly, South Africa's Anti-Apartheid Movement amongst others. BDS has opened up whole new ground for the Palestinian struggle for freedom, justice and human rights which is based on universally recognised principles. This time around the battle can, and must, be won.

NOTES

1. Staughton Lynd, Alice Lynd, Sam Bahour, *Homeland: Oral Histories of Palestine and Palestinians.* (Northampton, MA: Interlink Books, 1994), p. 276.
2. Ibid., p. 275.
3. Ibid., pp. 276–7.
4. Walid Khalidi, *Before Their Diaspora, A Photographic History of the Palestinians 1876–1948* (Washington, DC: Institute for Palestinian Studies, 1984), pp. 33–5.
5. BBC News, 'The Sykes-Picot Agreement' (29 November 2001) <http://news.bbc.co.uk/1/hi/in_depth/middle_east/2001/israel_and_the_palestinians/key_documents/1681362.stm> (accessed 28 June 2011).
6. Khalidi, *Before Their Diaspora*, pp. 33–5.
7. Julie M. Norman. *The Second Palestinian Intifada: Civil Resistance.* (Oxford: Taylor & Francis, 2010), pp. 18–19.
8. Ibid.

9. Ibid.

10. Ibid.

11. Khalidi, *Before Their Diaspora*, p. 189.

12. Gerald Butt, *Life at the Crossroads: A History of Gaza* (Nicosia: Rimal Publications, 1995), pp. 169–70.

13. Ibid., pp. 172–3.

14. Ibid., p. 173.

15. Sam Bahour, 'USAID Boycott Off Target', *Foreign Policy in Focus* (1 May 2002) <http://www.fpif.org/articles/usaid_boycott_off_target> (accessed 3 July 2011).

16. Ibid.

17. See 'Call for Academic and Cultural Boycott of Israel', *PACBI.org* <http://www.pacbi.org/etemplate.php?id=869> (accessed 3 July 2011).

18. 'South African school cuts ties with Ben-Gurion University in Israel', *Haaretz.com* (3 March 2011) <http://www.haaretz.com/news/diplomacy-defense/south-african-school-cuts-ties-with-ben-gurion-university-in-israel-1.351564> (accessed 3 July 2011).

19. See 'Palestinian Civil Society Call for BDS', *BDSMovement.net* <http://www.bdsmovement.net/call> (accessed 3 July 2011).

20. Ibid.

21. Adam Horowitz and Philip Weiss, 'The Boycott Divestment Sanctions Movement', *The Nation* (28 June 2010) <http://www.thenation.com/article/boycott-divestment-sanctions-movement?page=full> (accessed 3 July 2011).

2
Boycott, Bricks and the Four Pillars of the South African Struggle

Ronnie Kasrils

At a conference in London in 1959, Julius Nyerere, Tanzania's future president, called on the British public to boycott South Africa. Britain was South Africa's major trading partner at the time: 'We are not asking you, the British people for anything special. We are just asking you to withdraw your support from apartheid by not buying South African products.'[1]

By the 1970s, the extent to which the global boycott had unsettled the apartheid camp was illustrated by South African Prime Minister B.J. Vorster in a plaintive declamation: 'Every product we sell abroad is another brick in the wall of our existence.'

So effective was the educational and mobilisation activity of the Anti-Apartheid Movement (AAM) over the years that ordinary people around the world were able to see clearly where justice lay. The effectiveness of the AAM was directly linked to the policy, strategy and tactics of the struggle employed by South Africa's oppressed masses, led by the African National Congress (ANC).

FOUR PILLARS OF STRUGGLE

As history recalls, the international solidarity urged by Nyerere, became a fully-fledged Boycott, Divestment and Sanctions (BDS) campaign that assisted in the eventual triumph over apartheid in 1994. This campaign was an integral component of what came to be referred to as the ANCs 'Four Pillars of Struggle'.

The elements of this quartet were closely interwoven and constituted:

1. The mass internal political struggle of the oppressed South African people;
2. The underground political network;
3. Armed resistance, and
4. International boycott and solidarity.

Although these elements became a virtual organic whole over time, each had its own history and evolution.

Background

The ANC was established in 1912, with the objective of uniting the diverse tribal formations and kingdoms of the indigenous black peoples. Their armed resistance to colonial conquest had been extinguished by the superiority of modern European weaponry against spears and shields over the course of two centuries. Each of the indigenous kingdoms, such as Zulu, Xhosa, Sotho and Tswana – and independent Boer republics – were singled out for conquest one after the other in Britain's imperial doctrine of divide and rule. This came to a head at the end of the nineteenth century, following the discovery of diamonds and gold.

The ANC chose non-violent forms of struggle from its inception, deeming this the only feasible way of advancing the cause at the time. These methods were to become more and more militant and mass-based in support of demands for equal rights and freedom. This phase lasted until 1960 when the brutal repression meted out by the Apartheid regime culminated in the infamous Sharpeville massacre, in which 69 unarmed protestors were killed and over 200 wounded. The ANC and other organisations were banned and thousands were thrown into prison. Outspoken individuals and activists lost their liberty through draconian laws, bans and restrictions. These measures effectively obstructed the path to peaceful change. It then became a question of either submitting to brute force or fighting back.

None other than US President John Kennedy provided the moral basis for justified resistance in a much-celebrated quotation: 'Those who make peaceful change impossible make violent change inevitable.'[2] Regimes denying democratic rights, and those based on tyranny and occupation, need to mull over those words.

As a consequence, the ANC established an armed wing, Umkhonto weSizwe (MK or Spear of the Nation), which initially utilised sabotage operations to announce this new path of struggle. Methods of guerrilla warfare were later used, and played an important role in inspiring the masses, although remaining at a low level owing to the lack of suitable terrain in South Africa. Nevertheless, such actions gave the oppressed majority hope, disrupted the economy and acted as a psychological lever to undermine the regime and its support base. Over the years, however, armed struggle was secondary to a primary focus of mobilising the workers and masses through political organisation, strikes and protest actions.

Underground organisation grew slowly in strength and outreach from the 1970s onward. Liberation propaganda material was distributed in a situation where the regime was dominant and information heavily censored. Clandestine cells joined forces and gave guidance to emergent above-ground organisations of women, youth, trade unions, and cultural and religious groups. The resistance was provided with intelligence, refuge, food, transport and recruits; their chance of survival, which had been bleak in the early days, greatly improved.

By the mid-1980s, the international solidarity movement, and with it a BDS campaign, had expanded to significant levels, and the actions of all four contingents of struggle were working in concert. The term 'Four Pillars of Struggle' emerged. This entailed that in whatever sector an activist was involved – whether internally or internationally – it was with the knowledge and clarity of the bigger strategic picture. The importance of a clear-cut strategy for all to follow cannot be over-emphasised and is an essential ingredient for success.

GROWTH OF INTERNATIONAL SOLIDARITY

The international solidarity movement grew in response to the internal struggle against apartheid and the call from the ANC for the isolation of South Africa. This saw the growth of the Anti-Apartheid Movement in countries spanning five continents, uniting members of diverse political parties, trade unions, and ordinary people from all walks of life. The movement embraced supportive governments from Africa, Asia, Scandinavia and the socialist bloc. This global activity helped educate the international community and public everywhere and placed enormous pressure on South Africa and the countries supporting and trading with it. The AAM also pre-eminently focused on the United Nations, which became a significant vehicle for isolating apartheid. In August 1963, the UN Security Council adopted Resolution 181 which called upon all states to cease the sale and shipment of arms, ammunition and military vehicles to South Africa. This was soon followed by a General Assembly resolution of November 1963 that urged all states to refrain from supplying petroleum to South Africa. In December 1968, the General Assembly requested all states and organisations to suspend cultural, educational, sporting and other exchanges with the racist regime and with organisations and institutions in South Africa practising apartheid. The arms embargo was finally made mandatory in 1977.

It was an independent India that had first raised the illegality of apartheid at the United Nations, an initiative supported by the Soviet Union. By the 1960s, with much of Africa becoming independent from colonial rule, the strength of the anti-apartheid bloc of Afro-Asian states became compelling. Following the Second World War, the global community of nations and their people were revolted by racist laws. The US's racial bigotry buckled under the Civil Rights Movement and the African-American 'black lobby' became a vocal pressure group, forcing many changes in their country's position *vis-à-vis* South Africa. A milestone was achieved when African-American workers at Kodak forced the company to pull out of South Africa after the 1976 Soweto massacre.

The Apartheid regime and Zionist Israel both came into existence in May 1948, yet whilst the world recoiled at South Africa's mounting racist onslaught on its black majority, Israel was able to get away with the dispossession and ethnic cleansing of the Palestinian people with impunity. The sentiment in support of Israel following the catastrophic Nazi Holocaust and the fact that the western powers saw in the Zionist state an ally against the rise of Arab nationalism in the oil-rich Middle East both played their roles in this practice. It is extremely important therefore, in the winning of world opinion, for the duplicity and mythology of the settlers in Israel – as in apartheid South Africa – to be countered by the reality of the conquest of the indigenous peoples and the disaster of losing their land and birthright. To succeed in a boycott campaign requires the unmasking of injustice and ongoing crimes.

POTATOES, RUGBY, GUNS AND BANKS

The catalyst for the international campaign against apartheid South Africa emerged from the experience of the ANC's early domestic, internal boycotts. These were undertaken as part of the mass resistance to apartheid laws, associated with the 1950s Defiance Campaign, and exemplified in what was called the 'Potato Boycott'. This was directed against white potato farmers, who brutally exploited black pass offenders[3] – that is, those not in possession of the necessary documentation – as virtual slaves on their farms, where they were subjected to appalling labour and living conditions, beatings and even death.

In disgust at this cruelty, the call for a boycott on all potato products mobilised enormous pressure on the agro-business interests concerned. Taboo products included potato crisps, canned fruit and vegetables. This boycott was of limited success, owing to the fact that the ANC was soon banned and its activities hindered. However, the refusal to buy potatoes acted as a precedent for the global call to boycott South African products. Oranges and Cape grapes, drenched in blood, became iconic posters of the boycott call and the campaign began to swell, denting South Africa's economy and confidence. The boycott of easily identifiable products spoke to housewives and their children, taking the boycott into kitchens around the world, and was instrumental in mobilising and educating masses of people about apartheid.

One of the most dramatic boycott successes was the 1984 Dunne's shopworkers' strike in Dublin. It started when eleven assistants at the store walked out to join their trade union picket-line in support of a call for the store to stop selling South African fruit and vegetables. It ended after two years with the Irish government agreeing to ban the import of products from the apartheid state. By then, dockworkers around the world had refused to handle South African cargo. They joined students, academics, writers, artists and athletes who participated in the academic, cultural and sporting boycott in increasing numbers until a tipping point was reached.

Sport was an easily identifiable terrain to focus on. What began with an Olympic ban imposed in the 1960s was soon to be followed by the massive protests undertaken on many a cricket pitch and rugby field – in countries such as Britain, Ireland, New Zealand and Australia – which captured the world's attention. These events eventually resulted in apartheid South Africa being excluded from each and every major international sporting fixture. South Africa's white population was 'sports mad' – the game of rugby was a virtual religion for the white Afrikaaners, who were a mainstay of the Apartheid regime. Cricket was another key target. Protests began outside English cricket grounds hosting apartheid teams and soon grew in number. 'Apartheid is not cricket' was a favourite banner carried by protestors. 'Don't allow politics to interfere in sport' was the riposte from racist South Africa and those in Britain who chose to turn a blind eye to injustice. But with fair-minded people seeing that South African teams were the exclusive preserve of whites, it was easy to identify the source of injustice, and the campaign grew by leaps and bounds. The last South African rugby and cricket teams' visits to Britain were in the 1970s. Apartheid teams met similar opposition in the other traditional rugby and cricketing countries of Australia and New Zealand,

and the South African press came to refer to their country as 'the polecat of the world'.

Reflective of the way in which the sports boycott gained support was the fact that in 1966 the South African Springbok rugby team was greeted with adulation all over New Zealand. During the next tour in 1981, mass protests led to the cancellation of two games and pitch invasions at several others saw games being played under a massive police presence to control protestors. The controversy caused by the tour led to the cancellation of a planned 1985 tour of South Africa by the All Blacks as the boycott took hold; no further official fixtures between the two countries took place in any sport until after the Apartheid regime fell.

The sports boycott cut straight to the heart of white South Africans besotted by their love of rugby and cricket, and they finally voted in a 'whites only' referendum in 1992 to support the negotiations process. By then, they were thoroughly sick and tired of being treated like lepers on the sporting front and they craved 'normality'. Although white South Africans in the past used to angrily brag that they would not be intimidated by 'long-haired anarchists, communists and radical priests', isolation in fact hurt them deeply and this, together with the liberation struggle, opened their eyes. The business community also began to support a reform process when the BDS campaign began to hurt their pockets. Big business exerted great pressure on governing circles once they came to see reform as the means of deflecting revolution.

UN Resolution 181 proved to be particularly effective, with more and more countries refusing to export weapons to South Africa. The AAM in France built up huge pressure on its government for having exported Mirage fighter planes and Daphne submarines to South Africa. Public opinion and the UN ended this cooperation and South Africa turned to Israel to assist in its upgrading of fighter planes, to purchase naval craft, jointly build an arms industry and construct nuclear weapons.

Following the declaration of a State of Emergency by the Apartheid regime in 1985, sections of the international banking community, starting with Chase Manhattan in the US, stopped business and refused to renew South Africa's loan agreements. No longer able to raise funds abroad, the Apartheid regime plunged the country into a spiralling financial and economic crisis, from which it was unable to recover.[4] The last nail in apartheid's coffin was when the British Barclays Bank terminated business in 1988 after over a century as the most important overseas bank in South Africa. Britain's AAM members had been purchasing symbolic shares in order to attend Barclays Annual General Meetings and vote against its links with South Africa. After the demise of apartheid, certain South African cabinet members admitted that they were finally shocked into the realisation that they had to change course when Barclays, such a reliable trading partner historically, ceased business. This is a good example of initially focusing on the easier targets, such as oranges and rugby (as tough as even these might have been at times), and gravitating to banking and the nerve centres of business once a critical mass had been achieved.

No issue was ignored. No stone was left unturned. A campaign for the release of thousands of South African political prisoners, with Nelson Mandela as the iconic figure, was part and parcel of the international movement.

DETERMINED INTERNATIONAL PRESSURE

The AAM movement worked and grew for over thirty years until the Apartheid regime was ultimately crushed. In comparison, Palestine's BDS campaign which was only launched in July 2005, has accelerated at an even faster pace and gives much cause for hope.

In commenting on the significance of international solidarity and the similarities between the South African and Palestinian struggles, the distinguished Nobel Peace Prize recipient, Archbishop Desmond Tutu wrote:

> The end of apartheid stands as one of the crowning accomplishments of the past century, but we would not have succeeded without the help

of international pressure ... a similar movement has taken shape, this
time aiming at the end to Israeli occupation ... These tactics are not the
only parallels to the struggle against apartheid. Yesterday's South African
township dwellers can tell you about today's life in the occupied territories
... If apartheid ended, so can the occupation, but the moral force and
international pressure will have to be just as determined.[5]

The impact of such statements should never be under-estimated,
proving the old adage that '*The truth hurts.*' His statement
resulted in Archbishop Tutu becoming a prime target of the
Zionist propaganda machine, which branded this patron of
the South African Holocaust Centre an anti-Semite, simply
because he dared to speak the truth. These attempts at character
assassination became counter-productive as clear-thinking people
everywhere saw the falseness of these claims. It is generally
accepted that despite its strenuous efforts Israel has lost the
battle for ideas. Its aggression and punitive measures have come
to speak volumes.

This 'determined international pressure', whilst essential,
does not occur in a vacuum. This becomes apparent not only
in the case of the international campaign to isolate apartheid,
but also within the movement that called for the withdrawal
of American troops from Vietnam in the 1960–70s. This too
stands out as a latter-day twentieth-century example of the
international dimension being successfully invoked as part of
a broader struggle for freedom and independence. Indeed, the
approach adopted by the Vietnamese greatly influenced the
South African liberation movement, following an important
visit of an ANC delegation to Vietnam in 1978 which helped
give rise to the concept of 'Four Pillars of Struggle'.

In both instances, success lay in the fact that the appeal for
international solidarity was an important element of an overall
strategy. This strategy was multi-dimensional in nature, with all
elements primarily directed to securing the maximum unity of
and with the oppressed in their struggle for justice.

This unity was fundamental, as throughout history all manner
of tyrants have employed the strategy of 'divide and conquer'

to keep oppressed peoples weak and to crush their resistance. This unity stretched beyond the oppressed, who remained the focus and the leading force of the struggle, to include what we in South Africa termed 'isolating the centre of reaction', which involved reaching out to sections of the oppressor's social base, both nationally and internationally, in order to neutralise or win them over. The End Conscription Campaign amongst white youth – much like today's Israeli 'refuseniks' movement – saw growing numbers publicly refusing to participate in an unjust war. South Africa, like Israel, just did not have the numbers to indefinitely wage wars of aggression.

No element within the overall strategy was exclusive. The people's struggles inspired international support, just as international support in turn inspired the people's struggles, each coalescing and reinforcing one and other.

Success lay in the fact that the appeal for international solidarity was unequivocally made by the leadership of the liberation movement, on behalf of the oppressed, who through the manner in which they conducted their determined struggles, were able to demonstrate their moral superiority over the regime and the justice of their cause. In the prophetic statement of the Vietnamese revolutionary icon, Ho Chi Minh, echoed by ANC leaders: 'Our resistance war will be victorious because it is a just cause approved and supported by the people of the world.'[6]

These struggles were indeed supported, despite the challenging context of a divided Cold War world in which they occurred. Freedom-loving people were able to rise above the 'red, black or terrorist' propaganda peddled by the oppressors, enabling them to join together, collectively expressing their revulsion at the injustices perpetrated.

LESSONS

There are many lessons to be learnt from the South African experience as has been illustrated above. Some of the most important are cited below.

The all-important concepts of justice, the moral high ground and unity

If any element of an overall strategy is to be successful, it must flow from such central tenets. This I believe is distinctly relevant to the international mobilisation in support of the BDS campaign against Israel – which must also challenge the attitudes of Israelis. The analogy in the latter instance is threefold. It must reject the racist concepts of Jewish privileges and a 'Jewish state', which I believe run counter to the positive tenets of Judaism. It must also demonstrate international grass-roots unity inclusive of all religious persuasions. Finally, it must reject Zionist propaganda that equates opposition to Israeli policies with anti-Semitism.

The international boycott emerged from the early domestic and internal boycott

Internal boycott action demonstrated to the outside world that the call for international isolation stemmed from the oppressed people themselves. This is a message that was constantly emphasised, illustrating that the international movement was not simply working on behalf of oppressed South Africans, but in conjunction with them.

The explanation of the late ANC president, Chief Albert Luthuli, in his 1959 appeal to the British people is instructive here:

> It has been argued that non-white people will be the first to be hit by external boycotts. This may be so, but every organisation which commands … non-white support in South Africa is in favour of them. The alternative to the use of these weapons is the continuation of the status quo and the bleak prospect of unending discrimination. Economic boycott is one way in which the world at large can bring home to the South African authorities that they must either mend their ways or suffer for them.[7]

If one looks at Israel, the boycott of goods produced in the illegal settlements are a clear, appropriate and immediate target to mobilise around. The Dead Sea beauty products are a good example. However, it is important to link settlement products with the wider Israeli economy, since the former cannot survive outside the latter. This implies that a boycott should be against Israeli products and not simply those produced within the settlements. It should also be feasible to develop a boycott of international banking linked to settlement activity of all kinds. Similarly, campaigning for Israel's exclusion from European soccer competitions and the Eurovision song contest could also be considered as immediate, high-profile targets. An academic boycott of Israel's institutions is proving particularly effective, because this is such an important arena for the country and its intelligentsia. The time will come when more and more Israeli academics will contemplate taking a stand to avoid facing the stigma once felt by their counterparts in apartheid South Africa.

It takes time to build and sustain momentum

The vast anti-apartheid campaign against South Africa had modest origins. We have seen that it was initially established as a boycott movement in Britain in 1959, focusing specifically on South African products. It took time for the movement to build itself up into a formidable force. Initial boycott campaigns were built against easily identifiable targets such as oranges and rugby, and the subsequent move to divestment and sanctions grew out of that groundswell. Divestment by universities, trade unions and religious bodies can occur quite dramatically, but the successful application of sanctions at state level requires prolonged campaigning, as states make decisions based on their national interests; they resist acting against their allies although the South African case shows that it is possible. Pressure through the UN and the protests of civil society swung the balance against apartheid and must be equally unrelenting against Israel.

The Anti-Apartheid Movement's strength lay in the fact that it was mass-based and inclusive

The AAM drew its main support from the grass roots, especially in Britain, Western Europe, North America and Australasia, where governmental backing from South Africa's major trading partners for the campaign was less than forthcoming until much later.

The movement was able to galvanise this breadth of support because, much like the liberation movement that it flowed from, it was a broad and inclusive front, providing a home to all colours, creeds, classes and persuasions. All that was required was a commitment to working for apartheid's demise.

The AAM tapped into issues that those on the ground could easily identify with. For example, in Ireland it drew on the experience of the ravages of British colonialism, in America it evoked the legacy of slavery and racism, and in Holland on the fact that the country had been the first colonial power in South Africa. It was also able to readily adapt its campaigning methods, ensuring that they were relevant to specific conditions and recognising that strategies appropriate in one local or national context are not necessarily effective in others. Importantly, it had the support of the African states, which highlights the fact that the Arab states need to be far more assertive in their support of the Palestinian struggle – and of BDS – than they have been. The 'Arab Awakening' has sent shivers down Israel's spine, and that of its supporters, as well as autocrats throughout North Africa and the Middle East precisely because the so-called 'Arab Street' demands practical and positive action in support of their Palestinian brothers and sisters. Egypt, for example, cannot continue to connive at restriction of movement and goods across its border with Gaza, or heavily discounted fossil fuel sales to Israel. Such issues emerged as demands from the Egyptian masses from within the throes of revolution.

Education was an essential focus of the AAM's work

Education exposed the nature of apartheid and the myths and scare tactics propagated by the regime, which closely resembled those of its Zionist counterpart.

As the BDS campaign unfolds, we must ensure that we are thoroughly prepared to engage in a similar endeavour. We need to reject the claim that there should be even-handedness in dealing with the oppressed and the oppressor, rejecting the propaganda that Israel's brutality is motivated by understandable security concerns. We must bring to light Israel's entrenched system of colonialism, racism and denial of Palestinian national and human rights based on dispossession of their land – which is akin to that of apartheid South Africa. This is, after all, the fundamental source of the conflict.

It is this truth that resonates within one of Archbishop Tutu's testimonies:

> Some people are enraged by comparisons between the Israeli/Palestinian conflict and what happened in South Africa ... For those of us who lived through the dehumanising horrors of the apartheid era, the comparison seems not only apt, it is also necessary ... if we are to persevere in our hope that things can change.[8]

A campaign will pass through high and low points

A campaign must be sustained by constant commitment and energy. It requires an army of dedicated volunteers who are prepared to toil for long hours in organising meetings and rallies, handing out leaflets and pamphlets on street corners and outside department stores in all weathers. I recall times travelling long hours in Britain to address small meetings at seemingly obscure community halls. Often I would find an audience of no more than a dozen committed souls. It was important not to be down-hearted; if there were twelve people present, then they were a dozen who could become dedicated activists. In dire times when the struggle appeared endless, it was necessary to remember that the contradictions of apartheid, and a changing international situation, could bring about a sudden, dramatic upturn of fortune, opening up enormous possibilities. This occurred in South Africa with the student uprising of 1976. It also happened with the defeat of apartheid military forces in Angola at the Battle of Cuito Cuanavale in 1988, which opened the way to Namibia's independence, which had huge ramifications for South Africa. The recent popular uprisings in North Africa and the Middle East are a case in point, as they substantially affected the status quo in the region.

CONCLUSION

There are, undoubtedly, links and lessons to be drawn between the struggles of South Africa and Palestine, but the Palestinian BDS campaign is already earning its spurs and learning from its own rich experience. Through the BDS campaign, in conjunction with the internal struggles of the Palestinian people, we can ensure that those who have thus far refused to acknowledge the realities are eventually pressurised into accepting that they have no option but to do so – even if only in their own ultimate interests. Whilst the ANC's 'Four Pillars' included the armed struggle, the Palestinian people themselves must determine their own strategies and the specific focus given to each, according to what they deem most appropriate to achieving their ends – ends that must bring peace and security with justice and self-determination to all concerned. I have no doubt that the BDS campaign, together with the struggle of the Palestinian people, can succeed in bringing about the necessary change in the Holy Land, demolishing the walls of Zionist exclusivity so that all can live and thrive together in peace and harmony.

As South Africans, we pledge our unqualified support for this campaign, and expect our government to do likewise, not only because we ourselves are former beneficiaries of conscientious international support but also, as our former president, Nelson Mandela stated: 'We know too well that our freedom is incomplete without the freedom of the Palestinians.'[9]

NOTES

1. 'The Anti-Apartheid Movement: A 40-year perspective', 25–6 June 1999, South Africa House, London <www.anc.org.za>.
2. John F. Kennedy's 'Address on the First Anniversary of the Alliance for Progress', White House reception for diplomatic corps of the Latin American republics, 13 March 1962. *Public Papers of the Presidents* – John F. Kennedy (1962), p. 223 <http://www.presidency.ucsb.edu/ws/>.

3. Black South Africans were compelled by apartheid law to carry pass books; identification documents permitting them to be in designated 'white areas' for the purposes of employment only. Failure to produce the necessary documentation resulted in their immediate arrest.

4. Ibid.

5. Archbishop Desmond Tutu, 'Against Israeli Apartheid', *The Nation*, 15 July 2002 <www.thenation.com>.

6. Former Prime Minister of the Democratic Republic of Vietnam Pham Van Dong, Ho Chi Minh, *Thought Will Light Our Path Forever*, Vietnam: The Gioi Publishers, 2002.

7. Statement by Albert Luthuli, jointly with Dr G.M. Naicker and Peter Brown, Appealing to the British People to Boycott South Africa, December 1959, <www.liberation.org.za>.

8. Archbishop Desmond Tutu, 'Realizing God's Dream for the Holy Land', *Boston Globe*, 26 October 2007.

9. Nelson Mandela, International Day of Solidarity with the Palestinian People, Pretoria, 4 December 1997.

3
India's Freedom Struggle and Today's BDS Movement

Prabir Purkayastha and Ayesha Kidwai

It is well-known that the hallmark of the Indian national liberation movement was its successful use of boycott and civil non-cooperation as an essential component of the long struggle. What is less known is that the overwhelming popular support for these two classes of actions was sustained and fed by more radical social reform and revolutionary movements than the Congress/Gandhi-led movement at that time. Within the wider movement, the more conservative Congress and Gandhi played significant roles, as did the Communist Party, as well as the radical Tebhaga movement and the Telangana peasants' armed struggle amongst many others. India's freedom struggle was an inclusive one, in which many different people, movements and strategies of resistance figured. Amongst these strategies was the successful and powerful use of boycott.

Boycott and non-cooperation had two important aspects. First, they were closely tied to converting the movement against British Imperial rule from merely petitioning to active resistance. Secondly, they helped in building mass movements: boycott created a space in which people from all communities and classes could come together. It was an instrument of mass mobilisation and resistance, and these tactics demarcate this phase of the movement for Indian independence from earlier periods.

Interestingly, boycott in a social context existed at the local level in Indian society as a tool for social conformism – it was imposed by informal bodies called *Panchayats* for violations of social taboos, or caste barriers. It was directed at individuals or families, and even today exists as a retrogressive instrument.

The transformation of the strategy of boycott, from a social tool of exclusion into a progressive instrument of national struggle and all-inclusive mass mobilisation, was indeed a powerful development, and one that undoubtedly played a significant role in India's liberation movement.

The lessons that the Indian, and the international Boycott, Divestment, Sanctions (BDS) campaign can draw from this aspect of Indian history are many, but most importantly, that its effectiveness and appeal will only develop if it establishes mutually sustaining links and alliances with existing political and social movements within individual countries that are participating in the BDS movement.

BOYCOTT WITHIN INDIA'S FREEDOM STRUGGLE: A BRIEF OVERVIEW

As a strategy of protest, boycott first cut its teeth in 1896, when it was used to rally those affected by the countervailing excise duties on Indian cloth. However, the transformation of what was until then primarily a mode of agitation propelled by the interests of a nascent capitalist class into the prime strategy of social and political mobilisation came about only in 1905, with the development of the *Swadeshi* (indigenous) and *Swaraj* (self-rule) movements. At the simplest level, the concept of *Swadeshi* in this early phase demanded a boycott of British goods, particularly cloth, holding that it was the patriotic duty of both consumer and capitalist alike, to exercise a choice in favour of indigenous products irrespective of cost or quality. But as the movement against the partition of Bengal, announced in July 1905, shows, the call for *Swadeshi* very quickly became an integral part of the growing demand for self-rule.

Bengal was a major province in British-ruled India and was emerging as a major centre of protest against British rule. When the plan was announced in the first week of July, the country erupted in protest:

The weekly Sanjivani in Calcutta suggested a boycott of British goods ...
The boycott idea spread as two thousand public meetings were organized
in the cities and in hundreds of villages ... Societies [were] formed ... to
promote the boycott campaign. Shops selling foreign goods were picketed
... washer-men vowed not to wash foreign cloth ... [and] the boycott
developed a four-fold program that included not using English cloth and
other products, not using English speech, resigning [from] Government
offices, and socially boycotting persons who purchase foreign articles.[1]

The young Congress Party, which had until then engaged in
only 'passive resistance', was forced by public outrage against
the brutal repression to take a more radical position than it
had thus far. In December 1905, the Congress president, Gopal
Krishna Gokhale, denounced the partition of Bengal and defined
'self-government within the empire' as the goal.

In 1909, a young lawyer named Mohandas (Mahatma) Gandhi
returned to India (after leading successful non-cooperation
struggles of the Indian community in South Africa) and into
a milieu in which the public mood, fed equally by the more
conciliatory demeanour of the main Congress movement and the
revolutionary fervour of more radical groups, was for complete
political and economic freedom (*Swaraj*). It is to Gandhi's credit
that he was able to synthesise the range of peoples' emotions
and experiences of colonial rule into a coherent and inclusive
political strategy for complete independence; nevertheless, it
is also the case that Congress came to articulate this demand
partly because of the mobilisation effected by the more radical
political movements.

By the early 1920s, the leadership of the Congress was forced
to abandon its conservatism, and to launch its first 'non-violent
non-cooperation' movement. Termed *Satyagraha* ('insistence on
truth'), the movement was formally launched as a response to
the colonial administration's attempt to extend the emergency
powers of the war years beyond 1919. In reality, however, the
movement was the result of the success of the tax boycotts that
Gandhi had led in Kheda (Gujarat) and Champaran (Bihar)
in 1918. These agitations yoked together the cause of social
reform against the evils of caste and gender oppression with

the agrarian dissent against the colonial policies of compelling impoverished farmers to grow cash crops like indigo, tobacco and cotton, instead of food.

In this first nationwide anti-colonial movement, between 1920 and 1922, millions of Indians revolted against the British by boycotting the courts, government services and schools, and disavowing titles, pensions and British clothes and goods. However, Gandhi brought the movement to an abrupt halt in 1922, fearing a slide into violence and anarchy after a mob of protestors killed some policemen in Chauri Chaura. Although this suspension was greeted with dismay by many Congress leaders, Gandhi's arrest in the same year saw the Congress retreat from the struggle almost entirely. Even though Gandhi was released in 1924, after serving only two years of his six-year term, it was not to be the Congress who claimed the leadership of the anti-colonial mood in the country for the next six years. Rather, the public was to be radicalised by the growth of the revolutionary left and its actions against British colonialism.

It was this mood of public activism that eventually impelled Congress to adopt a resolution in favour of complete independence and to launch the second phase of non-cooperation and boycott. The success of Gandhi's famed Salt *Satyagraha* in 1930, which challenged the British monopoly on the collection and manufacture of salt and the salt tax, produced a mass upsurge. Across the length and breadth of the country, British cloth and goods were boycotted. Unpopular forest and tax laws were defied by peasants and tribal communities, and even when the British responded with violent repression, *satyagrahis* met the bullets with non-violent resistance. In Peshawar, a British Indian Army regiment, the Royal Garhwal Rifles, refused to fire on the crowds. The entire platoon was subsequently arrested and many received heavy penalties, including life imprisonment.

The civil disobedience in 1930 marked the first time women became mass participants in the struggle for freedom. Thousands of women, from large cities to small villages, became active participants in *satyagrahas*, inspired equally by the charisma of the Congress leadership and the nationalist sentiments and aspirations to equality of revolutionary ideologies. Although Gandhi had asked that only men take part in the salt march, a British government report noted that 'thousands of [women] emerged ... from the seclusion of their homes ... in order to join Congress demonstrations and assist in picketing: and their presence on these occasions made the work the police was required to perform particularly unpleasant.' A major consequence of this mobilisation, in turn, was that the cause of women's emancipation and access to rights and equality had to become an important concern of the national movement.

Throughout the 1920s and 1930s, workers' and peasants' struggles and rebellions also intensified. With the Congress in retreat for most of the 1920s, the opposition to British rule was led by the Workers and Peasants Party, the Communist Party of India and militant unions like the Girni Kamgar Union (Red Flag Union) of the Bombay textile workers.

The Naval Mutiny in Bombay in 1946 and the support it received from the working class made it clear that the instrument of British rule – the armed forces – were no longer reliable. Tebhaga, Punnapra Vayalar, the Worli *adivasis* (indigenous tribal peoples) and the historic Telangana peasants' armed struggle, were some of the non-Congress movements – at variance with the landlord-industrialist leadership – that played an important role in the final push for freedom.

During the national movement, what constitutes the Indian nation was hotly contested between those who sought to define it in narrow, linguistic, ethnic, or religious terms and those who gave it a much broader inclusive content, what Jawaharlal Nehru called 'unity in diversity'.[2] Those seeking a much more inclusive definition of the nation were also the ones who were interested in building a mass anti-colonial movement. For them, economic nationalism – freedom from the economic exploitation of the colonial power, control over the national resources and markets – became the major mobilising platform. Instruments such as boycotts of British goods and British institutions lent themselves much more readily to the ideas of economic nationalism and therefore became a powerful instrument of mass mobilisation.

India's freedom struggle was an inclusive movement, that mobilised men and women, conservatives and peasants, members of the armed forces and workers; it utilised boycott strategies, strikes and mass marches alongside armed struggle. Palestine's struggle too has historically been inclusive and its strategies of resistance wide-reaching, but the BDS movement may well offer one of the first collective and inclusive strategies through which the 'solidarity' of global civil society can be turned into 'active resistance' by people the world over.

THE INDIAN NATIONAL MOVEMENT AND PALESTINE

From the beginning, the Indian national movement was connected to the larger struggles outside India and was responding to various international events. The Indian national movement articulated its anti-colonial position on Palestine as well as its solidarity towards a number of national liberation struggles taking place elsewhere. It was this position that post-independence translated into India's foreign policy – a policy of non-alignment.

The 'official' Israeli standpoint (which is also echoed by some academics) is that India did not have diplomatic relations with Israel until 1992 because it was 'guided by Cold War alignments and politics, India's fear of alienating its large Muslim population, and New Delhi's strong ties to the Arab world'.[3] What such a view negates is that the Indian national movement had seen Palestine through the prism of its own struggle for liberation. In 1938, Gandhi wrote:

> Palestine belongs to the Arabs in the same sense that England belongs to the English or France to the French. It is wrong and inhuman to impose the Jews on the Arabs. What is going on in Palestine today cannot be justified by any moral code of conduct. The mandates have no sanction but that of the last war. Surely it would be a crime against humanity to reduce the proud Arabs so that Palestine can be restored to the Jews partly or wholly as their national home.[4]

Nehru echoed virtually the same sentiment:

> Towards the end of the nineteenth century this Zionist movement took gradual shape as a colonizing movement, and many Jews went to settle in Palestine ... During the World War the British armies invaded Palestine and ... declared that it was their intention to establish a 'Jewish National Home' in Palestine ... But there was one little drawback; one not unimportant fact seems to have been overlooked. Palestine was not a wilderness, or an empty uninhabited place. It was already somebody else's home. So that this generous gesture of the British Government was really at the expense of the people who already lived in Palestine, and these people, including Arabs, non-Arabs, Muslims, Christians, and, in fact, everybody who was not a Jew, protested vigorously at the declaration.[5]

For the Indian national movement, the imposition of a Jewish homeland was creating a 'settler state' on a land which was not empty but inhabited by Palestinians. The Indian national movement also saw in the creation of Israel as a Jewish state – a state based on religious identity, a policy that it had itself rejected for India.

There is a misconception, particularly in some schools of western academia, which views the entire post-colonial history as one of only Cold War politics. For them, the history after the Second World War was not one of de-colonisation but one of competition between the US-led and USSR-led blocs, the rest being only territories for contestation. They miss the entire point that for countries under colonial rule or emerging from it, the key issue was which countries were willing to support them in the critical exercise of de-colonisation. The Non-Aligned Movement (NAM) was not preaching a negative position of not aligning with any military bloc; instead, it was defending the desire of its members to emerge as *independent* countries. The NAM had a positive agenda for creating a committee of nations free from all forms of colonial rule. The Soviet Union, by and large, supported the newly independent countries and various de-colonisation movements, whilst the US was, in general, working with the historic colonial powers. The NAM saw the struggle of the Palestinians for a homeland as a genuine struggle against colonialism, as did the major Indian political forces. This was doubly reinforced after 1967, when all of the West Bank and Gaza Strip came under full Israeli military occupation. This was the continuity of policy in the Indian mainstream, not merely as foreign policy but also as a belief rooted in its views on colonialism which were based on its own history and experience.

The Indian policy towards Palestine underwent a radical shift in the 1990s. This was the period that India's Congress gave up economic nationalism which had been what defined the Indian national movement and its own past. It is this transition from self-reliance to integration with the global economic order – the neo-liberal economists' globalisation paradigm – that breathed new life into the concept of a nation based on religion. Once the concept of the sovereign national space, in which the state controls the resources and redistributes them based on a national agenda, is given up in favour of corporate-led globalisation, the nation then falls back on other forms of national identity, such as race, ethnicity, or religion.

The 1992 shift in Indo-Israeli relations was therefore not just a shift in policies towards Israel. It was a far deeper shift in how India would see itself in the future. Henceforth, the relationship with the US would be a major driving factor, Israel becoming a part of this overall matrix.

THE INDO-ISRAELI ARMS TRADE

In the aftermath of the Cold War, Israel was plagued by a shrinkage in its arms trade and export that forced it to become extremely proactive in seeking clients to sustain the industry. The establishment of Indo-Israel diplomatic relations in 1992 was of huge strategic significance for the Israeli Political-Military-Industrial complex, as it energised the overall performance of Israel's defence industry, making it one of the top five exporters of military hardware globally. According to Israel Defence Ministry reports, India currently accounts for more than 50 per cent of Israel's military exports. Israel overtook Russia as India's number one arms supplier in 2008. India has bought weapons from Israel that amount to over $8 billion since 1999 and is now Israel's biggest customer, buying more military and intelligence equipment from the industry than even Israel's own armed forces.

The growing influence of Israel through its defence contractors and commission agents are a long-term threat to India. The Israeli defence deals are mired in corruption, as documented both in India and in Israel. Even after public knowledge that 6–9 per cent commissions are being paid by the Israeli companies in violation of Indian laws, no steps have been taken by the Indian defence establishment to ban such companies. The penetration of India's government by Israeli agencies – paid for by Indian tax-payers' money through such defence contracts – obviously distorts India's foreign policy and hurts its national interests.

While India still provides lip service to the Palestinian cause, it has clearly changed its standing in the world from a position of solidarity with the colonised, to a friend of the coloniser. These facts undoubtedly present obstacles, at least at governmental level, for an official Indian position in support of BDS. A position akin to what India had during the heyday of the NAM where the Indian government actively pursued a policy of boycott and sanctions on South Africa and Israel is no longer likely. The Indian movements must therefore move into what is uncharted territory for them – a call for a boycott by the people themselves, of Israeli institutions and goods, and action to force the government to take action against Israel.

Here, the very structure of BDS as a 'bottom-up' movement dictates that it is the people who must fight the early battles in establishing and developing the campaign of boycott, and by this, put pressure on their governments. The nascent Indian BDS movement must tap into the historic grass-roots belief in, and practice of, boycott as a tool of struggle. It must relate the current boycott struggle to the history of support for the Anti-Apartheid struggle in South Africa. The Indian BDS movement therefore needs to relate the current BDS campaign to both the national as well as the international. If such a movement can be built with large mobilised support, the Indo-Israel arms trade represents a real and very strategic target. Any success on this front would significantly affect Israel economically and subsequently have a tangible knock-on effect in terms of Israel's ability to endlessly develop its own apartheid regime and continue its crimes against the Palestinian people.

THE BDS MOVEMENT IN INDIA

For now, the BDS movement in India remains in a fledgling form. Though a number of calls have been made by political parties and other organisations to break the arms deals with Israel as long as it continues its illegal occupation of Palestine, relatively little has taken place to date in terms of actual boycott action. Meanwhile, growing cooperation is visible between Indian big business and Israeli big business on a range of products and services.

The major political opposition to military and intelligence ties in India have come from the left. The Communist Party of India (CPI) and the Marxist Communist Party of India (CPI-M), India's two major leftist parties have led opposition to the military ties and the corruption in defence deals. An international conference entitled 'War, Imperialism and Resistance: West Asia' was organised in March 2007 by Indian civil society and backed by leftist parties, that included a Palestinian delegation. The conference passed a motion supporting the Palestinian BDS call: 'This Conference calls for boycott, disinvestments and sanctions on Israel as long as it continues its occupation of Palestinian and Arab territories.'

This was followed by the All India Peace and Solidarity Organisation (AIPSO) and the Committee for Independent Foreign Policy organising a convention on Palestine in May 2008. Key political and civil society figures participated in the convention, which launched a petition that called for the severing of Indo-Israeli military ties. The petition, when submitted to the Indian government, contained one million signatures.

Amidst a global grass-roots outcry against Israel during 'Operation Cast Lead' and its massacres in Gaza, a number of demonstrations were held in major cities and towns condemning Israel's atrocities and brutal attacks on Palestine's civilian population.

In June 2010, as a further protest against Israel's siege on the Gaza Strip, principled trade-union activism saw Indian dockworkers in the southern city of Cochin refuse to unload Israeli cargo and hold demonstrations near the office of Zim Integrated Shipping Services (India) Pvt. Ltd – the Israeli shipping line. This protest action was part of a global movement that saw similar actions held by dockworkers in South Africa, Sweden, Norway, Malaysia and the US, in the wake of the Israeli attacks on the Freedom Flotilla to Gaza.

This growing awareness of BDS began to take a more organised structure following the acceptance by renowned Indian writer Amitav Ghost of the David Dan Prize. In the presence of Israeli Prime Minister Shimon Peres, Ghost and Margaret Atwood jointly received the 2010 award at Tel Aviv University, despite international calls for them to boycott the prize. One of these calls was issued by a group of more than a hundred leading cultural and academic figures who subsequently officially formed ICACBI – the Indian Campaign for the Academic and Cultural Boycott of Israel. The establishment of ICACBI signalled the beginnings of the first organised BDS movement in India; together with the Committee for Solidarity with Palestine, the All India Peace and Solidarity Organisation, and the Palestine-based BNC (Boycott National Committee) alongside many other supporting organisations, a national conference was collectively organised in New Delhi in September 2010 entitled 'A Just Peace in Palestine'. The conference affirmed that 'the world must declare that Israel is an apartheid state. It must call for a global boycott and sanctions on Israel as long as it continues its illegal occupation of Palestine and its apartheid policies', and concluded with a statement that called for 'the Indian government to end its military ties with Israel and return to its earlier commitment to the cause of the Palestinian people'.

Although calls for boycott have now been made by various Indian organisations and there have been pressures brought within the Indian Parliament to break military ties with Israel, this has not yet resulted in a broad-based movement for boycott. The major reason for this is that the Palestine issue is not seen as one in which Indian people can play an effective role nor do they see it as an immediate issue for themselves. Here, there is a need to link the question of Israel's illegal occupation of Palestine to India's current foreign policy and also its own internal policy, along with its own colonial history. It is important to integrate the BDS movement into larger concerns that the Indian movements have regarding the secular character of the Indian state, India's alignment with the US as a subordinate ally, and the larger neo-liberal agenda which manifests itself in open plunder of the country's resources. While corruption has become a big issue in India currently, the corruption in defence deals and its links to Israel have yet to become the focus of real attention.

The BDS campaign in India therefore faces the task of aligning the international dimension of the movement with its national goals and struggles. It is this integration that gave the Indian national movement its international character. This is what we need to restore today – instead of considering Palestine as extrinsic, we must see it as integral to the Indian movements' task of fighting neo-liberalism at home, and the wider internationalist struggle against imperialist globalisation. The anti-colonial links between India's liberation movement and Palestine's struggle were, as we have seen, widely articulated during India's long battle for freedom, and also later within the post-colonial period. The current development of India's neo-liberal policies, which were intrinsic in the dramatic about-turn of India's foreign policy position on Palestine, have led India to look towards current imperial powers. This goes against everything that India struggled for, and for which so many Indians died. It is therefore the responsibility of the Indian people to once again build a boycott movement, as it did within its own liberation movement, to support the just struggle of Palestinians against colonial occupation.

NOTES

1. Sanderson Beck, *South Asia 1800–1950*, World Peace Communications (2008).
2. Irfan Habib, 'The nation that is India', *The Little Magazine*, III(2) <http://www.littlemag.com/faith/irfanhabib.html>.
3. D. Ronak Desai and Xenia Dormandy, 'Indo-Israeli Relations: Key Security Implications' Policy Briefing, Harvard University, 10 July 2008 <http://live.belfercenter.org/publication/18414/indoisraeli_relations.html?breadcrumb=%2Fexperts%2F1631%2Frona k_d_desai>.
4. Editorial in the newspaper *Harijan*, 26 November 1938.
5. Jawaharlal Nehru, *Glimpses of World History, 1934*, Oxford: Oxford University Press, 1985.

4

The US Civil Rights and Black Liberation Movement: Lessons and Applications for the Palestinian Liberation Movement

Kali Akuno

The Palestinian Boycott, Divestment and Sanctions, or BDS, movement, launched by Palestinian civil society to advance the cause of Palestinian self-determination following the various setbacks to the Palestinian liberation movement stemming from the Oslo Accords, is rapidly growing into a powerful international political force. As the movement continues to grow and expand, it is bound to encounter more and greater obstacles. To counter this, it can be valuable to study other people's movements that have employed BDS strategies and tactics on an extensive level and how they organised themselves to overcome or manoeuvre around the roadblocks on their path. One such movement is the Black Liberation Movement (BLM) in North America in its many phases. The BLM has employed BDS strategies and tactics extensively for the greater part of the last 200-plus years in its unfinished quest for true liberation.

The BLM has employed a broad range of strategies and tactics over the five hundred long years of its existence, including mass rebellions, emigration, work stoppages, mass strikes, armed struggle and international diplomacy.[1] Some of the most dynamic of the liberation strategies and tactics employed have centralised the comprehensive utilisation of boycotts, divestment initiatives and sanctions, commonly known as BDS. The most dynamic element of these BDS initiatives is that when they have been successful they have been able to engage masses of people and harness limited individual capacities and transform them, via collective activities, into powerful social and political weapons.[2]

They have often been able to accomplish this in creative ways that have reduced individual risk and minimised direct conflict with brutal and vastly more powerful enemies such as the Ku Klux Klan, the White Citizens Councils, the Southern Planter Elite, and the United States government.

It can be soundly argued that the employment of BDS strategies and tactics within the BLM have their roots in antebellum or pre-Civil War initiatives to end chattel slavery and secure basic human dignities. One of the earliest recorded successes of a combined boycott and divestment initiative was the protest of the Black Community in Philadelphia, Pennsylvania in 1787 led by Richard Allan and Absolom Jones against the racist practices and policies of the Methodist Episcopal Church. This initiative led to the creation of the order of the African Methodist Episcopal Church in 1816, which became a cornerstone in the institutional development of the Black Community in the United States.[3] Another exemplary model from the antebellum period is drawn from the Abolitionist movement (under black and white leadership on both sides of the Atlantic), which organised a boycott in the early 1790s of the strategic goods of the triangular trade such as sugar, rum, tobacco, cotton, coffee, and dyes that built the empirical economies of the Atlantic Ocean and laid the foundation for the capitalist world system. These boycotts played a major role in ending the transatlantic slave trade in the United States and the United Kingdom by 1808.[4]

BDS tactics within the BLM grew in considerable scope and application after the Civil War. As African-descendant people in the US have had very little access to capital until relatively recently, and even less substantive political power until the 1970s, boycotts, rather than divestment and sanctions, have been the primary weapon in the BDS arsenal employed by the BLM. Between the 1860s and the 1940s, a broad range of successful boycotts were organised by BLM forces that challenged the system of white supremacy and the institutions of oppression, including government and private pension programmes that excluded or exploited freed slaves and their descendants, lending agencies that exploited black farmers, discriminatory transport systems and laws established at the turn of the twentieth century, and businesses that refused to hire or serve black people such as the 'Don't Buy Where You Can't Work Campaign' led by Belford Lawson, Jr.[5]

Furthermore, the discriminatory policies of the US armed forces and their engagement in imperial conquest made them a target, alongside the US government directly via the original March on Washington Movement (MOWM), which was led by A. Philip Randolph against racial oppression and discriminatory hiring and contracting practices. Randolph's experience in union and grass-roots organising led to the creation of the MOWM in the 1940s. Whilst black soldiers were being encouraged to fight against Nazi fascism, they still faced segregation and institutional racism within the US military – a system that was happy to send young black men to die without valuing them whilst alive with even a semblance of equality. Randolph understood the need for independence from the inherently racist systems of white institutional power within the movement when he famously said 'If it costs money to finance a march on Washington, let Negroes pay for it. If any sacrifices are made for Negro rights in national defense, let Negroes make them … .' When Randolph's delegation met President Roosevelt and other officials in 1940 to present a memorandum demanding equality within the armed forces, the White House responded with a statement that included the following clarification of policy: 'the policy of the War Department is not to intermingle colored and white enlisted personnel in the same regimental organizations.' In the final days before the march, Roosevelt finally buckled to pressure and announced Executive Order 8802, which was the first federal action to promote equality and prohibit employment discrimination in the United States.[6]

The 1950s witnessed the maturation of the BLM's employment of boycott strategies. The Montgomery, Alabama Bus Boycott of 1955–56, generally considered one of the three primary catalysing moments of the high tide of struggle mounted by the BLM between the 1950s and the 1970s (the other two being the *Brown* v. *Board of Education* school desegregation decision and the murder of 14-year-old Emmett Till), dealt a critical blow to the legally sanctioned policies and practices of institutional racism. Although the Montgomery Bus Boycott is generally portrayed as being the product of a spontaneous act and for canonising the heroic actions and leadership of Rosa Parks and Martin Luther King, Jr., it was in all reality a deliberate and well-thought-out campaign based on years of preparation and planning. Montgomery was not the first boycott of its kind. Similar boycotts were organised in Mississippi, such as the one led by T.R.M. Howard in 1952–53 against the lack of restroom facilities for blacks on commuter buses, and the Baton Rouge, Louisiana Bus Boycott of 1953 led by Willis Reed and the Revd T.J. Jemison.[7] These earlier boycotts, and the wider people's movement, are the roots from which the Montgomery Bus Boycott grew. When Rosa Parks was arrested in December 1955 for refusing to give up her seat on a public bus to a white passenger, a widespread boycott was launched against the Montgomery public transport system. The boycott caused extensive financial damage to the Montgomery public transport system as its principle customers were blacks who were also the principle boycotters. The effectiveness of these boycotts, begun in earlier years but culminating with Montgomery, created intense pressure that led to a December 1956 United States Supreme Court decision that declared Montgomery and Alabama's transport segregation laws to be unconstitutional.

As previously noted, divestment strategies were not as widely employed in the BLM prior to the 1960s. But, when they *were* employed they tended to serve as catalysts for black institutional development. Most of the documented mass divestment initiatives employed within the BLM involved the removal of wealth, deeds and insurance policies from financial institutions and insurance companies that brazenly supported the oppressive policies and practices of American apartheid. The most successful of these divestment initiatives led to the establishment of independent black institutions such as banks, insurance companies and mutual aid societies, particularly before the Great Depression of the 1930s which liquidated most of the wealth amassed by black people after the Civil War. Two of the most successful divestment initiatives that translated into black independent institutions occurred in Natchez, Mississippi and New Orleans, Louisiana, where people of African descent acted en masse by taking their meagre savings from discriminatory institutions that denied them equal services in areas including loans, medical assistance and burial funds, and pooling them together to create independent mutual aid societies and banks. Initiatives such as this were employed after the Great Depression, more often to support a boycott initiative, but they tended to be quite short-lived and limited in their impact, as a result of capital restructuring after the Second World War and the creation of various welfare state institutions that provided essential social services.[8]

In the 1960s, the utilisation of boycotts and divestment initiatives became less prominent in the overall orientation of the BLM, primarily as a result of the successes of bringing down the legalised dimensions of American apartheid and the attainment of more political power and social influence in the United States as a direct result of the achievements of the mass resistance mounted by the movement. Sanctions however, began to grow in both utilisation and importance from the mid-1960s onwards. The sanctions typically employed by the BLM concentrated on exerting intense political and economic pressure on government institutions and corporate enterprises to force them to comply with various demands, such as access to jobs, educational opportunities, community investment and decent housing. A few of the more successful sanction initiatives of this period targeted the automotive industry, colleges and universities, and state social welfare agencies over hiring, safety, access and quality administrative issues.

One of the most memorable and celebrated BDS initiatives employed by the BLM was an international initiative in support of the Anti-Apartheid Movement of South Africa. The BLM and the South African liberation movement share a long and deep history of solidarity and strategic collaboration going back to the late 1800s. From the 1920s onwards, through the efforts of activists like Max Yergan and A.B. Xuma, the BLM and the South African liberation movement not only appealed to each other for inspiration and solidarity, but consistently shared strategies and tactics to aid their respective struggles. How to apply BDS strategies and tactics, particularly after the success of the Indian liberation movement – which the BLM and South African liberation movements both stood in active solidarity with – and that of the Montgomery Bus Boycott, became a common feature of their exchanges. Upon the founding of the international Anti-Apartheid struggle by activists from the African National Congress (ANC) in London in 1959, BLM activists and organisers were some of the first international supporters to take up the call and organise solidarity initiatives throughout the United States. These initiatives began to gain critical mass in the 1970s through the initiatives of formations like the African Liberation Support Committee (ALSC) and the Trans-Africa Forum. They played a major role in weakening the Apartheid regime economically and isolating it politically by persuading North American cultural workers (artists, academics and athletes) to honour the boycott call, forcing several major US corporations to divest from the South African economy, and by forming a solid political bloc in the US Congress around the Congressional Black Caucus (CBC) that pressed the US government to enforce international sanctions against the regime. This long history of solidarity played a critical role in the collapse of the Apartheid regime, and the subsequent transition to majority democratic rule in 1994.[9]

The BLM was not playing favourites in its international support of the South African liberation movement. It also employed BDS strategies and tactics in support of numerous national and social liberation movements in Africa – most notably those of Angola, Mozambique, Guinea-Bissau, Zimbabwe and Congo/Zaire – where it called on the US government and the North Atlantic Treaty Alliance (NATO) to stop arming and supporting the colonial empire of Portugal and the white settler regime in Zimbabwe (then Rhodesia), and for US government sanctions and multinational corporations to divest from the reactionary Mobutu regime in Zaire after the assassination of Patrice Lumumba.[10]

What the history of the BLM's employment of BDS strategies and tactics illustrates is that they can clearly be successful in advancing and attaining some of the critical objectives of a people's liberation movement. However, as the uncompleted struggle for black liberation in North America testifies, they, like all strategies and tactics, have their limitations. Where BDS strategies and tactics have tended to be most successful in the history of the BLM has been when mass self-reliant resistance was employed to confront a target that was either dependent on black labour or economic patronage, typically the utilisation of a service like transportation or the consumption of a product, or when boycott and divestment campaigns led to the establishment of black autonomous or independent institutions. Another critical factor in the success, or failure, of BDS tactics in the service of the BLM was the degree to which they shamed the US government in the context of the Cold War, or constrained the US government's operations in the Third World.[11]

However, it should be noted that while pan-Africanism and the eliciting of international solidarity have been central to the BLM since the era of slave rebellions, maroon societies and the Abolitionist movement, and was extensively mobilised in the 1880s–1900s, the 1920s–40s, and again in the 1960s–80s, the BDS initiatives of the BLM tended to be insular or self-reliant mobilisations that self-consciously depended on the strength of the black masses themselves.[12]

These historical and contextual lessons from the BLM are critical for the Palestinian BDS movement to internalise and incorporate if and where it sees them to be applicable. As the Palestinian BDS movement is currently modelled more on the example of the Anti-Apartheid Movement than the BLM (or the Indian) example, it possess some of the limitations of that particular movement, particularly the reliance on Palestinian exiles and descendants in the diaspora for leadership, and on non-Palestinians throughout the world for support and patronage. Exiles or their descendants in the diaspora can sometimes be out of touch with realities on the ground in their homelands, and non-Palestinians who engage the movement in various capacities sometimes cannot clearly appreciate the necessity of Palestinian self-determination for determining the course of the struggle. Thus, carefully considered direction and education from within Palestine is essential to lead the international movement. The balance of forces in the world must also be taken into strategic consideration. The lack of a critical mass of progressive nation states, as existed in the 1960s and '70s for instance, limits the threat of sanctions, and the general weakness of progressive social movements the world over (even with the powerful inspiration of the so-called 'Arab Spring') could possibly set some constraints regarding both reach and depth on the employment of boycott and divestment initiatives.

The primary limitation regarding the utilisation of a more BLM-oriented model pivots on the role of Palestinian labour in the interrelated and interdependent political economies of Palestine and the Zionist nation state. The Palestinian economy, namely that of Gaza and the West Bank, is severely constricted by what is in effect an Israeli and US-led embargo (which in the case of Gaza is actually a full-on military blockade), while Palestinian workers are rapidly joining the ranks of the world's excluded, dispossessed and disposable populations due to the embargo and wholesale replacement in the Israeli economy by super-exploitable migrant workers imported from South East Asia and Africa. Prior to the First Intifada, the Israeli economy was largely dependent on Palestinian labour. Israeli capital, in unison with the Israeli state, took deliberate steps after the First Intifada to make sure that Palestinian labour could never critically disrupt the economy again, hence their replacement. Palestinian labour's limited ability to disrupt the Israeli economy means that it is limited in its ability to employ many of the successful BDS methods employed by the BLM in the twentieth century.

However, as the example of the BLM illustrates, none of these challenges are insurmountable. The Palestinian liberation movement and its allies can and should learn a great deal from the BDS movements employed by the black, South African and Indian liberation movements amongst others, but, take heed that none of them can be copied whole cloth. In the final analysis, the Palestinian BDS movement needs, as it already has done in many ways, to blaze its own course to address the Palestine-specific conditions of the present era and those of the future. Those of us committed to the cause of Palestinian and human liberation, and who see the BDS movement as an essential tool to attain it, would do well to take stock of the lessons that can be gained from critically examining a protracted struggle like the BLM's alongside other relevant liberation movements and rights-based struggles. The day of justice will come, but we must prepare and organise ourselves effectively for the long march down freedom's road.

NOTES

1. Peter M. Bergman and Mort N. Bergman, *The Chronological History of the Negro in America*, New York: Harper and Row, 1969.
2. August Meier and Elliot Rudwick, 'Black Boycotts before Montgomery', *Ebony Magazine*, 1969 <http://books.google. com/booksid=09oDAAAAMBAJ&pg=PA154&lpg=PA154& dq=boycotts+before&source=bl&ots=8ovB72dlY9&sig=Xf YbDul8Lre4tHax_ZOmztjAu38&hl=en&ei=krI8Tu76K4bL gQfS9_DtBw&sa=X&oi=book_result&ct=result&resnum=1 &sqi=2&ved=0CBkQ6AEwAA#v=onepage&q=boycotts%20 before&f=false>.
3. John H. Bracey, Jr, August Meier and Elliott Rudwick (eds), *Black Nationalism in America*, Indianapolis, IN: Bobbs-Merrill, 1970.
4. Bergman and Bergman, *Chronological History of the Negro in America*, and Robin Blackburn, *The American Crucible: Slavery, Emancipation and Human Rights*, Verso Books, 2011.
5. Meier and Rudwick, 'Black Boycotts before Montgomery', *Ebony Magazine*, 1969, and Debbie Elliot, 'The First Civil Rights Bus Boycott: 50 years ago, Baton Rogue Jim Crow Protest Made History', National Public Radio, 19 June 2003 <http://www.npr. org/templates/story/story.php?storyId=1304163>.
6. August Meier, Elliot Rudwick and Francis L. Broderick (eds), *Black Protest Thought in the Twentieth Century*, New York: Macmillan, 1971, and Herbert Garfinkel, *When Negroes March: The March on Washington Movement in the organizational politics of the FEPC*, New York: Atheneum, 1969.
7. Elliot, 'The First Civil Rights Bus Boycott'.
8. Juliet E.K. Walker, *The History of Black Business in America: Capitalism, Race, Entrepreneurship*, Volume 1, 'To 1865', Chapel Hill: University of North Carolina Press, 2009; Meier, Rudwick and Broderick (eds), *Black Protest Thought in the*

Twentieth Century, and Bracey Jr, Meier and Rudwick (eds), *Black Nationalism in America*.

9. William Minter, Gail Hovey and Charles Cobb, Jr (eds), *No Easy Victories: African Liberation and American Activists over a Half Century, 1950–2000*, Trenton, NJ: Africa World Press, 2007, and Penny M. Von Eschen, *Race against Empire: Black Americans and Anti-Colonialism, 1937–1957*, Ithaca, NY: Cornell University Press, 1997; James H. Meriwether, *Proudly We Can Be Africans: Black Americans and Africa, 1935–1961*, Chapel Hill: University of North Carolina Press, 2002.

10. Minter, Hovey and Cobb, Jr (eds), *No Easy Victories*.

11. Von Eschen, *Race against Empire*; Carol Anderson, *Eyes Off the Prize: The United Nations and the African American Struggle for Human Rights, 1944–1955*, New York: Cambridge University Press, 2003; P. Henry (ed.), *Foreign Policy and the Black (Inter) National Interest*, Albany: State University of New York Press, 2000; Thomas Borstelmann, *The Cold War and the Color Line: American Race Relations in the Global Arena*, Cambridge, MA: Harvard University Press, 2001, and Mary L. Dudziak, *Cold War Civil Rights: Race and the Image of American Democracy*, Princeton, NJ: Princeton University Press, 2000.

12. Elliott P. Skinner, *African Americans and US Policy Toward Africa, 1850–1924: In Defense of Black Nationality*, Washington, DC: Howard University Press, 1992, and Henry (ed.), *Foreign Policy and the Black (Inter)National Interest*.

Part II
The Palestinian Call for BDS

5

The 2005 Palestinian Call for Boycott, Divestment and Sanctions – Official Text of the BDS Call

PALESTINIAN CIVIL SOCIETY CALLS FOR BOYCOTT,
DIVESTMENT AND SANCTIONS AGAINST ISRAEL
UNTIL IT COMPLIES WITH INTERNATIONAL LAW
AND UNIVERSAL PRINCIPLES OF HUMAN RIGHTS

9 July 2005

One year after the historic Advisory Opinion of the International Court of Justice (ICJ) which found Israel's Wall built on occupied Palestinian territory to be illegal; Israel continues its construction of the colonial Wall with total disregard to the Court's decision. Thirty eight years into Israel's occupation of the Palestinian West Bank (including East Jerusalem), Gaza Strip and the Syrian Golan Heights, Israel continues to expand Jewish colonies. It has unilaterally annexed occupied East Jerusalem and the Golan Heights and is now de facto annexing large parts of the West Bank by means of the Wall. Israel is also preparing – in the shadow of its planned redeployment from the Gaza Strip – to build and expand colonies in the West Bank. Fifty seven years after the state of Israel was built mainly on land ethnically cleansed of its Palestinian owners, a majority of Palestinians are refugees, most of whom are stateless. Moreover, Israel's entrenched system of racial discrimination against its own Arab-Palestinian citizens remains intact.

In light of Israel's persistent violations of international law; and

Given that, since 1948, hundreds of UN resolutions have condemned Israel's colonial and discriminatory policies as illegal and called for immediate, adequate and effective remedies; and

Given that all forms of international intervention and peace-making have until now failed to convince or force Israel to comply with humanitarian law, to respect fundamental human rights and to end its occupation and oppression of the people of Palestine; and

In view of the fact that people of conscience in the international community have historically shouldered the moral responsibility to fight injustice, as exemplified in the struggle to abolish apartheid in South Africa through diverse forms of boycott, divestment and sanctions; and

Inspired by the struggle of South Africans against apartheid and in the spirit of international solidarity, moral consistency and resistance to injustice and oppression;

We, representatives of Palestinian civil society, call upon international civil society organizations and people of conscience all over the world to impose broad boycotts and implement divestment initiatives against Israel similar to those applied to South Africa in the apartheid era. We appeal to you to pressure your respective states to impose embargoes and sanctions against Israel. We also invite conscientious Israelis to support this Call, for the sake of justice and genuine peace.

These non-violent punitive measures should be maintained until Israel meets its obligation to recognize the Palestinian people's inalienable right to self-determination and fully complies with the precepts of international law by:

Ending its occupation and colonization of all Arab lands and dismantling the Wall;

Recognizing the fundamental rights of the Arab-Palestinian citizens of Israel to full equality;

Respecting, protecting and promoting the rights of Palestinian refugees to return to their homes and properties as stipulated in UN resolution 194.

Endorsed by:
This call was endorsed by more than 170 Palestinian civil society organisations and institutions representing the three integral parts of the people of Palestine: Palestinian refugees, Palestinians under occupation and Palestinian citizens of Israel.

6

Why Palestinians Called for BDS

Raji Sourani

Injustice anywhere is a threat to justice everywhere
Martin Luther King, 1963

WHAT IS BDS?

The Boycott, Divestment, Sanctions (BDS) movement is rooted in the decades-old struggle for self-determination, the rule of law, and accountability. It is a mechanism used by individuals when their States fail them. It is a clear example of civil society acting as the conscience of the world, and standing up for human rights when those in power refuse to do so. BDS is a tool used, not to punish, but to promote compliance with human rights standards and the requirements of international law. It sends a clear message that violations of human rights are unacceptable, and that we, as concerned citizens of the world, will not reward those who are complicit in their perpetration.

It is essential that we never lose sight of BDS's true purpose. BDS is not an end, in and of itself. It is a powerful tool utilised by civil society to ensure that systematic violations of human rights end; to bring about a change in the overall system. This big picture is the key. Whether BDS be directed towards the end of apartheid in South Africa, of military rule in Burma, or of Israeli occupation, we must never allow ourselves to be sidetracked; the overall goal must always remain in focus, both to inspire and as a reference to guide our actions. Equally, BDS must always remain grounded in international law; this must be its marker and guideline. BDS is not an exclusively political tool, or an exclusively moral judgement, it is a clear response to violations of international law, and it is this which provides its legitimacy.

THE SITUATION IN PALESTINE

Israel's long-standing belligerent occupation of Palestinian territory has been characterised by two interconnected realities: systematic violations of international law, and total impunity for these illegal acts. The result has been the victimisation and suffering of the Palestinian civilian population, the so-called 'protected persons' of international humanitarian law.

The Israel–Palestine conflict is perhaps one of the most documented conflicts in the world. Dedicated and professional lawyers and fieldworkers – such as those at the Palestinian Centre for Human Rights – systematically document all violations of international law. Thousands upon thousands of cases have been prepared, with all necessary evidence and facts. United Nations resolutions, including those of the Security Council, have repeatedly called for an end to illegal activity, as well as Israel's withdrawal to its 1967 borders. The world's media frequently holds a magnifying glass to the occupation; during Israel's 27 December 2008–18 January 2009 offensive ('Operation Cast Lead') on the Gaza Strip, war crimes were broadcast live on television stations throughout the world. Few who saw it can forget the sight of white phosphorus raining down on Gaza City. The international press regularly report on the continued construction of illegal Israeli settlements, while in 2004 the International Court of Justice – the most important court in the world – ruled on the illegality of the Wall.

No one can claim that they do not know what is happening in occupied Palestine. However, the international community of States has turned a blind eye. Despite all States' legal obligation – *inter alia,* as High Contracting Parties to the Geneva Conventions of 1949 – to ensure respect for the law in all circumstances, and to search for and prosecute those suspected of committing grave breaches of the Conventions, nothing has been done. The clear demand for accountability has been met with stony silence, or at best, bland statements referring to unsustainable conditions, or actions non-conducive to peace. Simply put, Israel has been allowed to violate international law – and thus to undermine the international legal system – with complete, and pervasive, impunity. Not once has the State of Israel, or any individual Israeli suspected of committing war crimes, been held to account in accordance with the clear requirements of international law.

This impunity granted by the international community has resulted in continuing, and indeed, escalating, violations of international law. It is innocent civilians who have paid the price for States' inaction, double standards, and lack of political will.

THE PURPOSE OF SANCTIONS

Basically, sanctions are used as a means of ensuring respect for international law. They are a clear public statement that illegal behaviour is unacceptable, and that normal relations are impossible until this illegality is ended. The intent is to challenge the impunity enjoyed by perpetrators, and to ensure some form of accountability with respect to systematic violations of human rights. In this sense, sanctions have long been recognised, and utilised, as a means of securing respect for international law; as evidenced, for example, by numerous resolutions of the United Nations Security Council.

Again, it must be emphasised that the legitimacy of sanctions is dependent upon international law; they must be enacted on the basis of legal analysis and within strict guidelines to ensure that no abuse – whether intentional or unintentional – occurs.

THE OBLIGATION TO ENSURE RESPECT FOR INTERNATIONAL LAW

States' obligation to ensure respect for international law may be illustrated by reference to the four Geneva Conventions of 1949. However, it is noted that this obligation forms part of public international law more broadly, as evidenced, for example, by the rules on the Responsibility of States for Internationally Wrongful Acts.

Common Article 1 to the four Geneva Conventions of 1949 is one of the most significant components of international humanitarian law. Its position at the head of each of the four Geneva Conventions signifies its importance and, significantly, there have been no reservations or declarations made with respect to this Article. The Article itself holds that 'The High Contracting Parties undertake to respect and to ensure respect for the present Convention in all circumstances.'

The official ICRC *Commentary* notes that the inclusion of the phrase 'to ensure respect for' is deliberate, and is intended to emphasise the responsibility of the Contracting Parties. Therefore

> ... in the event of a Power failing to fulfil its obligations, the other Contracting Parties (neutral, allied or enemy) may, and should, endeavour to bring it back to an attitude of respect for the Convention. The proper working of the system of protection provided by the Convention demands in fact that the Contracting Parties should not be content merely to apply its provisions themselves, but should do everything in their power to ensure that the humanitarian principles underlying the Conventions are applied universally.

Importantly, ensuring respect for the Convention is not merely a right but also an obligation; Article 1 has been 'deliberately invested with imperative force'.

The Geneva Conventions now form part of customary international law. In confirming this status in *Nicaragua*, the International Court of Justice stressed the obligation inherent in Article 1:

> The Court considers that there is an obligation on the United States Government, in the terms of Article 1 of the Geneva conventions, to 'respect' the Conventions and even 'to ensure respect' for them 'in all circumstances', since such an obligation does not derive only from the Conventions themselves, but from the general principles of humanitarian law to which the Conventions merely give specific expression.

As confirmed by both the UN Security Council, and General Assembly, this obligation extends to third States, including those not directly involved in the conflict. As made explicit in the *Commentary*, 'no Contracting Party can offer any valid pretext, legal or otherwise, for not respecting the Convention in its entirety.'

RESORTING TO ENFORCEMENT MEASURES

Resorting to measures aimed at ensuring respect for the Fourth Geneva Convention is specifically envisioned in Article 1; 'Contracting Parties … should do everything in their power to ensure that the humanitarian principles in the Conventions are applied universally.' However, the duty to resort to such measures also emerges more broadly from international law. The International Law Commission (ILC) has recognised that 'some wrongful acts engage the responsibility of the State concerned … towards the international community as a whole.'

This was confirmed by the International Court of Justice in *Barcelona Traction*, where the court held that, with respect to *erga omnes* obligations, 'all States can be held to have a legal interest in their protection.' The *erga omnes* status of the Fourth Geneva Convention is evidenced *inter alia* by its universal ratification.

Article 41(1) of the ILC Articles on Responsibility of States for Internationally Wrongful Acts requires that 'States shall cooperate to bring to an end through lawful means any serious breach within the meaning of article 40.'

Consequently, States are under a 'positive duty to cooperate in order to bring to an end serious breaches', such as violations of customary international law and the Fourth Geneva Convention. The ILC emphasises that 'the obligation to cooperate applies to States whether or not they are individually affected by the serious breach.'

It is therefore evident, both from Article 1 of the Fourth Geneva Convention and international law more generally, that High Contracting Parties are under an obligation to take specific and effective measures aimed at ensuring respect for the Fourth Geneva Convention.

THE INITIAL CALL FOR BDS

The consistent failure on the part of the international community of States – in the face of overwhelming evidence demanding legal action – coupled with the requirement that States ensure respect for international law, resulted in Palestinian civil society's call for BDS. The demand first emerged in the context of the World Conference against Racism, held in Durban in 2001. At the conference, international civil society equated Israel's illegal policies of occupation with racism and apartheid, and called on the international community to sanction Israel with the intention of bringing about an end to these illegal practices, and ensuring compliance with international law. This move was inspired by the South African struggle against apartheid, and the recognition that BDS formed a component in the overthrow of the Apartheid regime. The call coincided with efforts intended to urge the European Union to activate Article 2 of the EU-Israel Association Agreement – the human rights clause – in order to suspend its privileged treatment of Israel.

Ultimately, however, the World Conference against Racism was overshadowed by the tragic events of 11 September 2001. In the disarray and the changed environment following this attack, all initial momentum was lost, and it took a number of years before BDS once more emerged as a topic of action and debate.

THE AFTERMATH OF DURBAN

The ten years since Durban provide an important time for reflection and analysis. What has happened to Palestinian and international civil society's call for sanctions, and what has been the impact on Israel's policies and practices?

In short, we are living through the worst period in the history of the occupation. As human rights organisations, we agitate for food, water, education, medicine and concrete. Broader, underlying issues, such as self-determination and an end to the occupation, have been overtaken by the pressing necessity of daily realities.

The Gaza Strip, East Jerusalem, and the rest of the West Bank have been cut off from each other – isolated, fragmented and disconnected. Palestinian civilians are denied access to family, friends, education and employment. Settlement activities continue to flourish to the extent that East Jerusalem is virtually isolated, while the rest of the West Bank has been broken down into a series of disjointed Bantustans encircled by settlements which deny any possibility of natural growth or development. Despite the 2004 Advisory Opinion of the International Court of Justice, the Wall continues to be built, solidifying the de facto annexation of land and resources, and cutting Palestinian communities in half.

Since 2007, the Gaza Strip has been subject to an absolute closure, severed from the outside world. In a situation worthy of Kafka, it is we, the civilian population of the Gaza Strip – the so-called 'protected persons' of international humanitarian law – who are subject – to a de facto and comprehensive regime of isolation and illegal sanctions. Unemployment, poverty and aid dependence have skyrocketed, undermining the entire spectrum of human rights. This collective punishment targets the very dignity of Gaza's 1.8 million inhabitants. Today, we demand an end to this collective punishment, and an end to the international community's complicity in its perpetration.

What then of justice? Of accountability? The Palestinian Centre for Human Rights has worked before the Israeli courts for over 15 years, representing thousands of victims in countless cases. It is our clear legal conclusion that justice is simply unobtainable within this system. Indeed, the Israeli Supreme Court itself characterises Palestinians as 'enemy aliens', who are 'presumed to endanger national security and public security'. For example, following Israel's 27 December 2008–18 January 2009 offensive on the Gaza Strip, the PCHR filed 490 criminal complaints – on behalf of over 1,046 victims – to the Israeli Military Advocate General. To date, over two-and-a-half years after the last complaint was filed, 469 have not been answered, while we have received only interlocutory responses with respect to a further 19 cases. The only two complaints which have reached a legal conclusion relate to the theft of a credit card.

This deserves emphasis. The PCHR represent the victims of the most horrific crimes of the offensive, and Israel's reaction to the offensive has been watched by the world. Yet, 488 of 490 cases – 99.5 per cent – have not been addressed. Despite frequent requests by the PCHR's lawyers, the victims have simply been ignored. This is the story of the occupation.

Justice has been denied to Palestinians. The rule of law has been replaced by the rule of the jungle, whereby force, violence and political manipulation are prioritised over fundamental human rights. The result is the complete and systematic denial of self-determination.

Despite this unprecedented deterioration in the human rights situation, the international community has continued to grant Israel pervasive impunity. The continued construction and expansion of settlements, the closure of Gaza, and the 2008–09 offensive on the Gaza Strip which killed approximately 1,181 civilians, have not been met with the accountability demanded by international law, but rather with bland statements, and effective acquiescence. The international community has become complicit in these violations of international law, including the institutionalisation of the closure of Gaza, through its inaction. By failing to hold Israel accountable, the international community is undermining the rule of law, and encouraging Israel to commit further violations. The extent of the impunity granted to Israel has reached the point where Israel feels confident publicly stating that it is waging 'economic warfare' against the people of Gaza, targeting them as a means of exerting pressure on the government.

This 'business as usual' approach must be challenged and ended.

THE ROLE OF THE STATES

As outlined above, the States are under an obligation to ensure respect for international law. However, with respect to Israel, it is clear that this obligation is consistently violated. Indeed, rather than enacting sanctions or other measures intended to ensure respect for the law, States turn a blind eye and adopt what is in effect a 'business as usual' approach. In many instances, Israel is in fact rewarded with preferential trade agreements, and other means of economic and military cooperation.

The EU-Israel Association Agreement is the most often cited example of this accountability-free relationship. Indeed, while Gaza was subject to an absolute closure, and only two weeks before the beginning of Israel's 2008–09 offensive on the Gaza Strip, EU-Israel relations were upgraded. However, though it is perhaps the most high-profile agreement, it is by no means the only one. Numerous States throughout the world, including Egypt, Jordan, Turkey and Tunisia, continue to engage in extensive economic and military cooperation with Israel, and to prioritise these arrangements over respect for international law, and civilians' fundamental human rights.

This is our challenge. Particularly in this, the era of the Arab Spring, States must be judged by the requirements of international law. We must demand that they stand up for human rights, the rule of law, and democracy, and that they act to ensure that States – and individuals – who violate international law are held to account. One of the means pursued by the PCHR to achieve this objective has been pressure to convene a Conference of the High Contracting Parties to the Geneva Conventions with the intention of ensuring Israel's respect for international humanitarian law.

BDS: THE CHALLENGE

BDS is a long-standing and valid tool. It has been successfully and effectively utilised in other contexts, and provides a useful rallying point for committed individuals around the world.

However, for BDS to be effective, it requires focus, clarity and unity. The goals of BDS must at all times remain clear. In the Palestinian case, our demand must be that Israel end its illegal practices. Indeed, it is precisely this point that marks the strength of the BDS message: BDS is not a unilateral measure, or a form of punishment, it is simply a clear demand that existing international laws be enforced: a demand that States live up to the obligations which they themselves wrote and ratified.

We must target illegality resolutely, and we must use the law as a guide for our actions. It is essential that in the fight for justice, we ourselves do not resort to injustice: the goals and methods must be spelled out clearly. This requires focus, consensus and leadership, the vital elements to an effective and just BDS campaign. Without such vision and leadership, the issue of BDS risks derailing the debate, turning the underlying problem – the occupation – into a side issue, while focus instead rests on superficial issues, capable of achieving only cosmetic results.

CONCLUSION

The need for BDS is clear; most recently the Russell Tribunal on Palestine found 'that 'Israel subjects the Palestinian people to an institutionalised regime of domination amounting to apartheid as defined under international law.' In 2011, no one can claim that they do not know the reality of the situation in occupied Palestine. The call for BDS must ring out as an impassioned cry for justice: for an end to the illegal closure of Gaza, for an end to the denial of civilians' fundamental human rights, for an end to the systematic perpetration of war crimes, for an end to Israel's belligerent occupation.

Human rights, the rule of law, and democracy are not luxuries, they are fundamental necessities: the oxygen of meaningful life. These are universal principles worth fighting for. This is not a Palestinian issue; it is one of equality, of justice, and it affects us all, for it is our shared humanity that hangs in the balance. It is the stand that we as individuals take, that defines us.

We must continue to reject all forms of human rights abuses. We must continue to work even for small changes. For the sake of the victims of injustice, we must carry out our work professionally and in a just manner. We must be vigorous and unyielding in our defence of the persecuted and bold enough to never stop opposing the victimisers, no matter who they may be.

Civil society has a huge role to play in this regard. It is through solidarity, and principled opposition to human rights abuses that empires fall and real change is achieved. We have seen the end of apartheid, Ben-Ali has been deposed, and for the first time in 7,000 years, the pyramids have moved in Egypt. True power is in the hands of the people. We must not give up.

7
Self-Determination and the Right of Return: Interlinked and Indivisible Rights

Nidal al-Azza

By looking at the Palestinian civil society's BDS Call, three interrelated and complementary components can be seen as a background to its language and goals. First, the failure of the international community to enforce its resolutions calling for the respecting of fundamental Palestinian human rights; secondly, the comprehensive meaning given to the right of self-determination within the Palestinian context; and third, the call upon international civil society and people of conscience all over the world to contribute effectively to the achievement of justice and the preservation of the fundamental rights of the Palestine people as a basis to build a durable and sustainable peace. This article tries to shed light on one of the three components mentioned above, namely, the Palestinian people's right to self-determination as stated in the BDS Call with a special focus on Palestinian refugees' right of return. Thus, this article argues that three precepts set into the Call – ending the occupation, ensuring equality, and the right of Palestinian refugees to return to their original homes – constitute the mechanism with which the Palestinian people's inalienable right to self-determination can be ensured. It concludes that the right to self-determination is meaningless and impossible without preserving the unity of the Palestinian people and ensuring the full implementation of all rights.

The Palestinian people are a fragmented national community, of which more than half live outside the area that is currently referred to as the Occupied Palestinian Territory (oPt). By stipulating three fundamental precepts within its text, the Call for BDS not only highlights this fact, but also demands that the rights of the entire national community are protected.

The BDS Call reads:

> These non-violent punitive measures [boycott, divestment and sanctions] should be maintained until Israel meets its obligation to recognise the Palestinian people's inalienable right to self-determination and fully complies with the precepts of international law by:
>
> 1 – Ending its occupation and colonisation of all Arab lands and dismantling the Wall;
>
> 2 – Recognising the fundamental rights of the Arab-Palestinian citizens of Israel to full equality;
>
> 3 – Respecting, protecting and promoting the rights of Palestinian refugees to return to their homes and properties as stipulated in UN Resolution 194.

Respect for the right to self-determination of peoples is enshrined in the UN Charter; it is presented as one of the fundamental purposes of the United Nations. Article 1, common to the two Covenants – the International Covenant on Economic, Social and Cultural Rights (ICESCR) and the International Covenant on Civil and Political Rights (ICCPR) – reaffirms the right of all peoples to self-determination, and obliges state parties to promote and to respect it. Its components have been articulated in the Declaration of Principles of International Law Concerning Friendly Relations and Co-operation Among States in Accordance with the Charter of the United Nations, which affirms:

> By virtue of the principle of equal rights and self-determination of peoples enshrined in the Charter of the United Nations, all peoples have the right freely to determine, without external interference, their political status and to pursue their economic, social and cultural development, and every State has the duty to respect this right in accordance with the provisions of the Charter.[1]

Although the Palestinian right to self-determination enshrined in the BDS Call fits within this common concept, it has been given broader and deeper meaning by determining its components in accordance with the specific nature of the Palestine question.

The BDS Call does not lay down the three inalienable rights exactly as stipulated in the UN General Assembly resolutions 3236 and 3376, in which inalienable rights of the Palestinian people refer to rights to self-determination without external interference, national independence and sovereignty, and Palestinian refugees' return to their homes and property from where they have been displaced. Instead of repeating the words of UN resolutions, the BDS Call emphasises the right of self-determination and gives it a comprehensive and practical meaning. This meaning extends the right as a principle and develops the vague and indistinct formulation of the official UN document. This is notable in clarifying the foundation and mechanism with which to facilitate self-determination in the Palestinian context.

Prior to the Oslo Accords, the inalienable rights of the Palestinian people were accepted to be indivisible rights in the relevant UN resolutions. In its 1976 plan, the Committee on the Exercise of the Inalienable Rights of the Palestinian People (UN-CEIRPP) developed a programme to implement Resolution 3236 (above). The plan was designed to create a two-state solution in historic Palestine and to resolve the question of Palestinian refugees. Although it was supported by the overwhelming majority of the international community, it was vetoed by the US and Israel. Moreover, it has never been backed by practical measures of state members of the UN. As a result, it ended on the shelves of the UN archives, like hundreds of other relevant resolutions, reports and statements of UN bodies and agencies addressing the Palestine question. The 'shelving' of UN resolutions which used to reiterate the confirmation of the inalienable rights, is a result of the lack of determined practical measures of enforcement which derives from a lack of political will. In practical terms, the UN has failed in enabling the Palestinian people to exercise their inalienable rights.

Following the Oslo Accords, the UN approach, under the dominance of US foreign policy, has noticeably confined its declarations of Palestinian self-determination by limiting them to the right to have a 'viable Palestinian state', or, in the words of the *Road Map for Peace*, to the creation of 'an independent democratic Palestinian state living side by side in peace and security with Israel and its other neighbours'. Irrespective of the legality and/or legitimacy of such confinement, the UN, including the Committee on the Exercise of the Inalienable Rights of the Palestinian People and other committees established specifically for Palestine, was noticeably affected by such restrictions. This dramatic retreat can be clearly seen in UNGA resolution 66/14 (2011), which not only refined the mandate of the committee to, and tied it with, the direct negotiations of the so-called Middle East Peace Process, the Quartet Road Map, and the 1967 borders, but it also omits the inherited affirmation of the inalienable rights, and the Right of Return. The significance of the linguistic subtleties that reduced 'reaffirms ... ' to 'requests ... ' and later (inalienability of the) 'right of the Palestinians to return' to (just resolution of) 'final status issues' must not be overlooked in this context:

The General Assembly ...
Requests the Committee to continue to exert all efforts to promote the realization of the inalienable rights of the Palestinian people, including their right to self-determination, to support the Middle East peace process for the achievement of the two-State solution on the basis of the pre-1967 borders and the just resolution of all final status issues and to mobilize international support for and assistance to the Palestinian people ... .

Given these facts, the BDS Call has not only addressed civil society actors, but also has revived and developed the complementary approach of the inalienable rights. The BDS Call presents the Palestinian right to self-determination as an approach combining three interrelated and complementary components which intrinsically protect the rights of the entire national community by taking into account the various political statuses and fragmented natures of the Palestinian people.

By looking at the three components, it becomes clear that the right to self-determination in the BDS Call is a comprehensive platform that is built upon many axioms: the unity of Palestinian people in places all over the world, the collectivity of Palestinian rights, the interdependence between individual and collective rights, and the failure of the approach that has attempted to divide and fragment Palestinian people and their rights. These avenues lead us to another important truth in the BDS Call, namely the unfeasibility of the achievement of national independence if any one of the axioms is excluded.

Ending the Israeli occupation of the Palestinian territory occupied in 1967 may be a prelude to a Palestinian political entity, although not necessarily an independent state, and may lead to a kind of normalisation between Israel and its neighbours. However, such a 'solution' may at best answer the questions of Israeli colonies constructed within the 1967 borders, the Apartheid Wall, and restrictions on freedom of movement in the oPt. It may establish an agreed arrangement on Jerusalem as well, but it will not end the institutionalised Israeli discrimination and apartheid systems targeting Palestinian citizens of Israel. Moreover, ending the Israeli military occupation may solve the question of the 1967 Palestinian refugees (approximately 1 million), but will not solve the question of 1948 refugees (approximately 6 million).

It could be argued that the Israeli Palestinian citizens' right to equality is, or will become irrelevant to the Palestinian right to self-determination, as it is an internal issue of the state of Israel. This argument may have some validity if the Palestinian people were not a collective national community, despite the fragmented nature of their existence. Such an argument assumes that Palestinian citizens of Israel are not seeking their national rights, even as a minority living inside Israel. This argument also ignores the increasing nationally motivated struggle of Palestinians inside Israel to confirm their Palestinian national identity as a basis for their right to equality. Many recent studies prove that their 'acceptance' of Israeli citizenship has not resulted in reducing their affiliation to their people or national identity.[2] Taking into consideration the family relationships and strong ties of kinship between Palestinians throughout the world, this argument becomes immaterial in that it initially denies the possibility of the extension of relations outside of the borders of the oPt. For example, I myself live in exile in a Palestinian refugee camp in the West Bank, but I have family members who are today Palestinian citizens of Israel. I also have family members in Jordan and in the US, as a result of their displacement. We all have the same national identity, culture and characteristics, and this fragmented story is the enforced story of our national community. We Palestinians, although hugely fragmented in geographical terms as a result of political actions, are one collective national people. This fact is a moral imperative, but it is also a fact that has always been recognised in the international context. The inalienable right to self-determination belongs to us as a people, and is indivisible within that collective body, irrespective of our current fragmented locations. The enforced nature of our fragmentation is intrinsically linked to this reality, and in this context, it must also be remembered that the displacement of Palestinians continues today en masse. More than 30,000 Palestinian Bedouins in the Negev area of southern Israel are facing imminent displacement, hundreds of Palestinian families in Jaffa are under eviction orders, whole villages in Area C of the West Bank are facing demolition orders, as is the al-Bustan neighbourhood of Silwan in Jerusalem. Such policies have been ongoing for more than 64 years under different guises, but this fact cannot deny our collective national identity.

Despite the dramatic retreat in its renewed mandate expressed in UNGA resolution 66/14 of 2011, the UN-CEIRPP has never restricted the inalienable rights to Palestinians living in the oPt; rights have always been attributed to the Palestinian people collectively.

The struggle for self-determination should in theory end when a people achieves its national liberation. Yet if Palestinian self-determination becomes relevant only within the oPt, and even then excluding Jerusalem as the current Zionist framework suggests, the so-called 'self-determination' of the Palestinian people in reality would only be tangible for approximately one-third of the entire Palestinian people. Within such a model, the idea of self-determination actually becomes meaningless, as it does not represent the entire people. Thus, the right to self-determination cannot exist in separation from the right of return. Self-determination is a collective right, not a selective one relevant only to a fraction of the national community. This is the framework as laid out in international law, and this position is also the only morally defensible structure. By restricting 'self-determination' to only those Palestinians within the oPt, Israel is in fact attempting to refute the right of return forever, and thus essentially 'erase' approximately two-thirds of the entire Palestinian people from any participatory role within, and any inherent links to, their own national community and individual and collective identity. In its study entitled *The Right of Return of Palestinian People* (1978), the UN-CEIRPP confirmed that '[In] the case of the Palestinian people, the individual or personal right of return assumes a special significance for without its restoration, the exercise of the collective or national right of self-determination, itself guaranteed by a variety of international instruments, becomes impossible.'

The inalienable right to self-determination of the Palestinian people and the right of return are interlinked and indivisible rights. The BDS Call and the current movement that has grown around it have revived and developed the well-established approach in international law and previous documents of the United Nations. It has drawn the comprehensive and practical way to achieve a durable and just solution based on human rights for all people of Palestine.

NOTES

1. The United Nation General Assembly Resolution 2625 (XXV): Declaration of Principles of International Law Concerning Friendly Relations and Co-operation Among States in Accordance with the Charter of the United Nations, 24 October 1970.
2. See Abdel Fattah Al-Qalqili and Ahmad Abu Goush, *Palestinian National Identity: The Foundations and Governing Framework*, BADIL, 2012.

8

Levelling the Scales by Force: Thoughts on Normalisation

Rifat Odeh Kassis

Anyone with any exposure to Palestine and Israel, or anyone who has ever had a conversation about our region, will also be exposed to certain words and phrases that are woven through such conversations like threads – or which are deployed around them like firecrackers. These words become markers, signals and judgements. They are written and spoken all the time, but they are not always clearly defined – despite being among the most important ideas to truly understand.

One such word is the term 'conflict' itself. 'Conflict' may seem like a simple noun, empty of motive or ideology. But the reality is subtly otherwise: the phrase 'Palestinian–Israeli conflict', for instance, leads its readers to think of an equal dispute between two equal parties. The usage and the effect of this word, then, is a first step toward *normalisation* – an essential concept to comprehend in any quest for justice, and the subject of this essay.

'Normalisation': when actors in the Palestinian struggle for a just peace use this term, what do they mean? What is the reasoning behind a refusal to work with an individual or group because of a 'normalising' attitude or act? And why is normalisation so damaging to the achievement of justice?

In order to clarify this goal – justice – it's also important to clarify normalisation. I'd like to start with a straightforward definition of normalisation as expressed by the first Palestinian BDS (Boycott, Divestment and Sanctions) conference, held in Ramallah in November 2007:

> Normalisation means to participate in any project or initiative or activity, local or international, specifically designed for gathering (either directly or indirectly) Palestinians (and/or Arabs) and Israelis, whether individuals or institutions; that does not explicitly aim to expose and resist the occupation and all forms of discrimination and oppression against the Palestinian people.

This definition can take many forms in daily life. Among the important ones succinctly defined in a document published by the Ma'an Development Center of Ramallah,[1] normalisation encompasses:

1. Projects that do not agree on inalienable rights for Palestinians under international law and the conditions of justice,
2. Projects implying equity between Israelis and the Palestinians in the responsibility for the conflict, or that claim that peace is achieved through dialogue and understanding and increased cooperation between both sides, without achieving justice,
3. Projects that hide the situation of the Palestinian people as victims of the Israeli colonial project,
4. Projects that refuse, ignore or dilute the right of the Palestinian people to self-determination, the right of return and compensation according to the UN resolution No. 194, and
5. Projects supported by or in partnership with the Israeli institutions that do not recognize the legitimate rights of the Palestinian people or projects receiving support or funding (in part or in whole) from the Israeli government such as cinema festivals, information technology exhibitions, etc.

To me, the second kind of normalisation – 'implying equity between Israelis and the Palestinians in the responsibility for the conflict, or claim that peace is achieved through dialogue and understanding ... without achieving justice' – is among the most important to understand. Indeed, it is among the most subtle, the most common, the most liable to be hidden under the trappings of good intentions – and, therefore, among the most difficult to stop.

Politicians are not the only ones who commit normalisation when it comes to the Israeli occupation. Newspapers do it, television does it, filmmakers and artists and pop singers do it, ordinary people talking politics over dinner do it. *Language* does it. Normalisation is the process, the instinct, the narrative that neutralises what can never be neutral, that renders over six decades of meticulously institutionalised Israeli military rule into an eternal and incorrigible spat between two groups of people who 'can't get along'. When it comes to normalisation, it is not only our dignity that is under threat; it is our reality, and it is our rights.

If only the Palestinians would just stop throwing rocks! If only the Israelis would just stop building settlements for a few weeks! Then the talking could begin; then peace would be just around the corner. This is the belief that lies below the surface of even the most well-meaning normalisation. Let's negotiate; let's send rock bands to Tel Aviv as long as they go to Ramallah too; let's send our children to summertime peace camps in the United States. Let's do everything we can to domesticate anger, to level the scales by holding one of them down by force, to position Israelis and Palestinians (civilians, politicians, jazz musicians, whoever they may be) in a 'dialogue' that disregards the fact that Palestinian civilians live without even the most basic human rights; that Palestinian national politicians do not represent any actual nation; that Palestinian jazz musicians cannot pass the necessary checkpoints in order to play where they please.

Normalisation is palatable and reassuring. It is the nervous, mollifying, conversation-stopping impulse behind the quick response I've so often heard when talk turns to the 'Palestinian–Israeli conflict': 'Oh, it's just so complicated!', or 'Both sides are at fault', or 'Both have suffered so much.' On the one hand, then, we can say that normalisation accommodates a basic human desire to pacify turbulence, to make each other (and ourselves) more comfortable in the face of deeply uncomfortable realities, and to express concern about hardship without getting our hands dirty around the roots of its causes. It's reductive, but it's explicable.

On the other hand, normalisation serves far more sinister ends than just graceful small talk. In the face of oppression, it permits us to turn a blind eye to it. In doing so, it *strengthens* oppression. It encourages us to forget how to recognise oppression in the first place. It allows us to believe that, by articulating our vague, earnest hope for equality in all things, this equality must also apply to oppressor and oppressed, must absolve the oppressor from its oppression, and must absolve us from condemning it as such.

As the saying goes, only free men can negotiate. Normalisation is what makes them – men and women who are not free in any sense of the word – do it anyway.

I must once again stress the importance of language in all contexts, both overtly political and not, when it comes to normalisation. In its most brutal forms, normalisation is what transformed the December 2008–January 2009 Israeli bombardment of the Gaza Strip, in which 1,400 Palestinians were killed, mostly civilians, including over 300 children, from a massacre into a 'war'. Normalisation is what turns the Apartheid Wall into a 'security fence'. Normalisation is what euphemises the 99 permanent military checkpoints, most of them *inside* the Occupied Palestinian Territory (oPt) rather than along any kind of border, into 'terminals'. And normalisation in its more comprehensive tonal sense is what weakens 'colonisation' into 'disputed land', what dismantles 'occupation' into 'security'.

This is crucial: normalisation prevents us from calling a spade a spade, from defining our reality as it is. If we cannot do that, we are lost.

To call it a spade, then – to deny the denial of our rights, and to demand those rights – we as Palestinian civil society organisations and as Palestinians in general must refuse to participate in this process that reduces us. In other words, we must refuse to participate in activities or collaborations with groups or individuals who perpetuate acts or atmospheres of normalisation.

One important manifestation of this philosophy is the global BDS campaign, which is by definition a struggle against normalisation. I'd like to address the BDS campaign further in this context: both the campaign itself and the importance of its opposition to normalisation, as well as the criticisms such a strategy often attract.

The global BDS campaign calls upon us to boycott – to refuse normalisation – with the full range of injustices perpetrated by the State of Israel against Palestinians. The Israeli occupation restricts the entirety of our rights, not only the ones you can exercise in a court or a voting booth: it affects our economy, our education, our mobility, our language, our health and our hope. It constitutes the geographic, economic, political, social, spiritual and psychological fragmentation of Palestinian communities and lives. There is nothing remotely normal about any of this. To dismiss injustice and inequality only in name – while continuing to fund Israeli companies or buy Israeli products or play a concert in an Israeli hall because to do so seems logistically convenient or ethically uncomplicated – misses the point altogether. The BDS campaign is a reminder that the Israeli occupation is an enormous and intricate apparatus that will only change if we refuse to support it. Which is to say, if we refuse to normalise with it.

Both within the Israeli community and around the world, there exists a great deal of discomfort and confusion about the tactics and intentions of anti-normalisation work. Many people find the BDS campaign, among others, to be 'imbalanced' or overly punitive; many believe the Palestinians should 'dialogue' with the Israelis about what's happening in the oPt, because the problem is just a lack of information and mutual understanding, while many believe that only a 'positive' approach will do, and BDS doesn't qualify.

Unfortunately, these claims are not only patronising and ineffectual, but also irrelevant. There is nothing 'positive' about more than 64 years of land appropriation, expulsion, military violence and systematic violations of human rights. Nor is there anything 'positive' in the way the Israeli state responds to dissent: targeted arrests, military brutality at non-violent protests, blacklisting human rights organisations, the deportation of activists. The goal of 'balanced dialogue' is impossible in a place where there is no balance, a place of forced silence. In short, it is absurd and offensive to advocate for 'positive engagement' with an apartheid state, to 'convince' it to be more empathic with the people it subjugates, to construe the ultimate goal as 'mutual understanding' rather than an end to oppression itself.

The BDS campaign, then, is the only way for the Israeli community – and the world – to truly see, experience and *know* what their government is doing in Palestine.

Moreover, time is running out. While the world stands by and discusses the effectiveness of the BDS movement, Israel continues – with undeniable effectiveness – its stranglehold of Gaza, its demolitions and evictions in East Jerusalem and elsewhere, its high-speed settlement construction, its entire range of oppressive policies. Israel, both on the ground and on the Knesset floor, is tilting more and more dangerously to the right and turning more and more irrefutably into an apartheid state. To delay opposition, to delay a boycott, is in itself dangerous.

Our responsibilities to the truth, for both Palestinians and Israelis, are at once collective and also deeply personal. Anti-normalisation work is a way to honour and act upon those responsibilities. It is powerful – and powerfully non-violent – resistance, with human solidarity as a tactic as well as a goal.

Let us remember that normality without honesty is meaningless, as is cooperation without justice. Let us care so deeply about our capacity for change that we will refuse to undermine ourselves, and each other, along the way.

NOTE

1. Ma'an Development Center, *Boycott, Divestment and Sanctions: Lessons Learned in Effective Solidarity* <http://bdsmovement. net/?q=node/574>.

9

International Law, Apartheid and Israeli Responses to BDS

Professor Richard Falk

INTRODUCTORY PERSPECTIVES

By now there are overwhelming confirmations that a just and sustainable peace between Palestine and Israel will not be achieved by traditional diplomacy or through the efforts of the United Nations. Justice will be eventually achieved, but only through the agency of struggle waged by, with, and on behalf of the Palestinian people. This is the primary lesson of more than sixty years of Palestinian dispossession resulting in massive exile and huge refugee encampments. Furthermore, since 1967, an oppressive occupation has morphed into an apartheid regime of colonialist governance and a creeping form of de facto annexation, facilitated by the establishment and expansion of unlawful Israeli settlements throughout the West Bank and East Jerusalem. The secondary lesson is that neither the United States nor the UN has been either able or willing to counter Israeli criminal defiance of international law and the related impunity of their leaders. Perhaps most tellingly, the world watched as helpless spectators while Israel mercilessly attacked Gaza for three weeks at the end of 2008 with its full panoply of modern weaponry, much of it supplied by the United States, to wage a one-sided war (code-named 'Operation Cast Lead' by Israel) that recalled the worst colonialist excesses.

With this experience of decades of Palestinian suffering and frustration, the cruel charade of a recurrent 'peace process' should no longer delude people around the world that an end to the Palestinian ordeal can be brought about by the leaders of these two embattled peoples, and their American intermediary, whose consistent partisanship contradicts its self-serving claim to act as an honest broker. At the same time, there are encouraging signs on the political horizons that give hope and direction to the Palestinian struggle: the 'Arab Spring' reminds us that even the most oppressive and abusive forms of political rule are potentially vulnerable to massive popular uprisings by brave and determined non-violent collective action; and there are increasing indications that if the regional push for democracy goes forward in the Middle East, it will almost certainly lead to a greater diplomatic engagement by neighbouring countries producing stronger support for achieving the long-deferred Palestinian right of self-determination. Most significantly, these regional developments seemed to have generated a surge of Palestinian energy disclosed in a renewed militancy that seems calibrated with the expanding and deepening global Palestinian Solidarity Movement (PSM) and it could, according to informed observers, also potentially lead to a third intifada, although what shape a new uprising may take is as yet unclear.

With this background in mind, we can assess this increasingly robust PSM that has as its central expression the BDS (Boycott, Divestment and Sanctions) Campaign. This campaign, initiated by a collective voice of Palestinian civil society, has been inspired by, but not copied from, the South African Anti-Apartheid campaign that was so effective in discrediting and isolating the racist regime in Pretoria, paving the way with minimal violence toward the establishment of a multiracial constitutional democracy led by Nelson Mandela. The South African experience, while different in crucial respects, does underscore the degree to which the militarily weaker and politically oppressed side in a prolonged conflict can prevail if its cause is just, if it persists in struggle, and if it relies on appropriate tactics.

Launching the BDS Campaign represented a shift in the priorities of resistance for Palestinian society, featuring a reduced reliance on governmental initiatives (politics from above) and a new confidence in the historical agency of popular movements (politics from below), without rejecting some combination of the two in the final phases of a push toward peace and self-determination. BDS, although seeking a political climate more conducive to balanced diplomacy at the level of sovereign states, presently asserts that only the mobilisation and activism of civil society can uphold Palestinian rights. In this regard, BDS represents a major commitment to soft power approaches to conflict resolution, although not necessarily involving the unconditional renunciation of armed resistance. BDS is itself a non-violent form of political activism that relies on the voluntary participation of people at all levels of society, regardless of their national or ethnic identities, and without geographical limitations. Its origins, leadership and orientation are Palestinian, but its recruitment and range of actions are ecumenical and flexible, with respect to the degrees of commitment that are understood to reflect the diverse outlooks of participating actors and their programme. The campaign is as wide as the world, issuing a special welcome to its ranks to members of Israeli society. Indeed, Israeli participation is valued highly in the BDS movement. It has an enhanced symbolic and substantive status because the defection of Israelis, whether rightly or wrongly, tends to lend an added measure of perceived authenticity to the justice and reasonableness of Palestinian claims, demands and tactics.

Although the movement supporting BDS is global in scope and composed of peoples of many national, ethnic and religious identities, it is important for non-Palestinian supporters to accept that its direction and political approach should always remain under the direction of its Palestinian organisers. It is important in this regard that those of us who are not Palestinian, yet lend support to BDS, reject Orientalist efforts to substitute our West-centric guidance for theirs. In this regard, non-Palestinians active in the PSM have a political responsibility to defer to the lead of Palestinian civil society, who currently best represent Palestinian democratic aspirations.

LEGALITY OF BDS

The essential character of the international BDS campaign is an expression of citizens in a free society to demonstrate their moral concerns, and to appeal to others to join them. Seeking to promote the rights of the Palestinian people under international law is thus integral to the functioning of a democratic society. It is non-violent and relies on persuasion to achieve its desired results. It is also educational as it needs to convince people of why BDS is appropriate. International law does not explicitly validate BDS by name, although clearly it stands as an expression of fundamental civil and political rights that are enumerated in the Universal Declaration of Human Rights and subsequent treaty instruments.

The imposition of sanctions by governments does raise some legal issues, although these are not normally viewed as serious impediments to the adoption of sanctions. It can be argued that sanctions violate the non-intervention norm in international law if imposed by government action, as was the case during the last stages of the anti-apartheid campaign. If sanctions are decreed by the UN Security Council, as is presently the case with respect to Iran, it constitutes a controversial challenge to Article 2(7) of the Charter that prohibits UN intervention in matters essentially within the domestic jurisdiction of a state unless international peace and security are found to be seriously at stake.

A TOOL AGAINST APARTHEID (AGAIN)?

At the same time, the South African precedent is relevant in several respects, especially in giving its legitimating blessings to non-violent forms of global initiatives against a racist regime by a member state that failed to abide by international law, ignoring a variety of UN initiatives, including the disregard of the International Crime of the Suppression and Punishment of the Crime of Apartheid (1973). The BDS campaign argues that among the most serious Israeli forms of criminal unlawfulness is the multi-dimensional imposition of an apartheid regime that consists of the discriminatory separation of Palestinians into such subordinated categories as occupied, refugee, terrorist and minority in a Jewish state. It is important to appreciate that international law treats 'apartheid' as a universal crime, and not one that necessarily resembles the forms of drastic discrimination that prevailed in South Africa.

The generalising of the crime of apartheid was given treaty form in the International Convention on the Suppression and Punishment of the Crime of Apartheid, which came into force in 1973 with adherences now numbering 107 states. The crime of apartheid is defined in the Convention as 'inhuman acts for the purpose of establishing and maintaining domination by one racial group of persons over any other racial group and systematically oppressing them'. The Rome Statute of the International Criminal Court treats apartheid as one of seven forms of Crimes Against Humanity, describing its essence as consisting of an 'institutionalized regime of systematic oppression and domination by one racial group'.

The most obviously apartheid structure has evolved in the West Bank, where a dual system of administration accords full legal protection to Israeli settlers, while subjecting Palestinians to a non-accountable Israeli administrative regime of military occupation that was established in 1967, and has gradually matured into de facto annexation.[1] The apartheid character of this occupation regime is associated with several features of the Israeli–Palestinian relationship:

- Preferential citizenship, visitation, family unification, and residence laws and practices that prevent Palestinians who reside in the West Bank or Gaza or elsewhere in the world from reclaiming their property lost in 1948, 1967, or at other times, or from acquiring Israeli citizenship or even residence rights, as contrasted to a Jewish Law of Return that entitles Jews anywhere in the world with no prior tie to Israel to visit, reside, obtain property and become Israeli citizens;
- Differential systems of authority in the West Bank favouring Israeli settlers (inhabiting settlements that were established in flagrant and continuing violation of Article 49(6) of the Fourth Geneva Convention), who enjoy full rights under Israeli law, as opposed to Palestinian residents living in the same geographic space and with full legal rights to be

there, who are governed by military administration that is arbitrary and abusive;

- Dual and discriminatory arrangements for movement in the West Bank and to and from Jerusalem, including an Israeli-only road network and a Separation Wall determined to be unlawful by the World Court in 2004; discriminatory policies on land ownership, tenure and use; extensive burdening of Palestinian movement, including checkpoints involving long waits and frequent humiliations for Palestinians while Israeli settlers and visitors have unrestricted mobility facilitated by different coloured registration plates on cars; also, there are onerous permit and identification requirements imposed only on Palestinians, and

- Palestinians are subject to punitive house demolitions, expulsions, deportations and restrictions on entry to and exit from all three parts of Occupied Palestine. Israel exercises full control over approximately 60 per cent of the West Bank area ('Area C' of the Oslo Accords), and has recently been imposing a variety of conditions on Bedouin communities near Jerusalem and in the Negev with the thinly disguised objective of dispossessing them. In contrast, Israeli settlers live securely including those who have established settler outposts, which although illegal under Israeli law as well as international law (major settlements, as opposed to settler outposts, are illegal under international law but not under Israeli law), receive protection from Israeli military forces and are awarded subsidies from government ministries involved in housing.

In short, Israeli apartheid structures, policies, and practices are pervasive in their dual character, producing gross economic, social and political inequality between Israelis and Palestinians. These structures evolve over time and assume different forms in the West Bank and East Jerusalem, as well as in Israel itself. With some irony, blockaded Gaza is the only portion of Occupied Palestine that does not have to cope with everyday apartheid, although the oppressive and multiply dangerous quality of life in Gaza makes its 'imprisoned' population possibly the most victimised of all Palestinian constituencies at the present time. It should be remembered in the BDS context that apartheid is universally treated as an international crime, and that by making support for BDS a civil wrong, Israel is seeking to discourage non-violent opposition to crime by imposing harsh penalties.

There is also the related issue of the Palestinian minority within Israel. The increasing insistence by the Israeli government that it be recognised as 'a Jewish state', not only by the leadership representing the Palestinian people in international negotiations and the international community, but even by its 1.7 million Palestinian Israeli citizens, who comprise about 20 per cent of Israel's total population. These Palestinian citizens of Israel are subject to a large variety of discriminatory laws and regulations, to open discussion of their being transferred to a Palestinian entity without their consent, and to greater scrutiny than Israelis with respect to mobility. This may or may not amount to 'apartheid', but it illustrates and confirms the systematically racist nature of the treatment inflicted upon the Palestinians for more than six decades.

CONTENDING THAT BDS IS ANTI-SEMITIC OR 'RACIST'

Some critics of BDS insist that by focusing on Israel there is a selectivity of concerns that targets the 'Jewish state' of Israel while neglecting comparable or worse infringements on international law and human rights elsewhere in the world, and that as result BDS should be viewed as anti-Semitic or racist. The literature and rationale for BDS is based on the rights of Palestinian people and stands or falls on its own. The entire international community has been preoccupied with the Israel–Palestine conflict for some decades, and the whole foundation of Israel's existence rests on initiatives of the United Nations and external actors. In 2004, the International Court of Justice issued a near-unanimous Advisory Opinion, expressing the clear conclusions that Israel had a solemn obligation to abide by international law in its relations with the Palestinian people. Israel repudiated this authoritative judgment, and continued to flaunt international law, and thus the rights of the Palestinian people.

There is also the initial colonialist commitment of the Balfour Declaration in 1917, that looked with favour at the establishment of 'a national home for the Jewish people' (not state) in historic Palestine, 'it being clearly understood that nothing should be done which may prejudice the civil and religious rights of existing non-Jewish communities'.[2] In this manner, Britain conditioned the fulfilment of the Zionist project by reference to the protection of Palestinian rights (at least officially if not necessarily in practice), an obligation that was later transferred to the UN when Britain ended their role as mandatory power. It is the failure to uphold this obligation over such a long period that has both generated Palestinian resistance and struggle, and led over time to a widening circle of global civil society initiatives undertaken in solidarity with the Palestinian people, of which BDS and the Freedom Flotillas are recent examples.

It is pure diversion on the part of supporters of Israel to play the 'anti-Semitic card' under these circumstances. Israel's flagrant violation of international law, its refusal to respect Palestinian rights, its strong linkage to the United States, and the unfulfilled UN role fully justify the attention given to the conflict. BDS is fully consistent with international law, and reflects the values of democratic engagement of peoples beyond borders in struggles for global justice.

ISRAELI RESPONSES TO BDS

It is worth noting that the more seriously framed Israeli objections to BDS are not based on appeals to international law, but are rather political and moral arguments contending that BDS, despite its claims to be promoting human rights and global justice, is actually part of an effort to delegitimise Israel's 'right to exist'. A further claim is that BDS supporters often call for the resolution of the conflict by way of a one-state solution which is arguably premised on the replacement of the present Israeli state by a secular bi-national state,[3] although in actuality the campaign itself focuses on the realisation of inalienable Palestinian rights without taking a position on the shape of the future Palestinian state.

Israel has increasingly associated the BDS campaign with what it refers to as the 'delegitimisation' of Israel. The most analytical and comprehensive assessment along these lines has been prepared by the Reut Institute, an Israeli think tank.[4] The basic contention is that the BDS campaign, whether consciously or not, is seeking to question the legitimacy of Israel, as now constituted, and in their words 'supersede the Zionist model with a state that is based on the "one person, one vote" principle'. Given the BDS emphasis on Palestinian rights as the necessary precondition for a sustainable peace, the Reut Institute's position makes a reasonable case, although there is some ambiguity present. Shlomo Aveneri, the prominent Israeli philosopher and political personality, has commended the distinction between challenging specific policies of Israel as illegitimate and questioning the Israeli state as such. In effect, Israel will aggravate its problems of positive branding if it treats critics of its specific policies as equivalent to delegitimisers that question the viability of the Israeli state as now constituted. It seems difficult at this stage of the conflict, given Israel's deliberate policies of expansionist settlement in the West Bank and East Jerusalem, to envisage any satisfactory resolution of the conflict except through the establishment of some form of bi-national secular state that is not organised along religious or ethnic exclusivist principles, although establishing homelands for both Jews and Palestinians.

The Reut analysis also calls upon Israel to mount a counter-campaign that rebrands Israel positively in world public opinion, and reaffirms the Zionist essence of the Israeli state. It criticises Israel's current foreign policy and security doctrine for its failure to respond appropriately to the 'existential threat' posed by BDS, and more generally 'the delegitimisers,' reminding readers that powerful regimes have been undermined in the past, citing the South African experience during the apartheid period. The Reut call is for a worldwide counter-campaign that aims to isolate and discredit the delegitimisers, and restore the image of Israel by a global public relations (*hasbara*) mobilisation, including activating Zionist communities throughout the world. It also calls for reform in the Ministry of Foreign Affairs so that it can defend Israel against soft-power tactics, and not limit security to its traditional hard-power dimensions. In this regard, the Reut approach recognises the shift in Palestinian strategy, as exemplified by BDS, and complains that the Israeli government has not reacted appropriately. I believe Tel Aviv has heeded this message, and is now itself making an all-out effort along the lines proposed by Reut, above all seeking to confuse this non-violent struggle for Palestinian rights under international law by labelling BDS supporters as extremists and by insisting that systemic criticisms of Israel amount to a contemporary form of anti-Semitism.

In this sense, the battlefield associated with the Israel–Palestine issue has been expanded in two dimensions: from a fundamentally territorial encounter between occupier and occupied to a worldwide struggle without boundaries, and from an emphasis on hard-power oppression and hard-power modes of resistance to a soft-power competition based on controlling the heights of moral and legal authority as reinforced by public opinion and media sympathies.[5] It is not surprising that in this new phase of the struggle, legal and moral issues such as the Goldstone Report, the Freedom Flotilla incidents, and the BDS campaign have substantially displaced the dynamics of violent encounter. In one sense, this itself is a victory for BDS, both by its recognition that Palestinian prospects depended on redefining the forms of engagement in the battle and by the Israeli admissions that they needed to change their own strategic orientation toward the conflict to avoid isolation and potential defeat. It could be also observed that such Israeli military initiatives as the Lebanon invasion of 2006 and Operation Cast Lead of 2008–09 reached 'frustrating outcomes' in the words of the Reut report, and reflected an outdated and evidently dysfunctional militarist approach to Israel's true security and foreign policy interests.

Other purportedly moderate critics of BDS have emphasised such issues as scaring off mainstream peace advocates, undermining the Israeli peace movement that is generally opposed to boycott and divestment initiatives, and somehow feeding accusations of anti-Semitism through actions seen as highly critical of Israel.[6] Suffice to say after such prolonged failures at the inter-governmental level to secure fundamental Palestinian rights by relying on diplomatic approaches, it would seem entirely justifiable for those in solidarity with the Palestinian struggle and for Palestinian civil-society activists to resort to such non-violent coercive approaches to encourage compliance with international law. BDS represents an extraordinary campaign to address an extraordinary situation of prolonged oppressive occupation, colonisation, apartheid, refugee and exile confinement, and denial of human rights, including the right of self-determination. As was the case with South Africa, apologists for Israel's policies seek to invoke such diversionary arguments to avoid the build-up of pressure for changes in governmental policy.

The latest Israeli response, reflecting the rightward drift of Israeli politics, was to pass by a Knesset vote of 47–38 an anti-boycott law on 11 July 2011 entitled 'Bill for Prevention of Damage to the State of Israel Through Boycott 2011'. It makes supporters of BDS, including NGOs and even consumers in any form, subject to serious civil penalties of various kinds, and gives the sellers of boycotted goods a civil law remedy by showing damages. The scope of the law is very broad, penalising any person or organisation that advocates an 'economic, cultural or academic boycott', and extending its reach explicitly to include settlement-only boycotts by saying that the penalties and rights of lawsuits apply if the boycott is directed towards products or services from 'an area under its [Israel's] control'.

Under the new law, individuals or organisations promoting a boycott, even if limited to settlement products, can face lawsuits, denial of tax exemptions and other benefits from the state, and exclusion from bids for government contracts.[7] The removal of tax-exempt status, which can be decreed by the Israeli government, would make it difficult for some Israeli human rights groups to survive, and this may be a collateral goal of the legislation. The law explicitly protects a range of named settlement goods. It also prohibits the government from dealing with a foreign government or any company anywhere in the world that complies with any facet of the 'anti-Israel' boycott.

The backers of the anti-boycott law do not stress economic concerns as much as viewing this push-back against BDS as part of an effort by Israel to resist any further delegitimisation, but I would think that this crude anti-boycott push-back measure will instead produce a surge of support for BDS initiatives around the world. Ironically, the unintended result of the anti-boycott law may be to lend an extra degree of legitimacy to the BDS campaign.

This Knesset action, legally controversial in Israel and among its international supporters, raises new issues about the branding of Israel as 'the only democracy in the Middle East'. This was never a credible claim but rather a triumph of Israeli *hasbara*, although much of Israel's new legislations, including the anti-boycott bill, exhibit increasing hostility to the freedoms associated with a genuine democracy.

CONCLUSION

The Palestinian BDS campaign owes its inspiration to the Anti-Apartheid Movement that adopted similar tactics from 1959 onwards which were seen as instrumental in reconstituting the political climate in such a manner so as to lead to an abandonment of racism, and the peaceful transformation of the South African constitutional structure in the direction of a multiracial democracy. The South African outcome represents an extraordinary victory for soft-power militancy, overcoming the cruel and comprehensively repressive Apartheid regime. The BDS dimensions of the global solidarity movement was greatly strengthened by near-universal support in the United Nations, and through the success of grass-roots anti-apartheid pressures in the United States and the United Kingdom in turning the two most important strategic allies of South Africa into supporters of international sanctions against the regime.

Even as the Palestinians are winning in the struggle for legitimacy in relation to their rights, and their demands for a just and sustainable peace, there are concerns about the political outcome of this latest phase of struggle. So far, Israel has been able to retain the support of the United States and significant parts of Europe, and has been able to neutralise the United Nations to a large degree, particularly though US vetoes in the Security Council and by its leverage within the UN bureaucracy. Furthermore, the Israeli leadership and public opinion show no signs of any willingness to consider options that acknowledge fundamental Palestinian rights, although this was also true in South Africa until an abrupt shift of opinion took place that had been entirely unexpected by informed outside observers. It should be realised that winning the 'Legitimacy War' may not be enough. It has not been enough, for instance, to emancipate the people of Tibet or Chechnya.

At the same time, we cannot know the future. These non-violent initiatives encompassed by BDS provide a legally and morally appropriate means to carry on the struggle for Palestinian rights. Such soft-power tactics give Israel the opportunity to reconsider its approach to relations with the Palestinian people. The BDS mobilisation, assuming that its momentum continues to build, creates incentives for Israel to consider more benign alternatives for its own future social, economic and political development. In these respects, the BDS movement is a creative and constructive response to the challenges associated with the continuing denial of the most basic of Palestinian rights, and deserves the support of individuals and governments supportive of human dignity and conscience throughout the world.

Such a conclusion is bolstered by the degree to which Israel has itself attuned its tactics to fighting against what it calls the 'Delegitimisation Project' of its opponents. In effect, Israel is recognising that the main war zone is now subject to an encounter between soft-power capabilities, and has started to appreciate that its hard-power disposition and inclinations are no longer functional, although reliance on hard-power tactics continues to dominate Israeli security thought and practice, as the 2011 encounters at the borders with Lebanon and Syria exhibited.[8] The Palestinian refugees who were injured and killed by Israeli forces on Nakba Day (15 May) 2011 and also in June of the same year were attempting to implement their rights as laid out by UN resolutions, international law and human rights legislation to return to their homes.

Always, the oppressed are waging an uphill battle against the structures and techniques of oppression. The Palestinians have been engaged in this struggle for many decades, but seem finally to have adopted an approach that takes advantage of their control of the moral and legal high ground. Israel foolishly reinforces this advantage by their consistent refusal to comply with international humanitarian law and human rights law, as well as their unwillingness to address Palestinian rights. History has normally vindicated perseverance in the struggle for basic rights, and the Palestinian movement for peace and justice is from one perspective the last major unfinished chapter in the anti-colonial narrative that was the dominant development supportive of human well-being in the last century. The BDS campaign is a hopeful way of writing the future history of Palestine in the legal and moral language of rights rather than in the bloody deeds of warfare. Such struggles, rooted so firmly in the arena of rights, deserve support from all of us.

NOTES

1. For elaboration, my report to the UN General Assembly, 'Report of the Special Rapporteur on the situation of human rights in the Palestinian Territories occupied since 1967', 30 August 2010, see especially para. 5 on apartheid features of the Occupation.
2. 'The Balfour Declaration', 2 November 1917.
3. 'The BDS Movement Promotes the Delegitimization of the State of Israel', The Reut Institute, 10 June 2010.
4. 'The Delegitimization Challenge: Creating a Political Firewall', The Reut Institute, 14 February 2010.
5. It is correct that the Palestinians attempted from the 1970s a form of hard-power globalisation of their struggle via a variety of violent tactics, including the hijacking of planes and ships, shootings in public places, and seizing hostages at the Olympic Games. Such tactics did expand the battlefield, but alienated world public opinion and involved relying on unlawful attacks on civilians, and were abandoned.

6. For effective responses to these lines of criticism of BDS, see Omar Barghouti, *Boycott, Divestment, Sanctions: The Global Struggle for Palestinian Rights*, Chicago, IL: Haymarket Books, 2011, Note 1, pp. 143–50.

7. See the helpful exposition of the law by Joel Greenberg, 'Israeli anti-boycott law stirs debate on settlement products', *Washington Post*, 22 July 2011; also statement of Human Rights Watch, 'Israel: Anti-Boycott Bill Stifles Expression', 13 July 2011 <http://www.hrw.org/en/news/2011/07/13/Israel-anti-boycott-bill-stifles-expression?print>.

8. In May and June 2011, Palestinian activists, joined by some international supporters, sought to reclaim their right of return on the anniversaries of the Nakba (1948) and Naksa (1967), and were met by Israeli lethal violence resulting in more than 40 deaths and hundreds of injuries. Israel's excessive use of force was condemned by the Special Envoy of the UN Secretary General to the Middle East. See *Haaretz*, 6 June 2011.

10
Towards a Just and Lasting Peace: Kairos Palestine and the Lead of the Palestinian Church

Archbishop Atallah Hanna

Editor's note: In 1985, a group of black South African theologians issued the 'Kairos Document'. The document was a principled example of liberation theology that aimed to challenge the churches' response to the policies of the South African Apartheid regime. In later years, other international theologians followed the South African lead by producing subsequent Kairos Documents relating to specific situations and conditions in Europe, India, Zimbabwe and Latin America. In December 2009, Kairos Palestine was launched.

As the global BDS movement against the Israeli occupation grows in scope and impact, global conversations about its objectives and methods also continue. Those of us, whether Palestinian or international and including both individuals and communities, who endorse and practise BDS activities are often called upon to explain why we do so. Sometimes such questions are asked in a spirit of curiosity and solidarity, whilst at other times they are asked in a spirit of hostility and defensiveness: *What is BDS actually for? What does it accomplish that negotiations cannot? How do you know what to boycott? How do you know when to stop?*

Kairos Palestine – comprised by the co-authors of 'A Moment of Truth' which is Palestinian Christians' word to the world about the Israeli occupation and a call for solidarity in ending it in order to establish a just peace – often receives requests to describe our position on BDS. I would like therefore, to discuss

Kairos Palestine's official stance from both a political and a theological perspective, addressing some of the questions above.

In our document 'A Moment of Truth', Kairos Palestine always connects BDS first and foremost to the basic fact of Israel as the occupying power of our land. We urge people to 'engage in divestment and in an economic and commercial boycott of everything produced by the occupation' (4.2.6); '… with regards to Israel's occupation of Palestinian land. As we have already said, we see the boycott and disinvestment as tools of non-violence for justice, peace and security for all' (6.3); '… the beginning of a system of economic sanctions and boycott to be applied against Israel … in order to reach a just and definitive peace that will put an end to Israeli occupation of Palestinian land … and will guarantee security and peace for all' (7.1).

In Kairos Palestine's theological and political advocacy work, we support a complete boycott of Israel (economic, academic, cultural, political, and so on) rather than a narrower boycott of products generated by settlements, or of products in general. The Israeli occupation affects, or rather constricts, every single aspect of Palestinian life. Its policies amount to nothing less than apartheid in the most technical, demonstrable sense. In 2009, a fact-finding committee of South African social scientists compiled a report that concluded, among other things, that the 'three pillars of apartheid in South Africa' are all implemented by Israel in the occupied Palestinian territory (oPt): distinguishing groups of people along racial lines and allocating superior rights, privileges, resources and services to the dominant one; dividing people into distinct geographic regions and restricting their mobility, and quelling any and all dissent against the regime by means of censorship, banning, torture, administrative detention and assassination.[1]

Even in ways that become daily routines, the Israeli occupation controls our economic reality and professional options. In restricting our mobility, it also restricts our access to education, travel, adequate health care and even members of our own families. It prevents many of us from owning land or seizes land that many of us already own. It subjects us to the constant threat and frequent reality of military violence and arbitrary arrest and it also prevents us from visiting our holiest places of worship. It is a total, not partial, occupation. In this way, we believe in the need for a total boycott.

When met with this reasoning, some people ask us, 'But is the BDS movement directed against the occupation or against Israel?' To this we must answer first that our fundamental goal remains the end of the occupation. However, it must be understood that the occupation does not and cannot operate independently from the policies of the Israeli governments, whether past or present. The Israeli regimes have not only always supported but also expanded the occupation, have systematically taken control of and colonised Palestinian land (through the Apartheid Wall, illegal settlements, land seizures, forced displacement, and so on), and have further fragmented the Palestinian people. Israel has taken great pains to ensure that occupation is virtually synonymous with the state; these two issues are indivisible.

This brings me to another important element of Kairos Palestine's position on BDS: *BDS is not a goal in itself*. Rather, it is a means by which to pressure the Israeli government, and encourage other governments and communities to do the same, to end the occupation and work toward a genuinely just peace. Moreover, the Kairos Document is not primarily about BDS; it *is* primarily about the importance of true solidarity, social equality and non-violent resistance, with love as its guiding logic. In this way, Kairos Palestine recommends BDS as a non-violent tool, thus implying that this is one of many such tools to be used. They are valid if implemented in the spirit of faith, hope and love.

After all, the most important goals of BDS are justice, peace and security for *everyone*, both Palestinians and Israelis. By affirming this objective and its non-violent tactics, we refuse to be dominated by the cycle of bloodshed, we reject revenge, and we advocate peaceful ways of ending the occupation and securing our rights. BDS is designed to establish justice and freedom for Palestinians as well as peace and security for Israelis. As is written in 'A Moment of Truth': 'We call on the Israelis to end the occupation. Then they will see a new world in which there is no fear, no threat, but rather security, justice and peace' (1.4).

For the Israelis to end the occupation, of course, they must accept responsibility for what it has already wrought. This accountability is a large part of what BDS seeks to engender. As Ran Greenstein, a sociologist who teaches at the University of the Witwatersrand in South Africa, writes, 'The challenge is to get [Israeli Jews] thinking about what they take for granted (that they are a majority in Israel legitimately, that the boycott reflects anti-Semitism, and so on) ... .'[2] Later, he writes:

> The goal would not be to convince the [Avigdor] Liebermans (impossible task), but to create a critical mass of minority dissidents: even in [South Africa] the majority of whites were opposed to change or indifferent, and only a small but crucial minority got involved in the struggle ... Pressure from the outside must not replace work from within: both are essential and need to be conceptualized in such a way that they reinforce one another rather than act at cross-purposes. There is no magic formula: it took decades in SA to reach a balance and it can be achieved in our case here as well.

Mr Greenstein's points reinforce our belief that BDS is a powerful means of solidarity not only between Palestinians and the international community, but also among Israeli, Palestinian and international peacemakers. The leftist movement within Israel remains weak and is often ignored on the international stage, partly because (as Mr Greenstein also mentions) many people fear accusations of anti-Semitism. This atmosphere of hesitation undercuts Israeli-led efforts (and there are some strong and deeply principled ones) to end the occupation; if the world continues to dismiss them as traitors, the Israeli government can safely claim that the world rejects their calls, especially for BDS. This provides all the more reason for Israeli activists to raise their voices along with Palestinians and internationals in support of boycott, which encourages advocacy that unifies both pressure from the outside and work from within. Mr Greenstein speaks to the need for:

> ... a focused campaign that would clarify the link between crime and consequences: certainly, BDS is a way for the Israeli state and society to see, feel, and know the toll the occupation has taken – and then to take responsibility by ceasing to perpetuate it – as the international community refuses to condone the injustices of apartheid.

Palestinians hold the right to self-determination; this is a human right and a tenet of international law that has been violated by the state of Israel for over 64 years. Resistance, too, is a right enshrined by international law for 'conflicts in which peoples are fighting against colonial domination and alien occupation and against racist regimes in the exercise of their right of self-determination'.[3] Palestinians have historically employed numerous forms of resistance, some of which were armed and others inherently non-violent; some acts of resistance were organised, whilst other examples were entirely spontaneous. All of these strategies of resistance have been rejected, repressed and often brutally punished by the occupation regime and its international supporters. Kairos Palestine stresses once again that BDS is an utterly non-violent, peace-seeking, solidarity-inducing, ethically consistent form of resistance; we believe that it is one of the most productive, generative and collaborative manifestations possible of our right, as Palestinians, to define our struggle and articulate our freedom. Repressing the BDS movement means repressing the chance for non-violence to succeed, and all of us, Palestinians and Israelis, *need* it to succeed in order to attain a just and lasting peace.

Kairos Palestine maintains that faith, hope and love do not merely await us at the end of the road to justice, but that they are also the very road we walk upon. As human beings, as Palestinians, and as Christians, we believe that BDS is a meaningful and essential part of this path.

NOTES

1. 'SA academic study finds that Israel is practicing apartheid and colonialism in the Occupied Palestinian Territories', Human

Sciences Research Council, 2009 <http://www.hsrc.ac.za/Media_Release-378.phtml>.

2. Ran Greenstein, Comments on Uri Avnery's article 'Tutu's Prayer', 29 August 2009 <http://gush-shalom.org.toibillboard.info/RanGreen.htm>.

3. Article 1(4) of Protocol 1 (additional to the Geneva Conventions), International Humanitarian Law.

Part III

Economy, Academia and Culture

11

BDS:
Perspectives of an Israeli Economist

Shir Hever

HISTORY OF THE ECONOMIC BOYCOTT

Critics of the Boycott, Divestment and Sanctions (BDS) movement would do well to remember, amidst their accusations of discrimination and anti-Semitism, that amongst the earliest uses of the economic boycott tool in the struggle for the fate of Palestine was the 'Hebrew Labour' policy of the Zionist movement. In the early twentieth century, Zionist immigrants to Palestine developed the concept of 'Hebrew Labour' which effectively meant boycotting Palestinian labour and products.[1] This practice, although today officially illegal in Israel, still persists in thousands of Israeli businesses, which advertise their commitment not to employ Arab workers; the law is not enforced against these businesses.[2] This discriminatory practice bears nothing in common with today's BDS movement, which explicitly embraces Israeli participation. In 1945, a significant boycott was adopted by the Arab states, even before Israel was officially founded, known as 'the Arab Boycott'. This entailed boycotting not only Zionist companies, but later also companies which traded with Israel. More embargo than boycott, this policy dissuaded companies like Coca-Cola, McDonald's, Mitsubishi, Toyota and others from selling to Israel or opening branches there for many years.[3]

The US government enacted a law to put pressure on companies not to cooperate with the Arab Boycott, and companies who maintained the boycott were required to pay fines. During the 1990s, the Arab Boycott began to fall apart. The beginning of the Oslo negotiations was used to put pressure on Arab states to abandon their boycott, and many companies began to open branches and trade with Israel. The rise of the World Trade Organization (the WTO, of which Israel is a member) further undermined the Arab Boycott. Because the WTO demands that each member of the organisation will treat all other members equally, countries like Saudi Arabia (one of the most important countries practicing the boycott into the 1990s) had to give up the boycott or be left out of the organisation.[4]

These two forms of boycott should not be confused with the BDS Call. Unlike BDS, neither Hebrew Labour nor the Arab Boycott adopted a rights-based approach, neither was in keeping with respect for international law, and neither was focused on protesting specific crimes committed by the boycott target. From a Palestinian perspective, the historic use of boycott swelled during the First Revolution (1936–39), when tax revolts and boycott of the institutes of British Mandatory rule reached a peak. Various low-level boycotts were attempted through the following half-century until, during the First Intifada (1987–91), Palestinian activists called on Palestinians to boycott Israeli goods, to stop paying taxes to Israel and to cut economic ties with Israel. Considering the heavy dependency of the Palestinian market on the Israeli economy, this call was extremely difficult to follow. Nevertheless, it was undertaken by many Palestinians, causing Israeli companies to lose valuable business from the captive Palestinian market, but also causing extensive economic damage to the Palestinians who pursued the boycott.[5]

ECONOMIC CULPABILITY AND THE REASONS FOR ECONOMIC BOYCOTT

The use of boycott as a tool to fight against the occupation began with a call to boycott the products of the Israeli colonies (often called 'settlements') in occupied lands: in the Gaza Strip (these colonies were removed in 2005), in the Golan Heights, and in the West Bank and East Jerusalem. Activists prepared lists of products to be boycotted, arguing that economic support to the colonies inevitably funds the occupation.

The call to focus the boycott on colony products is strengthened by a legal argument. According to the Fourth Geneva Convention (to which Israel is a signatory), it is forbidden for the occupying power to settle its own population in occupied territory. All Israeli colonies are therefore illegal, and buying their products can be considered to be supporting criminal activity. Israeli colonists who export agricultural products, for instance, grown on stolen Palestinian land, watered with stolen Palestinian water and often nurtured with exploited Palestinian labour – are a very clear-cut example of illegal activity.

This is compounded by the fact that Europe (Israel's main trading partner) gives Israel advantageous trade benefits (lower tariffs and duties) but only recognises Israel in the 1967 borders. Thus, products from the colonies should not receive the same benefits. However, Israeli companies consistently lie about the true source of the product, and with direct support from the Israeli government, the products are falsely labelled as 'made in Israel', for example, the company Soda Stream, which sells carbonated water machines in Europe under a false label.[6]

Israeli companies have a strong incentive to open factories, warehouses and offices in the colonies. They receive extensive government subsidies, pay lower taxes, are subject to far more lenient environmental regulation (after all, the waste is spilled onto nearby Palestinian villages who have very little say on the matter) and have the option of exploiting cheap Palestinian workers who are not fully protected by Israel's labour laws.[7] These same companies also have an incentive to keep their operation in the colonies secret, in order to retain preferential trade conditions from Europe, and in order to avoid being boycotted. A common practice used by the companies is to retain facilities in the colonies, but print an address on the product for a small office rented within Israel's recognised borders, for the purpose of giving the false impression that the company is located on the Israeli side of the Green Line. This actually means that customers have no way to be certain whether a product that they see in a store labelled 'made in Israel' is truly from Israel, or from the colonies. This is an important argument against a selective boycott focusing only on colony products. For those who truly wish to avoid the risk of supporting Israeli colonisation, the only safe course of action is to stop buying all Israeli products until Israel stops its policy of deception.

But as the Women's Coalition for Peace has noted, through their extensive research team called 'Who Profits?', the occupation seeps into almost every aspect of Israel's economy. Even companies that don't have any facilities physically in the colonies are often involved deeply in the occupation. They often provide services and products to the colonies, purchase raw materials and machinery from the colonies, and hire staff including colonists and soldiers who do their reserve duty in the Occupied Palestinian Territory (oPt). All of Israel's major telecommunication companies, transportation companies, and infrastructure companies routinely violate international law by providing services to illegal colonies. Furthermore, Israeli companies still enjoy benefits from using lands that were confiscated from Palestinians in 1948 as they were expelled, and many Israeli companies discriminate against non-Jewish workers. For example, the average wage of Palestinian citizens of Israel is only 67 per cent of the Israeli average.[8]

In fact, the companies which play the most significant role in shoring up Israel's occupation are not the settlement companies, but the large and influential Israeli corporations. These companies' taxes help fund Israel's military budget, and the owners of these companies exert extensive power over the Israeli political sphere. Because of their significant influence over Israel's policies, Israel's capitalists also share responsibility for these policies. Boycott and divestment are tools to remind these capitalists of their responsibility, and to apply pressure on them to create positive change.

Israeli colonisation of Palestinian land does not and cannot exist as a separate and distinct entity from the rest of Israel. They are all part of the same economy and policies, and colonisation is just one aspect of Israel's crimes against the Palestinian people. Therefore, an economic campaign of BDS must target all Israeli products and companies and not simply those who are directly active within colonies themselves.

DIVESTMENT

One of the three aspects of the BDS campaign, and the one easiest to misunderstand, is the divestment aspect. While boycott can be organised by consumers, and sanctions require government policy, divestment is something done by 'investors'. Often, activists forget that they are investors themselves.

While the bigger investors are usually capitalists and corporations (which are unlikely to be swayed by moral arguments), everyone with a pension fund is invested in a portfolio. Students in universities might be interested in the portfolios held by their universities (paid for with their tuition money), while people who belong to a religious denomination might take interest in investment portfolios held by their church, mosque, synagogue, or other religious centre, paid for with the community's donations. Trade unions also sometimes hold investment portfolios.

The first case for divestment is a case for avoiding responsibility for a crime. Companies sell stocks and bonds to investors in order to raise capital for their operations. When a company (either Israeli or international) violates the human rights of Palestinians, or violates international law, it is using investors' money. As investors are the actual owners of the company, they also share responsibility for the company's actions. In contemporary capitalist society, corporations have limited liability ('Ltd') so that investors can avoid legal culpability by tearing up their stocks. But they cannot avoid moral responsibility this way.

Divestment can be taken as a 'clean-hands' policy for investors not willing to take part in criminal activity. But large-scale divestment also has significant impact on the ability of Israel to commit crimes. Companies will become paralysed without ready cash-flow, and in extreme cases, a drop in its stock value could lead a company to bankruptcy. Most importantly, when activists begin a divestment process for moral and political reasons, they create a momentum which affects non-political investors. Investors who are interested only in profits are likely to withdraw their investments from a company which they perceive is in the process of losing its value because of political pressure.

'Africa Israel' is a good example of such actions and their results. The company's construction projects in the oPt made it a prime target for BDS campaigns, but as a property company it was not easy to boycott. Activists opted for divestment, and convinced the Norwegian Pension Fund to divest from the company. This was followed by Swedish banks who were pressured by their customers, and eventually by the Blackrock financial company who divested for economic, rather than political, reasons.[9] Following this, Africa Israel owner Lev Leviev had to convene a press conference and admit that the company could not meet its payments to debtors.[10] Although Leviev never admitted that the company's financial trouble was caused by divestment, it certainly was a decisive factor that helped push an already deeply indebted company over the edge. About 15 months later, Africa Israel announced that it would no longer build in the oPt.[11]

THE DIFFERENCE BETWEEN BOYCOTT AND EMBARGO

It is worth mentioning not only what BDS is about, but also what it is not. Although BDS may be presented by pro-Israelis as an attempt to destroy Israel's economy, it is in fact an attempt to put measured pressure on Israeli society through economic, cultural and academic avenues in order to give the government a path to change its policies and thus bring about the end of BDS.

A quick comparison between the Israeli siege on Gaza and the BDS movement brings forward the differences between an embargo and a boycott. While the people in Gaza may not import or export freely, BDS requests only one limitation on sales to Israel: not to sell Israel military equipment. Companies may export to Israel (meaning that Israelis can purchase any item other than weapons of their choice), although opening up shops in Israel would involve buying buildings and equipment and therefore would be a violation of BDS. Even if BDS is implemented on a very wide scale, it will not cause a shortage in basic needs for the Israeli population, unlike the siege on Gaza. This reservation is critical, and demonstrates that the Palestinian organisers of BDS are very selective in the pressure which they wish to apply. BDS remains a tool, not an end in itself, and by setting its limits, campaigners have demonstrated that the rights-based goals of BDS remain the focus of the campaign at all times.

In fact, realistically BDS cannot destroy the Israeli economy. It is highly improbable that sufficient support will be generated for BDS anytime soon that Israel's international trade will come to a halt. It is far more likely that BDS will achieve a measurable and painful impact on Israel's exports, enough to make Israelis realise that their country's apartheid policies are no longer sustainable.

THE COST OF OCCUPATION TO ISRAEL

The social disintegration brought by decades of occupation has had a deeper impact on Israel than the economic costs, but economic factors can still serve as an indicator to demonstrate the heavy burden on Israeli society. Of course, the economic damage inflicted on the Palestinian population from the occupation is much deeper, but understanding the cost of the occupation to Israeli society is significant in appreciating the role of BDS.

The occupation of the oPt was a profitable venture for the Israeli economy in the first two decades after 1967. But the Palestinian rebellion in the First Intifada shook the Israeli economy, forcing the Israeli government to redouble its efforts to control the Palestinians and their land, and turning the occupation into a massive expenditure.[12] The cost of the occupation is difficult to calculate, because it is hidden under hundreds of budget titles. Much of it is hidden within the budget of the Ministry of Defence, which is a state secret. Numerous mechanisms are employed by the Israeli government for hiding these costs – both from international accountability and from the Israeli public itself. Nevertheless, numerous studies have been published by Israeli economists over the years in an effort to estimate the cost of the occupation, which can be divided into two main categories: civilian costs and security costs.

The civilian costs include subsidies to the colonies (in housing, infrastructure, services and taxes), and cost Israel nearly US$3 billion annually. Military costs (including Border Police deployment, imprisoning Palestinians, protecting the colonies, the Separation Wall, and so on) are approximately double that figure, at nearly US$6 billion. These costs (a rough estimate based on multiple studies) are increasing rapidly, at a rate of about 7 per cent per year.[13]

The growing cost has forced the Israeli government to cut back on public services and liquidate the welfare state, which has turned Israel into an extremely unequal society. The 2011 'social justice' protests across Israel, the largest the country had ever seen, are a sign that Israelis are certainly feeling these cuts, although at present the public has not yet made the link between these economic cutbacks and the cost of occupation. Economic burden itself cannot bring social and political change; it can only prepare the ground for it. As the Israeli government is dragged into ever-growing spending on maintaining the unsustainable occupation, it pays not just with money but with the currency of social solidarity in Israel.

ISRAEL'S VULNERABILITY TO BDS

The cost of the occupation has made Israel more vulnerable to BDS. Unlike South Africa, Israel's is a highly globalised economy. In 2010, exports comprised 36.9 per cent and imports 34.9 per cent of GDP, demonstrating that Israel is highly dependent on foreign trade.[14] Also, Israel is short on natural resources and must import raw materials from abroad. In 2009, 67 per cent of imports to Israel were raw materials and fuels.[15] This means that Israel's policymakers would be unable to conceal the effects of BDS from the general public. Although BDS does not prevent Israel from importing raw materials and finished goods (except weapons), effective boycott and divestment could cause a collapse in the value of Israeli currency.

As BDS grows, Israelis will feel a difference in their ability to take either leisure or business trips abroad, and to consume imported goods. This is especially significant for a society which considers itself to be part of the 'West' albeit isolated in the Middle East, and whose main trade connections are in Europe and the US.

Divestment also affects Israelis' pensions and savings. Although the effects have so far been relatively minor, every collapsed company or company which chooses to leave Israel has immediate repercussions for pension funds, insurance portfolios, and so on. The credit default of Africa Israel (described above) affected the vast majority of Israeli citizens.

It should be noted that, due to Israel's stark inequalities, BDS is most likely to affect the elites in Israel first. The lower classes in Israel are more likely to purchase locally produced goods and can rarely afford travel abroad. Thus, BDS affects the large exporting corporations and the influential elites in Israel. This is an argument for both the effectiveness of BDS as well as its moral justification. BDS activists would like to focus their efforts on those in Israel who are most likely to benefit from the exploitation of the Palestinian economy, as well as those most likely to be able to bring about a change in government policy. In May 2011, Idan Ofer, son and heir to one of Israel's most powerful economic empires, and CEO of the Israel Corp company, assembled approximately eighty senior Israeli businesspeople to an emergency meeting to discuss the possibility that the dead-end Israeli position in the peace negotiations will lead to a 'South Africa-style boycott' and how to prepare for that.[16]

Israel's vulnerability should not be mistaken to mean that BDS itself can win the struggle for Palestinian freedom. However, we can imagine a scenario in which BDS reaches the point where it takes a significant toll on the profits of Israel's larger corporations. If a large company or two chooses to leave Israel because of BDS, and if the business community comes to a consensus that the 'Israel' brand name does more damage than good, then the general public's illusion that the status quo can be maintained by force of arms will be shattered. Soldiers and officers will have to be careful about shooting live ammunition at unarmed Palestinian demonstrators, because of the consequences for murdering innocents in the form of international pressure (symbolised by, but not limited to, BDS). The boost to the Palestinian struggle will be such that it is reasonable to assume that many Israelis and eventually the government will realise that no other option exists but to give up the inherent elements of injustice in Israel's political system.

REACTIONS IN ISRAEL TO BDS

Since BDS is a rapidly growing threat to Israeli businesses, it may seem surprising that the reactions to it in the Israeli media are muted. Although BDS is mentioned (mostly indirectly) in the news on a daily basis, the information presented is often inaccurate, incomplete and outdated. A quick search in the international media brings much better information about BDS. The reason for this is that BDS is a sensitive subject, from which many Israeli journalists shy away. Companies who feel the effects of BDS are loathe to discuss them for fear of bolstering the movement, and because they could be perceived as unpatriotic for discussing it. Journalists are encouraged to present BDS as part of an anti-Semitic agenda against Israel, within a conceptual framework that tries to shift BDS from its actual demands (for justice, human rights and equality) to unrelated issues of racist hatred of Jews. This reframing of BDS allows the Israeli government, business community and media to portray BDS as a force of nature, something which cannot be understood or addressed seriously, and thus enables the denial of the actual reasons for the campaign. Because of this, Israel's propaganda efforts (called 'Hasbara') do not attempt to confront BDS and initiate an argument, but to change the subject instead, to speak about other aspects of Israel (like technology and tourism) and leave BDS's questions unanswered.

Internally, Israelis cannot remain oblivious to the international pressure. Merely mentioning it could mark one as unpatriotic, but thoughts cannot be censored, and the culture of silence and obfuscation that evolves around BDS only serves, in the long run, to prove its significance to Israelis.

COUNTING SUCCESSES AND FAILURES

Pausing to take a look at the successes of BDS, one could argue that so far, BDS has not had a significant impact on companies that do not operate directly in the oPt. Also, the determination of certain companies to persist in their dealings with Israel even when losing money may give the impression that international corporations are willing to subsidise Israeli policies. However, considering that the campaign is only six years old, there are already some very impressive successes. Apart from Africa Israel (discussed above), a few examples are cited below.

Asa Abloi, the Swedish corporation, decided to close its Multilock factory in the Barkan colony industrial zone.[17] As one of the first BDS successes, this development paved the way for other companies to follow suit. Unilever, the gigantic food corporation, followed suit as it removed its Beigel & Beigel factory from Barkan.[18] Unilever at first failed to sell the factory, thus highlighting the fact that BDS made investments in the colony industries unappealing to corporations.

Caterpillar, which continues to provide Israel with bulldozers to demolish Palestinian homes, has suffered from divestment and stockholder uproar. Eventually, the company moved its 2011 annual shareholders meeting from the Chicago area to Little Rock, Arkansas in an attempt to avoid protests,[19] and the Caterpillar brand has also suffered because of the company's involvement in the occupation. These actions demonstrated the effectiveness of the public education campaigns launched by BDS activists and the internal effects that Caterpillar is suffering due to BDS activism. Activists also purchased Caterpillar stocks in order to attend stockholder meetings for internal disruption and subsequent divestment proved the effectiveness of those actions.

After being nationalised by Belgium during the recent global economic crisis, Dexia Bank was exposed for having provided loans to colonies in the West Bank. The bank came under increasing pressure, and eventually had to announce its intention to sell Dexia Israel and disconnect from its operations in Israel.[20] The Belgian government realised that it would be held responsible for criminal activity if it continued to hold onto the bank, and Dexia Bank was given no option by the Israeli government to continue its operations only within the Green Line. This highlighted the importance of a comprehensive boycott of Israel and the futility of trying to focus the boycott only on colony products.

The German railway company Deutsche Bahn pulled out of a project to build a line between Jerusalem and Tel Aviv that would go through the West Bank.[21] Germany is one of the most difficult countries in which to carry out BDS activism, due to the country's history of Jewish persecution and the contemporary fear of being associated with its dark past, yet the actions of Deutsche Bahn proved that even in Germany the unquestioning support of Israel has cracked.

The greatest economic success of BDS so far, however, has been Veolia. The company participated in the construction of a light railway in Jerusalem (including occupied East Jerusalem) and also in bus lines and garbage disposal in the colonies. It became the target of massive international protests, and has lost billions of dollars in contracts and tenders because of its illegal activity. Veolia eventually sold its share in the light railway, but still continues to lose contracts around the world as it refuses to give up its bus and garbage contracts in the colonies. Veolia serves as a warning post for any international company that considers making money through contacts with the Israeli government.[22]

WHY DO I SUPPORT BDS?

The Palestinian civil society call for BDS specifically mentions that Israelis are invited to support the movement, but are themselves exempt from boycotting their own economy (it would be impossible, after all, for Israelis to stop buying Israeli-made goods). This, I believe, creates a greater responsibility for Israelis. Not only have I been born into a privileged class, and have enjoyed preferential rights over Palestinians since the day I was born, but I am also not expected by Palestinians (nor able) to actively participate in the boycott of Israeli products. As an Israeli citizen, I am not reminded daily of the urgency of resolving the injustice in Palestine; I do not live in a refugee camp and do not have to struggle to survive. However, morally and politically, it is just as urgent for Israelis to end the injustice that has become the hallmark of their government and state.

I firmly believe that BDS is an effective tool that can begin to make Israel accountable for its crimes, and that can open the door for a real change in the situation. It is a moral duty for Israelis to speak out for BDS – because their voice is needed to clarify that democracy and justice will not emerge from within Israel's internal political process.

Finally, I believe that every colonial regime, of which Israel is undoubtedly one, must eventually fall. Israel's Apartheid regime will collapse either in bloodshed or through non-violent struggle. BDS is the most powerful tool of the non-violent struggle, it is wholly inclusive for all people and is entirely rights-based; as a human being and an Israeli, I have every reason to prefer a non-violent end to the ongoing injustices perpetuated against the Palestinian people.

NOTES

1. Anita Shapira, 1977, *The Lost Struggle: Hebrew Labor [Hama'avak Hanikhzav, Avoda Ivrit]*, Tel Aviv: Hakibutz Hameukhad.
2. Alternative Information Center, 'Israel's Yellow Pages Publishes Ads Promoting "Hebrew Labour" – Only Businesses', 17 February 2011 <http://www.alternativenews.org/english/index.php/news/israeli-society/3315-israels-yellow-pages-publishes-ads-promoting-hebrew-labour-only-businesses-html>.
3. Martin A. Weiss, 'Arab League Boycott of Israel', *CRS Report for Congress*, 19 April 2006.

4. Ibid.
5. Ma'an Development Center, 2009, *Boycott, Divestment & Sanctions; Lessons Learned in Effective Solidarity*, p. 6.
6. Who Profits, *Soda Stream; A Case Study for Corporate Activity in Illegal Israeli Settlements*, Case Study No. 1., January 2011.
7. Shlomo Swirski, 2008, *Is There an Israeli Business Peace Disincentive?*, Adva Center, Tel Aviv.
8. Shlomo Swirski, Eti Konor-Atia and Hala Abu-Khala, *Israel: A Social Report 2010*, Adva Center, Tel Aviv, December 2010, p. 15.
9. Press Agencies, 2009, 'Blackrock Following the British Embassy, UNICEF and Oxfam – Withdraws from Investing in Africa Israel', *Kalkalist*, 25 August 2008.
10. Gilad Shalmor, 'Leviev: "Preparing as if the Crisis isn't Over"', *Channel 2*, 30 August 2009 <http://www.mako.co.il/news-money/economy/Article-1414167385a6321004.htm>.
11. Coalition of Women for Peace, 'Press Release: Israeli Holding Company Africa Israel Claims it Will Not Build in Settlements', *Coalition of Women for Peace*, 1 November 2010 <http://www.coalitionofwomen.org/?tag=africa-israel-investments&lang=en>.
12. Shlomo Swirski, *The Burden of Occupation; The Cost of the Occupation to Israeli Society, Polity and Economy, 2008 Update*, Adva Center, Tel Aviv, p. 10.
13. Shir Hever, *Political Economy of Israel's Occupation: Repression Beyond Exploitation*, London: Pluto Press, 2010, pp. 68–71.
14. Israeli Central Bureau of Statistics (ICBS), 2011, 'E.1.1 Expenditure on Gross Domestic Product, and Uses of Resources', *Statistical Reader*, 2001 <http://www1.cbs.gov.il/reader/>, accessed July 2011.
15. Israeli Central Bureau of Statistics (ICBS), 'Imports and Exports, by Group of Goods (net)', *Statistical Reader*, 2011 <http://www1.cbs.gov.il/reader/>, accessed July 2011.
16. Zvi Zarchia, 'Idan Ofer: Without a Negotiation Initiative – We Will Soon Become South Africa', *The Marker*, 14 May 2011.
17. Noam Sheizaf, 'Citing Anti-Settlement Pressure, Multilock to Close W. Bank Factory', *+972 Magazine*, 22 December 2010 <http://972mag.com/major-success-for-the-anti-settlements-campaign-multilock-to-close-west-bank-factory/>.
18. Alternative Information Center, 'BDS Success: Unilever to Move Factory out of West Bank', 12 October 2010 <http://www.alternativenews.org/english/index.php/topics/

economy-of-the-occupation/2916-bds-success-unilever-to-move-factory-out-of-west-bank>.

19. Chicagoans Against Apartheid in Palestine, 'Caterpillar Moves Meeting to Little Rock to Avoid Protests', *WeDivest.org*, 8 June 2011 <http://wedivest.org/2011/06/caterpillar-moves-meeting-to-little-rock-to-avoid-protests/>.

20. Nora Barrows-Friedman, 'BDS Victories: Dexia Bank to Sell Israeli Subsidiary; Veolia Loses Another Contract', *Electronic Intifada*, 20 May 2011 <http://electronicintifada.net/node/9991.

21. Tobias Buck, 'Deutche Bahn Pulls Out of Israel Project', *Financial Times*, 9 May 2011.

22. Adri Nieuwhof, 'Pressure Continues on Veolia and Alstom to Halt Light Rail Project', *Electronic Intifada*, 4 February 2010 <http://electronicintifada.net/content/pressure-continues-veolia-and-alstom-halt-light-rail-project/8665>.

12
Colonialism, the Peace Process and the Academic Boycott

Ilan Pappe

I have been a political activist for most of my adult life. In all those years, I believed deeply that the only way to change the unbearable and unacceptable reality in Israel and Palestine was to work for change from within. This meant that I have tried to be constantly involved in an attempt to persuade the Jewish society – to which I belonged and into which I was born – that its basic policy in the land was wrong and disastrous. Like so many others, for me the options were clear: I could either join politics from above, or counter it by activism from below.

I began by joining the Labour Party in the 1980s and then the Democratic Front for Peace and Equality (*Hadash*) – where I was offered but declined to be a member of the Knesset. Parallel to these efforts, I turned my energies to work within educational and peace NGOs and even chaired and headed two such institutions, first a Zionist one, the Institute for Peace Studies in Givat Haviva (belonging to the 'Left Zionist' movement), and then a non-Zionist one, the Emil Touma Institute for Palestinian Studies. Inside and outside of the Zionist framework, I and many of my more veteran and younger colleagues were toiling to engage in a constructive dialogue with our compatriots in the hope of making a modicum of impact on the policy in the present so as to enhance the chances for reconciliation in the future. It was mainly a campaign of information about crimes and atrocities committed by Israel in, and since, 1948 and a plea to accept a future based on equal human and civil rights for all.[1]

For any activist to come to the conclusion that change from within is unattainable is not just an intellectual or political process – it is more than anything else an admission of defeat. And it was this fear of defeatism that led me to procrastinate for a very long time before adopting a more resolute and less ambivalent position on the matter.

But after almost thirty years of activism and historical research, I was convinced in around 2002–03 that the local balance of power in Palestine and Israel pre-empted any hope for a transformation from within the Israeli Jewish society in the foreseeable future. This realisation coincided with the initial gelling of the roots from which the Boycott, Divestment and Sanctions (BDS) campaign was born.

Two impulses produced the BDS option. One was historical and the other was activism on the ground. Historically, the recent and illuminating example of South Africa seemed to inspire most of the constructive thinking of what pressure should look like or mean. On the ground, activists and NGOs under occupation were seeking non-violent means not only as a way of resisting the occupation, but also in order to expand the resistance options beyond the armed methods which had achieved limited success.

BDS began as a call from the civil society under occupation, was endorsed by other Palestinian groups and then translated into individual and collective actions worldwide. These actions differ in their poignancy and form, and vary from boycotting Israeli products to the severance of ties with Israeli academic institutes. What they have in common is that they send a message of outrage that feeds a willingness to take a strong stance against the atrocities on the ground in Palestine. Some have chosen an individual display of protest whilst others opted for an organised campaign, and it seems that the elasticity of these choices produced a sweeping process that was powerful enough to instigate a new public mood and atmosphere.

ACCEPTING THE COLONIALIST PARADIGM

Late in the day for me, and much earlier on for some of my more astute and perceptive colleagues, came the realisation that the problem in Israel was not a particular policy or a specific government. There was a principled problem rooted deeply in the ideological infrastructure that fed Israeli decisions on Palestine and the Palestinians ever since 1948 – an ideology, which elsewhere I described as a hybrid dogma that fuses together colonialism and romantic nationalism.[2] In the twenty-first century, Israel became a formidable settler colonialist state unwilling to transform or compromise with the reality around it – a state that was willing, using the most lethal weapons at hand, to crush any resistance to its control and rule over what used to be historical Palestine. It began with the ethnic cleansing of nearly 80 per cent of Palestine in 1948, expanded with the imposition of harsh military rule on the Palestinian minority in Israel (1948–67), and then continued with the occupation of the remaining 22 per cent of the land in 1967. Ever since then, the Palestinians living there were enclaved in mega-prisons, Bantustans and sieged cantons. This ideological infrastructure also fed the vile discriminative policies towards the Palestinian citizens in Israel and still prevents today any reasonable and just solution for the millions of Palestinian refugees scattered around the world. If time is a factor in any historical process, in the case of Israel it contributed to the weakening, if not total disappearance, of any internal challenges to this ideological infrastructure. The number of people willing to question the wisdom of the policies pursued by successive governments ever since 1948 has remained insignificant and low.

While the ideological infrastructure can be described as a hybridity between colonialism and romantic nationalism, the reality on the ground is of a settler state that continues today colonising and uprooting the indigenous people of Palestine wherever they are. This reality has therefore to be decolonised before anything else is attempted. A successful decolonisation would remove most of the injustices and oppressions that are intact today in the relationship between Israelis and Palestinians.

Admittedly, Israel is not a straightforward case study of colonialism. It is in many ways a unique sample of the phenomenon, but it is beyond the scope of this chapter to delve into that question; others have done so in a very succinct and illuminating way.[3] Nor is the term 'decolonisation' easily applied to any solution of either the Israeli occupation of the 1967 Palestinian territories or for the question of Palestine as a whole. And yet the colonialist/anti-colonialist paradigm is the best we have for both analysing the reality in Israel and Palestine today, and for finding ways forward towards a comprehensive solution.

With the help of this twin paradigm, I would like in this chapter to tackle two of the more important counter-arguments made against BDS. The first is that negotiations between the two sides are a preferred way forward in the search for peace and reconciliation, and secondly, that the BDS initiative would entrench the Israelis even deeper in their intransigence and unwillingness to compromise. Both these counter-arguments are examined here from within the double prism of colonialism/ decolonisation in an attempt to show that this particular vantage point is the best explanation and justification for the BDS option so many of us have endorsed in the last decade or so. I will also try and show that the academic boycott component in this campaign is also justified and understood better from within this dual prism.

BDS VERSUS THE 'PEACE PROCESS'

It almost seems superfluous to expose the fiasco called the 'peace process' these days. But it is important to show the vitality and validity of BDS through a close examination of the damage caused by the futile strategy of peace.

In 1936, the Zionist settlement enterprise covered less than 10 per cent of Palestine, whereas today, after nearly a century of declarations, resolutions and assorted 'peace initiatives', it stretches over approximately 90 per cent of the country. These decades of diplomatic 'efforts' have only deepened the Zionist colonisation of Palestine. Thus it seems that the message from the peace brokers, mainly Americans since 1970, was that peace can be achieved without any significant halt or limit to the colonisation of Palestine. True, there was an eviction of settlers from Gaza in 2005 and some isolated outposts in the West Bank, but this did not alter the overall matrix of a colonial control with all its systematic daily abuses of civil and human rights, and this was more than compensated for by settlement construction in the West Bank and East Jerusalem. The occupation of the West Bank, the strangulation of the Gaza Strip, the oppression of the Palestinians inside Israel and the denial of the refugees' right of return continued as long as this policy was packaged as a comprehensive peace settlement to be endorsed by obedient Palestinian and Arab partners.

The reason for these international failures and Zionist successes are the faulty premises on which the 'process' was based from very early on but in particular since 1967, when it became an exclusively US-led western initiative.

The basic formula, apart from the idea of a two-states solution as a final objective of the process – is that an Israeli withdrawal from areas it occupied in 1967 would signal the end of the conflict. This meant that once all the Israeli concerns about the state's security would be satisfied, the Israeli Army would withdraw from the lives of the Palestinians. These concerns nowadays are summarised by Prime Minister Netanyahu as the recognition of Israel as a Jewish state, and by everyone else in the Israeli political centre in the demand for the creation of a de-militarised future Palestinian state over only parts of the Occupied Territory. The consensus is that after the repositioning of the military presence, the army could still keep an eye on the future Palestine from Jewish settlement blocs, East Jerusalem, the Jordanian border, and from the other side of the Separation Walls and fences surrounding the West Bank and the Gaza Strip.

While it is possible that the 'Quartet' and even the Obama administration would wish to see a more comprehensive withdrawal and a sovereign Palestinian state as the basis for a future solution, no one in the international community challenges the sequence and the endgame proposed by the Israelis: no withdrawal before Israel's concerns are met and satisfied, and the creation of two enclaved Bantustans, controlled from the outside by Israel as the final geopolitical map of what used to be historical Palestine. This final settlement offers no viable solution to the refugee or Jerusalem question; nor does it refer at all to the plight of the Palestinian citizens inside Israel.

So while the 'process' deepened the colonisation it also produced a roadmap that would perpetuate it forever. Moreover, the internal logic of the 'process' is based on anticipation for a change in the Palestinian agenda and not in the Israeli one. In other words, the message from abroad to Israel was that peace does not require any transformation from within. The inevitable refusal of even the most fragile Palestinian leadership to accept this rationale enabled the Israelis to say that the anticipated change in the Palestinian position has failed to mature and therefore Israel is entitled to pursue unilateral policies that would safeguard its national security (the famous 'ingathering' policy as it was coined by Ehud Olmert).[4]

Therefore, it may now be safe to conclude that the peace process served as a disincentive for internal transformation in the mentality and ideology of the coloniser and occupier. This meant that the most brutal occupation since the Second World War was kept alive, and will be sustained, as long as the international community awaits a transformation in the positions of the oppressed and accepts as valid those upheld by the oppressor since 1967.

The annals of colonialism, and in particular those of decolonisation, teach us that the end of military presence and occupation was a *condito sine qua non* for the commencement of meaningful negotiations that would lead to a closure and new relationship. The unconditional end of the Israeli military presence in the lives of more than 3 million Palestinians should be completed before any negotiations about the future commence. For genuine negotiations to develop, the oppressive nature of the relationship between the two sides should be substituted by some sort of equal footing and presence around the discussion table. History also teaches us about the folly of piecemeal agreements and attempts to ignore the heart of the matter in ethnic, national, or colonial conflicts. Hence, peace must include *all* the Palestinians, inside and outside, and refer to the *whole* of historical Palestine, not just a mere 22 per cent of it.

In most cases, occupiers and colonisers were forced to leave, rather than make the decision for themselves. This was usually brought about as a result of prolonged and bloody armed struggle. This has been attempted with limited success in the Israel–Palestine conflict. A less common feature, applied in the very last stages of decolonisation, was the exertion of external pressure on the rogue power or state. The failure of the former and the wish to move forward with as little bloodshed as possible make the latter strategy more attractive. In any case, the Israeli paradigm of 'peace' is not going to shift unless it is pressured from the outside and/or forced on the ground, to do so.

BDS AS AN EMPOWERMENT OF PEACE

Even before one begins to define more specifically what such outside pressure entails, it is essential not to confuse the means – pressure – with the objective – finding a formula for joint living. Or put differently, it is important to chart clearly the perception of the pressure as a trigger for meaningful negotiations rather than a substitute for it.

Therefore, despite my growing doubts about the effectiveness of the option from within, it still remains for me the best way of bringing about a lasting solution to the question of the refugees, the predicament of the Palestinian minority in Israel and the future of Jerusalem. There are necessary steps to be taken on the way toward the realisation of such a solution – better served, in my opinion, by a one-state structure rather than a two-states solution. Given the total stalemate at the level of the political elite negotiations, those of us who are active 'from below' or on the margins of world politics, must contemplate and ponder further on how best to incorporate all the outstanding problems while including in the dialogue whoever is willing to, or should, be part of the future state or two-states solution.

For people who are not Jewish citizens of Israel, the hesitations and internal debates about the justification for the boycott may seem spurious. But they are not, since any member of Israeli Jewish society who would put at the top of the priority list the call for outside pressure is willing to be totally alienated from his or her own society (and only very recently be outlawed by new legislation). Those of us who choose this way are not expecting, nor should they expect, to be rewarded or even praised. But there is here a very essential element of actively putting yourself in a direct confrontation with your state, society and quite often friends and family, whilst Palestinians of course, will always pay a much higher price for the struggle.

On the other hand, any other option away from such a struggle – from indifference, through soft criticism and up to full endorsement of the Israeli policy – is far worse. It means a wilful decision to be an accomplice to crimes against humanity. In this respect, the responsibility of Jewish society in Israel is far greater than for anyone else involved in this discussion about how to advance the chances of peace in Israel and Palestine.

This realisation, I think, explains the increasing number of Israeli Jews who support pressure from the outside on Israel as the best way forward. It is undoubtedly still a very small group but it does form the nucleus for a potential future Israeli peace camp. This is also why the Israeli Knesset passed a law criminalising anyone who supports BDS in Israel – which in its turn increased the number of those endorsing the movement from within.

For the few Israelis who decided to be early sponsors of BDS, it was a defining moment of posing ourselves in the clearest way possible *vis-à-vis* our state, its origins, its nature and policies. It also seems, in hindsight at least, to have provided a moral sponsorship which has been helpful for the success of the campaign.

Supporting BDS remains a drastic act for an Israeli peace activist. It excludes one immediately from the consensus and the accepted discourse in Israel. For all intents and purposes, this is the crossing of the final red line, a farewell to the tribe. But there is really no other alternative. The closing of the public mind in Israel, the persistent hold of the settlers over Israeli society, the inbuilt racism within the Zionist population, and the dehumanisation of the Palestinians and the vested interests of the army and the industry in keeping the Occupied Territory, mean that we are in for a very long period of callous and oppressive occupation.

Much was to be learned from the Oslo process, when a discourse of peace was employed in order to help the Israelis to find a more convenient way of maintaining the occupation (unfortunately, for a while, with the help of Palestinian leaders who fell prey to the US-Israeli deception tactics). It meant not only that the 'hawks' vetoed the end of occupation, but also that the 'doves' were not really interested in stopping it. In such circumstances, and in order to shorten as quickly as possible the human misery and tragedy wrought by this occupation, a concentrated and effective pressure on Israel should be applied by the world at large. Such pressures proved themselves in the past, particularly in the case of South Africa. In many ways, the Zionist model is worse than South Africa's Apartheid regime. Both forms of control demand the world's response and rejection.

The pressure is also needed in order to prevent the possibility of even worse scenarios; although after the massacres in Gaza in January 2009, it is hard to see how much worse it can get. But it can: from the possible ethnic cleansing of Palestinians in Israel and in the Greater Jerusalem area to genocidal policies in Gaza and elsewhere – the Israeli state repertoire of evil has not yet been exhausted.

The problem is that the governments of Europe and especially the US administration are not likely to endorse BDS. But one is reminded of the trials and tribulations of the boycott campaign against South Africa, which emanated from civil societies and not the corridors of power. In many ways, the most encouraging news comes from the most unlikely space: American college campuses. The enthusiasm and commitment of local students has helped in the last decade to disseminate the message of divestment to American society – a society that was regarded as a lost case by the global campaign for Palestine. They are facing a formidable task against both the effectiveness and cynicism of AIPAC (the American Israel Public Affairs Committee) and the fanaticism of Christian Zionism. But they offer a new way of engagement with Israel, not only for the sake of Palestinians, but also for the sake of humanity itself.

In Europe, an admirable coalition of Muslims, Jews, Christians and atheists is pushing forward this agenda against fierce accusations of anti-Semitism. The presence of Jews amongst those who campaign help to fend off these vicious and totally false allegations.

The moral and active support of Israelis like myself is not the most important ingredient in this campaign, but it is vital to keep in touch with progressive and radical Jewish dissidents in Israel. They are a bridge to a wider public in Israel, which eventually would have to be brought in, after the pariah status of Israel would hopefully persuade them to abandon their policies of support, or at best silence, about war crimes and abuses of human rights. We hope to empower Palestinians themselves and those on the outside who are now engaged in the campaign, and we are empowered ourselves by such an action. The millions of Jews in Israel are a fact to reckon with. It is a living organism that will remain part of any future solution. However, it is our sacred duty to end the oppressive occupation as soon as we can and to prevent another Nakba – and the best means for this is obviously a sustained campaign of BDS.

THE UNIQUE NATURE OF THE ACADEMIC BOYCOTT

One of the reasons given at the announcement of the initial academic boycott was my own treatment by the University of Haifa.[5] At the time, I was annoyed that my own plight was compared to the actual suffering of Palestinian academia under occupation. I thought that the abuse of academic life in the Occupied Territory was a good enough reason to single it out as an important reason for outside pressure.

But in hindsight I can see the relevance. My own case study, of a lecturer who was ousted because of his resistance to the policies of the state and the continued harassment of my colleagues with similar views by the universities, illustrates forcefully why the boycott of Israeli academia abroad was justified, not just as part of the overall pressure on the Jewish state to end its brutal occupation, but also as a warning to the scholarly community in Israel that its protracted moral cowardice had a price tag on it. As long as this academia went on exercising a reign of intimidation and tyranny in its own campuses, and was silent about the destruction of academic life in the Occupied Territory, it could not be part of the enlightened and progressive world to which it wanted so eagerly to belong.

In 2011, I am afraid that not much has changed. My colleagues still find it difficult to support me or show solidarity for the beliefs I represent, and have failed to learn the historical lessons of the past. Today it is me, tomorrow it is them. Many of them come from families who experienced the same incremental process of silencing in Nazi Germany, Fascist Italy and Spain, and in the military regimes of Latin America. They still live in self-denial, believing it will never happen to them.

So particular pressure on Israeli academia is justified because of the way it does not allow the few principled members in it the right to stand alongside the oppressed and occupied.

But the culpability of the Israeli academia goes deeper than that. It provides in all kinds of ways the scholarly and scientific scaffolding for the criminal policies perpetuated against the Palestinians. From the provision of the personnel that run the occupation, graduating from special university programmes catering for such missions, through to the technological institutes that invent some of the world's most lethal weapons employed against a civilian population, and ending with the human scientists who provide the historical narrative, Orientalist justification and political strategy for the perpetuation of the colonisation and occupation – the verdict on this academia is loud and clear: guilty as charged.

This can be understood if the colonialist nature of Zionism is recognised. By connecting Zionist ideology and the policies of the past with the present atrocities, we are able to provide a clear and logical explanation for the campaign of Boycott, Divestment and Sanctions. Non-violently challenging a self-righteous ideological state that allows itself, aided by a mute world, to dispossess and destroy the indigenous people of Palestine, is a just and moral cause. It is also an effective way of galvanising public opinion not only against the present genocidal policies in Gaza and colonisation of the West Bank and East Jerusalem, but hopefully one that would prevent future atrocities.

But more importantly than anything else it will puncture the balloon of self-righteous fury that suffocates the Palestinians every times it inflates. It will help end the western immunity to Israel's impunity. The Israeli academia plays a crucial role in fuelling this self-righteousness and in propagating for western immunity. Without that immunity, one hopes that more and more people in Israel will begin to see the real nature of the crimes committed in their name, and that their fury would be directed against those who trapped both them and the Palestinians in this unnecessary cycle of bloodshed and violence.

The validity of the Boycott, Divestment and Sanctions option is a first step in triggering a process of disarming Israel from its lethal ideology and its real material arms. Boycotts and external pressure have never been attempted on this level in the case of Israel, a state that wishes to be included in the civilised democratic world. Israel has indeed enjoyed such a status since its creation in 1948 and, therefore, has succeeded in fending off the many United Nations resolutions that condemned its policies and, moreover, has managed to obtain a preferential status in the European Union. Israeli academia's elevated position in the global scholarly community epitomises this western support for Israel as 'the only democracy in the Middle East'. Shielded by this particular support for academia and other cultural media, the Israeli Army and security services can go on, and will go on, demolishing houses, expelling families, abusing citizens and killing men, women and children almost daily without being called to account, regionally or globally, for their crimes.

Military and financial support is significant in enabling the Jewish state to pursue its policies. Any decrease in such aid is most welcome in the struggle for peace and justice in the Middle East. But the cultural image Israel enjoys feeds the political decision in the West to unconditionally support the Israeli destruction of Palestine and the Palestinians. A message that will be directed specifically against those who officially represent Israeli culture (spearheaded by the state's academic institutes which have been particularly culpable in sustaining the oppression since 1948 and the occupation since 1967), can be the start of a successful campaign for disarming the state from its ideological constraints (as similar acts at the time had activated the Anti-Apartheid Movement in South Africa).

External pressure is effective in the case of a state in which people want to be regarded as part of the civilised world, but whose government, with their explicit or implicit help, pursues policies that violate every human and civil right. Neither the UN, nor the US and European governments, have sent a message to Israel that these policies are unacceptable and must be stopped. It is up to international civil societies to send messages to Israeli academics, businessmen, artists, hi-tech industrialists and every other section in society, that there is a price tag attached to such policies.

THE FUTURE OF BDS

There are encouraging signs that global civil society, and particular professional unions, are willing to intensify their pressure. The achievements are symbolic in legitimising a demand for disarming the state from its practices and ideological prejudices.

However, pressure is not enough if an effective dismantling of the ideology that produces the weaponry is desired. It should be complemented by a process of re-education in Israel itself, though, as noted in the beginning of this chapter, the chances for a change from within seem slim. Pressure from the outside is called for because there is an urgent need to prevent the continued destruction of Palestine and the Palestinian people. However, that does not mean that one should give up the attempt to dismantle the ideological weapon by education and dissemination of alternative knowledge and understanding; the two are actually interlinked. Those very few who toil relentlessly in Israel to re-educate their society from a pacifist, humanist and non-Zionist perspective, are empowered by those who pressure the state to act along these lines and leave behind the old habits of aggression and militarism.

The Palestinians, of course, have an agency in this as well. Non-violence, rather than armed struggle, can have a less immediate effect on alleviating an oppressive reality, although it can also have long-term dividends. But at this stage no one can interfere in the affairs of a liberation movement torn by different visions and haunted by decades of struggle without the achievement of justice. What is essential is to seek and address a Palestinian contribution to a post-conflictual vision free of retribution and revenge. A non-militarised vision for both Jews and Arabs, if transformed from the realm of utopia and hallucination into a concrete political plan, together with the outside pressure and the educational process from within, can help enormously in ideologically disarming the state of Israel.

Finally, the Jewish communities in the world, and in particular in the western world, have a crucial role to play in this disarmament. Their moral and material support for Israel indicates endorsement of the ideology behind the state. It is not surprising, therefore, that in the last few years the voice of the non-Zionist Jews is increasingly heard under the slogan 'Not in my name'. The main weapon official Israel uses against outside pressure, or any criticism for that matter, is that any such stance is anti-Semitic. The presence of Jewish voices in the call for peace and reconciliation accentuates the illogical and immoral way in which the state of Israel tries to justify its crimes against the Palestinians in the name of the crimes perpetrated in Europe against the Jews.

As this chapter tries to argue, learning about the past and its fabrication is an essential part of the activism generated by BDS. It begins by asking people concerned with the realities in Palestine and Israel, in whatever context, to learn the history of the Zionist project, to understand its *raison d'être* and its long-term impact on the indigenous people of Palestine. Hopefully, such knowledge would associate the violence raging in that land with the historical roots and the ideological background of Zionism as it developed through the years. Recognition of the role of the ideology that necessitated the building of a fortress with one of the most formidable armies in the world, and one of the most flourishing arms industries, enables activists to tackle tangible goals in the struggle for justice in Israel and Palestine, and in the general struggle for disarmament in the world.

An efficient process of ideological disarmament should avoid unnecessary demonisation, should clearly distinguish between political systems and 'people' as the BDS campaign does, and should clearly perceive how reality is distorted, information manipulated, how educational systems and other socialisation organs can indoctrinate, and how governments misrepresent and demonise whomever they wish.

This is in essence a strategy of activism that would initiate a very tough dialogue with a state that wishes to be part of the 'civilised' world, while remaining racist and supremacist. In this state lives a society that does not wish, or is unable, to see that its ideological nature and its policies locate it within the group of rogue states of this world. For better or for worse, what academics in the West teach about Israel, what journalists report about it, what conscious and conscientious people think about it and what eventually politicians would decide to do about it, is the key to change in the reality in Israel and Palestine. This dismal reality has repercussions not only for peace in the Middle East but in the world as a whole. But it is not a lost cause, and now is the time to act. Within this framework, BDS represents the most powerful and constructive tool available to us all, and it is a tool that we must utilise to the utmost.

NOTES

1. I describe this trajectory in *Out of the Frame*, London and New York: Pluto Press, 2010.
2. Ilan Pappe, 'Zionism as Colonialism: A Comparative View of Diluted Colonialism in Asia and Africa', *South Atlantic Quarterly* (Duke University Press), 107(4), 2008: 611–33.
3. Gabi Piterberg, *The Returns of Zionism; Myths, Politics and Scholarship in Israel*, London: Verso Press, 2009.
4. Ilan Pappe, 'Ingathering', *London Review of Books*, 28(8), 20 April 2006: 15.
5. See Pappe, *Out of the Frame*.

13

Faithless in the Holy Land – A Musician's Journey to Boycott

David Randall

It was a formidably hot August morning in Tel Aviv and I was more than a little hung over. Faithless had played at a rave on a beach somewhere south of the city the night before and the after-show had become a haze of mojitos, merriment and late-night swimming in the Mediterranean. Most of the band drifted slowly back to the beaches of Tel Aviv the following morning for our day off, but I had different plans. I'd heard a bit about the political situation in the region and I wanted to see for myself what life was like for Palestinians. So I stepped out into the rising heat to begin the short, but complicated journey from Tel Aviv to Gaza. This was 1999 and although the Erez crossing into the Gaza Strip was frequently closed for Palestinians, the Israelis didn't yet have a policy of trying to exclude international visitors like me.

What I saw on that short visit made a huge impact on me. Even then, long before the blockade imposed on Gaza following the elections of 2006 and the brutal siege of late 2008, the poverty was stark. Just off Al Nassar Street, scrawny teenagers guided donkeys along sand-covered lanes and craftsmen fixed shoes and fashioned tools on ancient-looking machinery. In the rubble of one of Gaza's refugee camps, groups of men, prevented from travelling to work in Israel, crowded around games of backgammon, while ragged-looking children kicked oranges around or played tag in the dirt. It was obvious Gaza got few visitors – I was eyed with friendly curiosity. 'Welcome to Gaza' was shouted from a passing car and everywhere I went seats were pulled up for me and small cups of sweet mint tea poured.

There seemed to be a sense of approval and appreciation that I had bothered to visit. When it was established that I was from Britain, I was sternly lectured about the Balfour Agreement and Britain's role in this whole mess. In a shabby-looking park with a large new monument to martyred soldiers, a young woman wearing a hijab approached me, keen to practise her English. She explained that the Israelis had turned Gaza into a prison – a prison for people whose only crime was that they were Palestinian. I rejoined the band in Tel Aviv that evening with a determination to find out more.

In 2005, Faithless returned to play a music festival in Haifa. By this time I had made several trips to Palestine – mostly to the West Bank where I had worked with members of a hiphop crew called the Ramallah Underground. Their rapper, Boikutt, featured on the second of my Slovo albums. Since Ramallah was so close, I invited Boikutt to come to the Faithless show. He thanked me but explained that the checkpoints, Separation Wall and Israeli-only roads that dissect the West Bank would make the short journey impossible. He added that as a supporter of the cultural boycott of Israel, he would prefer that we weren't performing there at all. At that time I knew of no western bands or artists who supported the boycott. Many had been persuaded that Israel was more often the innocent victim of regional politics rather than the perpetrator of state terrorism and apartheid. After all, that was the view peddled by most of the mainstream media who faithfully echoed the attitudes of the UK and US governments. Since at least the 1950s, both have seen it as in their strategic interests to give political cover to Israel – as well as economic and military support. However, soon after that conversation with Boikutt, public attitudes started to change, due mainly to the brutal actions of the Israeli state itself.

First came Israel's massive assault on Lebanon in 2006 – allegedly in retaliation to the abduction of two Israeli soldiers by Hezbollah. The conflict cost at least 1,200 lives – mostly Lebanese citizens – and ended in a humiliating defeat for the Israeli Army. Over a million Lebanese civilians were displaced by the war and parts of South Lebanon are still uninhabitable due to unexploded Israeli cluster bombs. Next was 'Operation Cast Lead' – Israel's shocking bombardment of Gaza in December 2008–January 2009, in which 1,385 Palestinians were killed – 318 of them children.[1] Just one year later, an international flotilla of boats attempting to bring aid to besieged Gaza suffered a vicious attack by the Israeli Army while in international waters. A UN report concluded that Israeli Defense Force soldiers opened fire with live rounds before they illegally boarded the ship. Nine activists died, six of them – one American and five Turkish citizens – in execution-style killings. There were no Israeli fatalities.

Anger at each of these events erupted in demonstrations and student occupations across the world. What was interesting about the reaction to the Lebanon war was that so many people saw it as an extension of the same western imperialist project that had led the US and UK into the disastrous wars in Afghanistan and Iraq. The attack was an attempted pre-emptive strike against Hezbollah, many activists argued, intended to clear the way for a US attack on Iran.

But it was the siege of Gaza that affected me most deeply. It was described by a UN fact-finding mission as 'a deliberately disproportionate attack designed to punish, humiliate and terrorise a civilian population, radically diminish its local economic capacity both to work and to provide for itself, and to force upon it an ever increasing sense of dependency and vulnerability'.[2] I learned more about the horrors of this attack following an offer from my friend Jen Marlowe – a filmmaker, writer and activist from the US. She asked me to compose music for her short film 'One Family in Gaza', which tells the story of the Awajah family – one among thousands subjected to 'Operation Cast Lead'. In the film, Waffa Awajah describes how her son Ibrahim – an unarmed 9-year-old boy – was executed by an Israeli soldier at point-blank range in front of his family. When Waffa pleaded with the soldier to spare the lives of the other children, the soldier laughed. Unable to retrieve Ibrahim's body for fear that they might be killed, the family hid through the night. Waffa could only look on while Israeli soldiers used her son's body for target practice.[3]

Mounting public awareness of Israel's crimes meant that increasing numbers of ordinary people felt the need to speak up – among them musicians, writers and artists. Palestinian civil society was calling for boycott, divestment and sanctions of Israel (BDS) and the potential to make that a reality was growing.

In 2010, Faithless were once again invited to perform in Israel. It was our vocalist, Maxi Jazz, who first raised the question of whether we should boycott. He did so one evening on tour, at a dinner attended by all but one of the band members. After some discussion, everyone at the dinner agreed that we should join the boycott and that Maxi should write a statement explaining to fans why we had taken that decision:

> 'All Races All Colours All Creeds Got The Same Needs.'
> Hi, this is Maxi Jazz and these are just some of the lyrics I perform every night with my friends known as Faithless. And this short note is for all fans and family of the band in Israel. It's fair to say that for 14 years we've been promoting goodwill, trust and harmony all around the world in our own small (but very loud!) way. Ok. We've been asked to do some shows this summer in your country and, with the heaviest of hearts, I have regretfully declined the invitation. While human beings are being wilfully denied not just their rights but their NEEDS for their children and grandparents and themselves, I feel deeply that I should not be sending even tacit signals that this is either 'normal' or 'ok'. It's neither and I cannot support it. It grieves me that it has come to this and I pray everyday for human beings to begin caring for each other, firm in the wisdom that we are all we have. We Come 1.
> maxi[4]

Around this time, several other established artists honoured the boycott, including Elvis Costello, the Pixies, Massive Attack, Gil Scott Heron, Santana, Roger Waters, Devendra Banhart, the Tindersticks, Pete Seeger, Cassandra Wilson and Cat Power. I decided to meet with members of the Palestinian Campaign for the Academic and Cultural Boycott of Israel (PACBI),[5] as well as with other musicians, to draft a declaration which we hoped would encourage the growing movement among musicians. It was first published on the *Wall of Silence* website and reflects my views on how the cultural boycott should be defined:

We have one declaration:

Not one note of music will be played within Israel until every last piece of its Apartheid Wall is removed, the blockade of Gaza is lifted, and Israel withdraws from the Occupied Palestinian Territories.

We are DJs and musicians and we love music. We welcome musical projects and collaborations that cross borders. We will continue to welcome our Israeli colleagues to join us in our concerts, clubs, recording studios, parties, homes and lives – unless they allow themselves to be used to promote Israel.

And we encourage all musicians to visit and perform in the Occupied Territories – the West Bank and Gaza.

But we refuse to play one note of any piece of music in Tel Aviv, West Jerusalem, Haifa, Eilat, or any other part of Israel, until every last piece of the illegal Apartheid Wall is removed and the Occupation ends.

THE BEATS DROP WHEN THE WALL FALLS.

One Love.[6]

The growth of the Boycott, Divestment and Sanctions (BDS) movement has worried both the Israeli government and Zionists internationally. In early 2012, a group of thirty leading music executives, agents and lawyers were invited for lunch at the law offices of Ziffren Bittenham in Los Angeles by an organisation calling themselves 'Creative Community for Peace'. The well-funded group was set up by former chairman and CEO of Universal Music Publishing Group, David Renzer, and worldwide head of music for EA video games, Steve Schnur, with the sole objective of preventing artists from joining the boycott of Israel.[7] When singer Macy Gray expressed serious doubts about whether she should perform in Israel, Renzers and Schnur stepped in. They argued that the act of performing in Israel is good for both Israelis and Palestinians, and added that if she went, they would fund the donation of an ambulance to United Hatzalah – an organisation of Israeli medical volunteers. Macy agreed to go.

Some critics of the boycott ask why Israel is singled out when so many states behave badly. It's worth pointing out that it's a perverse logic that says we can't criticise a particular state just because there may be another that's even worse. Often, the people who ask the question are implicitly making the charge of anti-Semitism. They claim that to criticise Israel is to be anti-Jewish. This idea conflates Zionism with Judaism. Zionism itself has systematically attempted to make such a conflation. I completely reject it. As the editors of the Independent Jewish Voices book *A Time to Speak Out* state:

> It is because successive Israeli governments claim to represent Jews in general, a claim that is as groundless as it is injurious, that it is vital to speak out. Moreover in the United Kingdom those who claim to speak for British Jews collectively (or allow that impression to go unchallenged) tend to reflect only one position on Israel's conflicts: that of the Israeli government. In reality, however, there is a broad spectrum of opinion among Jews in Britain – just as there is among any other Jewish population in the world – on Israel and on Zionism. Many Jews refuse to view these subjects through a narrow ethnocentric lens. They base their opinions instead upon universal principles of justice and human rights. And they refuse to accept that Israel alone offers a viable identity for Jews.[8]

Labelling all critics of Israel anti-Semitic is like labelling all opponents of apartheid in South Africa anti-white. In fact, the struggle against anti-Semitism is undermined by Zionists who claim to represent all Jews and who denounce all opposition to Israeli government policy as anti-Semitic. Theirs is a bullying tactic used to suppress opposition. As David Clark, former adviser to the Labour government in Britain in the 1990s, puts it;

> When I hear people argue that Israel is unfairly singled out, I wish I could persuade myself that what they mean is: 'If only people cared as much about the people of Tibet/Darfur/Zimbabwe as they do for the Palestinians'. But … I suspect that what they often mean is: 'If only people cared as little for the Palestinians as they do for the people of Tibet/Darfur/Zimbabwe'.[9]

Besides, the absence of calls for boycotts elsewhere is not necessarily evidence of Israel being singled out for criticism. Boycott is not a universal principle that can be applied in every situation – it is a political tactic. In most situations, it would be the wrong tactic. For example, I opposed the UK and US governments' invasions and occupations of Iraq and Afghanistan. To build an effective cultural boycott of the UK or the US would be extremely difficult. Both countries have huge domestic music industries, so for a boycott to be noticed it would have to be big. And building that critical mass would be a very hard task, since so many musicians are based in those countries or have careers which rely on sales within them. There are many things that musicians can and have done to oppose their own government's policies and to support the Stop The War movement – but boycott is not one of them. Conversely, it's hard to impose an effective boycott on somewhere you never had any contact with anyway. I completely oppose the brutal regimes in Saudi Arabia and Bahrain, but it's a bit meaningless to refuse to play there if you've never been asked to do so in the first place. (I did wholeheartedly support calls to cancel the 2012 Grand Prix in Bahrain.)

Israel by contrast, is a country in which the tactic of cultural boycott can have a real impact. For one thing, Israel is carefully branded by its government as the regional centre for all things cool, sexy and western. Tel Aviv is promoted as a hedonistic, open-minded party city – an image made credible by frequent visits by many of the world's best-known bands and DJs. This manufactured image matters to Israel. The implicit message is that the country is liberal and progressive. Music fans can dance, drink and party long into the night, blissfully distracted from the suffering endured by Palestinians. In effect, music helps to drown out the cries of the oppressed in a society wilfully in denial of its role as oppressor. The cultural boycott is a refusal to be complicit in this crime. It is a non-violent and effective way to highlight the reality of what is going on and to apply pressure for change. Perhaps most importantly, boycott is what Palestinian civil society – those on the sharp end of oppression – has asked of us.

Opponents of the cultural boycott sometimes argue that it punishes the wrong people – that music fans are among those most likely to oppose their government's policies. But gigs do not take place in a political or economic vacuum. No matter how enlightened an artist's particular fans may be, or how progressive the band's message is, a show in Israel can only too easily be interpreted by the wider world as an endorsement of business as usual in an apartheid state.

Other critics have claimed, rather patronisingly, that musicians have only honoured the cultural boycott because of pressure from political activists. But artists make up their own minds – there's nothing wrong with activists bringing important issues to their attention. Coercive pressure is more likely to be exerted from the other side.

When Faithless decided to join the boycott, our manager and one leading band member strongly disagreed with the decision. They put considerable pressure on Maxi to change his mind, believing that the rest of us would follow. It turned out that the manager has extensive business connections in Israel and thus a significant financial incentive to bury his head in the sand and continue to conduct business as usual. I've spoken to other established artists who have also faced pressure from managers or others in the industry to avoid publicising their support of the boycott. Many arrive at the rather pointless compromise of refusing invitations to perform in Israel, while never publicly stating why.

Threats from opponents outside the music industry can be even more serious. In February 2011, I agreed to record a radio advert for 'South African Artists Against Apartheid' to coincide with a Faithless tour there. In the advert I said, 'Twenty years ago I would not have played in apartheid South Africa; today I refuse to play in Israel. Be on the right side of history. Don't entertain apartheid. Join the international boycott of Israel. I support southafricanartistsagainstapartheid.com.'[10]

When the advert aired on mainstream pop radio station SABC's 5FM, the radio station and our concert promoter were inundated with complaints from Zionists. We were warned to expect protests outside the gig and the promoter brought in a lot of extra security to screen those coming in, raising suspicions that veiled death threats were also made. As I waited to go onstage, my guitar technician slapped me on the back and said 'I won't take the bullet for you Dave, but don't worry – I'll clean the blood off your guitars.' I thanked him and we laughed nervously. The threats were idle scaremongering – there wasn't a single protestor and the raucous Cape Town audience emanated nothing but love. The point remains that there is an overwhelming pressure on artists, both from within the industry and from without, to ignore or refuse the call to boycott Israel. It is a pressure that we must resist. The more of us that do, the easier it will be for others to join us.

Our call for BDS resonates with a mood of change that has spread around the world in recent years. The Palestinian Intifada provided inspiration for the revolutionaries of Tunisia and Egypt, who in turn inspire the students and workers at the forefront of the struggle against austerity in Europe. Increasingly, people are asking why the world is organised in the way that it is. Increasingly, people are asking how we can change it. BDS and the internationalism in which it is rooted is part of the answer. Our cause has never been more timely.

NOTES

1. B'Tselem, 'One and a Half Million People Imprisoned', 27 December 2009 <http://www.btselem.org/gaza_strip/20091227_a_year_to_castlead_operation>.
2. 'The Goldstone Report', United Nations Fact Finding Mission on the Gaza Conflict to the Human Rights Council, 29 September 2009 <http://www2.ohchr.org/english/>.
3. Jen Marlowe's film, 'One Family in Gaza', can be viewed at <http://vimeo.com/18384109>.
4. <http://www.wallofsilence.org/>.
5. The Palestinian Campaign for the Academic and Cultural Boycott of Israel.
6. <http://www.wallofsilence.org/news.html>.
7. Danielle Berrin, 'Music Moguls to Artists: Don't Boycott Israel', *JewishJournal.com*, 25 April 2012 <http://www.jewishjournal.

com/hollywoodjew/item/music_moguls_to_artists_dont_boycott_israel_20120425/>.

8. Anne Karpf et al. (eds), *A Time To Speak Out: Independent Jewish voices on Israel, Zionism and Jewish Identity*, London: Verso, 2008.

9. David Clark, 'A Response to David Hirsh', *Engage* website, 15 March 2006 <http://www.engageonline.org.uk/blog/article.php?id=297>.

10. The advert and more information can be found at <http://www.southafricanartistsagainstapartheid.com/2011/07/legal-victory.html>.

14
Our People

Iain Banks

I support the Boycott, Divestment and Sanctions (BDS) campaign because, especially in our instantly connected world, an injustice committed against one, or against one group of people, is an injustice against all, against every one of us; a collective injury.

My particular reason for participating in the cultural boycott of Israel is that, first of all, I can; I'm a writer, a novelist, and I produce works that are, as a rule, presented to the international market. This gives me a small extra degree of power over that which I possess as a (UK) citizen and a consumer. Secondly, where possible when trying to make a point, one ought to be precise, and hit where it hurts. The sports boycott of South Africa when it was still run by the racist Apartheid regime helped to bring the country to its senses because the ruling Afrikaaner minority put so much store in their sporting prowess. Rugby and cricket in particular both mattered to them profoundly, and their teams' generally elevated position in the international league tables was a matter of considerable pride. When they were eventually isolated by the sporting boycott – as part of the wider cultural and trade boycott – they were forced that much more persuasively to confront their own outlaw status in the world.

A sporting boycott of Israel would make relatively little difference to the self-esteem of Israelis in comparison to South Africa; an intellectual and cultural one might help make all the difference, especially now that the events of the 'Arab Spring' and the continuing repercussions of the attack on the Gaza-bound flotilla peace convoy have threatened both Israel's ability to rely on Egypt's collusion in the containment of Gaza, and Turkey's willingness to engage sympathetically with the Israeli regime at all. Feeling increasingly isolated, Israel is all the more vulnerable to further evidence that it, in turn, like the racist South African regime it once supported and collaborated with, is increasingly regarded as an outlaw state.

I was able to play a tiny part in South Africa's cultural boycott, ensuring that – once it thundered through to me that I could do so – my novels weren't sold there (while subject to an earlier contract, under whose terms the books were sold in South Africa, I did a rough calculation of royalties earned each year and sent that amount to the ANC). Since the 2010 attack on the Turkish-led convoy to Gaza in international waters, I've instructed my agent not to sell the rights to my novels to Israeli publishers. I don't buy Israeli-sourced products or food, and my partner and I try to support Palestinian-sourced products wherever possible.

It doesn't feel like much, and I'm not completely happy doing even this; it can sometimes feel like taking part in collective punishment (although BDS is by definition aimed directly at the state and not the people), and that's one of the most damning charges that can be levelled at Israel itself; that it engages in the collective punishment of the Palestinian people within Israel, and the Occupied Palestinian Territory, that is, the West Bank and – especially – the vast prison camp that is Gaza. The problem is that constructive engagement and reasoned argument demonstrably have not worked, and the relatively crude weapon of boycott is pretty much all that's left. (To the question, 'What about boycotting Saudi Arabia?' – all I can claim is that cutting back on my consumption of its most lucrative export was a peripheral reason for giving up the powerful cars I used to drive, and for stopping flying, some years ago. I certainly wouldn't let a book of mine be published there either, although – unsurprisingly given some of the things I've said about that barbaric excuse for a country, not to mention the contents of the books themselves – the issue has never arisen, and never will with anything remotely resembling the current regime in power.)

As someone who has always respected and admired the achievements of the Jewish people – they've probably contributed even more to world civilisation than the Scots, and we Caledonians are hardly shy about promoting our own wee-but-influential record and status – and felt sympathy for their suffering, especially in the years leading up to and then during the Second World War and the Holocaust, I'll always feel uncomfortable taking part in any action that – even if only thanks to the efforts of the Israeli propaganda machine – may be claimed by some to target them, despite the fact that the state of Israel and the Jewish people are not synonymous. Israel and its apologists can't have it both ways, though: if they're going to make the rather hysterical claim that any and every criticism of Israeli domestic or foreign policy amounts to anti-Semitism, they have to accept that this claimed, if specious, indivisibility provides an opportunity for what they claim to be the censure of one to function as the condemnation of the other.

The particular tragedy of Israel's treatment of the Palestinian people is that nobody seems to have learned anything. Israel itself was brought into being partly as a belated and guilty attempt by the world community to help compensate for its complicity in, or at least its inability to prevent, the catastrophic crime of the Holocaust. Of all people, the Jewish people ought to know how it feels to be persecuted en masse, to be punished collectively and to be treated as less than human. For the Israeli state and the collective of often unlikely bedfellows who support it so unquestioningly throughout the world to pursue and support the inhumane treatment of the Palestinian people – forced so brutally off their land in 1948 and still under attack today – and to be so blind to the idea that injustice is injustice, regardless not just on whom it is visited, but *by* whom as well, is one of the defining iniquities of our age, and powerfully implies a shamingly low upper limit on the extent of our species' moral intelligence.

The solution to the dispossession and persecution of one people can never be to dispossess and persecute another. When we do this, or participate in this, or even just allow this to happen without criticism or resistance, we only help ensure further injustice, oppression, intolerance, cruelty and violence in the future.

We may see ourselves as many tribes, but we are one species, and in failing to speak out against injustices inflicted on some of our number and doing what we can to combat those without piling further wrongs on earlier ones, we are effectively collectively punishing ourselves.

The BDS campaign for justice for the Palestinian people is one I would hope any decent, open-minded person would support. Gentile or Jew, conservative or leftist, no matter who you are or how you see yourself, these people are our people, and collectively we have turned our backs on their suffering for far too long.

15
Why We Back the Boycott Campaign

Ken Loach, Rebecca O'Brien and Paul Laverty

When we decided to pull our film *Looking for Eric* from the Melbourne International Film Festival [in 2009] following our discovery that the festival was part-sponsored by the Israeli state, we wrote to the director, Richard Moore, detailing our reasons. Unfortunately, he misrepresented our position and [then] did so again [publicly] on the *Guardian*'s 'Comment is free' [blog] by stating that 'to allow the personal politics of one filmmaker to proscribe a festival position ... goes against the grain of what festivals stand for', and claiming that 'Loach's demands were beyond the pale.'

This decision was taken by three filmmakers – director, producer, writer – not in some private abstract bubble, but after a long discussion and in response to a call for a cultural boycott from a wide spectrum of Palestinian civil society, including writers, filmmakers, cultural workers, human rights groups, journalists, trade unions, women's groups and student organisations. As Moore should know by now, the Palestinian Campaign for the Academic and Cultural Boycott of Israel (PACBI) was launched in Ramallah in April 2004, and its aims, reasons and constituent parts are widely available on the Net. PACBI is part of a much wider international movement for Boycott, Divestment and Sanctions (BDS) against the Israeli state.

Why do we back this growing international movement? During the last sixty years, Israel, backed by the United States, has shown contempt for hundreds of UN resolutions, the Geneva Convention and international law. It has demonstrated itself to be a violent and ruthless state, as was clearly shown by the [2008–09] massacres in Gaza, and was even prepared to further challenge international law by its use of phosphorus weapons.

Israel continues to flout worldwide public opinion; the clearest example of its intransigence is its determination to continue to build the Wall through the Palestinian territory despite the 2004 decision of the International Court [of Justice at the Hague].

What does the international community do? Nothing but complain. What does the United States do? It continues to voice its 'grave concern' while subsidising the Israeli state to some $3 billion a year. Meanwhile, 'on the ground' – a good title for a film – Israeli settlers continue to take over Palestinian homes and lands, making a viable Palestinian homeland an impossible dream. Normal life, with basic human rights, has become a virtual dream for most Palestinians.

Given the failure of international law, and the impunity of the Israeli state, we believe there is no alternative but for ordinary citizens to try their best to fill the breach. Desmond Tutu said:

> The end of apartheid stands as one of the crowning accomplishments of the past century, but we would not have succeeded without the help of the international community – in particular the divestment movement of the 1980s. Over the past six months, a similar movement has taken shape, this time aiming at the end of the Israeli occupation.

At a BDS event in the West Bank town of Ramallah, author Naomi Klein made a very good point when she argued that there is no exact equivalency between Israel and South Africa:

> The question is not 'Is Israel the same as South Africa?' It is, 'do Israel's actions meet the international definition of what apartheid is?' And if you look at those conditions which include the transfer of people, multiple tiers of law, official state segregation, then you see that, yes, it does meet that definition – which is different than saying it is South Africa. No two states are the same. It's not the question, it's a distraction.

Not long after the Gaza invasion we spoke to the head of a human rights organisation there who told us that the Israelis were refusing enough chemicals to adequately treat the civilian water supply, a clear example of vindictive collective punishment delivered to one-half of the population.

Neve Gordon, a Jewish political professor teaching in an Israeli university, argued, 'The most accurate way to describe Israel today is an apartheid state.' As a result, he too is supporting the international campaign of divestment and boycott. We feel duty bound to take advice from those living at the sharp end inside the Occupied Territory. We would also encourage other filmmakers and actors invited to festivals to check for Israeli state backing before attending, and if so, to respect the boycott. Israeli filmmakers are not the target. State involvement is. In the grand scale of things, it is a tiny contribution to a growing movement, but the example of South Africa should give us heart.

A version of this essay was originally published by the Guardian's 'Comment is free' in 2009, and is republished here with the authors' permission.

Part IV

Activists and Activism

16
Derailing Veolia
Adri Nieuwhof

The French multinational cooperation Veolia Environnement caught the attention of a mobilising Palestinian civil society and international human rights advocates several years ago for its involvement in the Jerusalem Light Rail project. Its subsidiary, Connex, participates in the City Pass Consortium that was contracted to build and operate an Israeli light rail system in 2005. Veolia holds a 5 per cent stake in City Pass and a 30-year contract as the operator of the light rail. The City Pass consortium consists of Veolia's subsidiary Connex, the French company Alstom and four Israeli companies.

The Jerusalem Light Rail (JLR) is a component of the 'Jerusalem Transportation Master Plan' sponsored by the Israeli government and the Jerusalem municipality. The first line of the JLR connects West Jerusalem to Jewish settlements in occupied East Jerusalem, such as Pisgat Ze'ev, French Hill, Neve Ya'akov and Gilo. Without consulting Palestinians, the JLR is designed to meet the needs of settlers who live on occupied Palestinian land.

Israeli settlements in the Occupied Palestinian Territory (oPt), which includes the annexation of East Jerusalem, are illegal under international law. Numerous UN resolutions and the 2004 advisory opinion of the International Court of Justice on Israel's Separation Wall in the West Bank have confirmed that settlements violate Article 49 of the Fourth Geneva Convention – which states 'The Occupying Power shall not deport or transfer parts of its own civilian population into the territory it occupies.' Through its involvement in the JLR, Veolia is directly implicated in maintaining illegal settlements in the oPt.

On 17 July 2005, eight days after Palestinian civil society released the call for BDS, City Pass signed the Jerusalem Light

Rail contract at the offices of then Prime Minister Ariel Sharon. On that occasion, Sharon made it clear that the JLR would 'sustain Jerusalem for eternity as the capital of the Jewish people, the united capital of the state of Israel'. The JLR had been years in planning, and the Palestinian Liberation Organization (PLO), well aware of the Zionist vision and implications of the rail system, had protested against land confiscation for the JLR as early as 2001. In a 22 October 2007 press release by the French delegation, the PLO reiterated its rejection of the JLR because 'it harms the Palestinian population and its rights to self-determination.'

Campaigns against the JLR offer the opportunity to expose Israel's violations of international law and the human rights issues that are intrinsically linked to the project. In addition, Veolia is an excellent target for the BDS campaign because it is a global multinational corporation that is highly visible in many countries through its delivery of public services.

BUILDING THE DERAIL VEOLIA AND ALSTOM CAMPAIGN

In its first two years, the Veolia campaign began with a few uncoordinated actions in Europe. Solidarity activists in France protested Veolia's involvement in the JLR on several occasions, including at the company's annual shareholders' meeting.[1] Swiss activists also demonstrated their principled resolve by blocking a Connex shuttle bus to the renowned 'Autosalon' in Geneva in March 2006.[2] Five months later, in Ireland, solidarity activists united with trade unions to force Veolia to cancel plans for training Israeli engineers and drivers in Dublin.[3]

Meanwhile, the media attention in Geneva triggered activists in the Netherlands to call on the socially responsible ASN Bank to divest from Veolia. A few clients, supported by the Jewish lobbying group A Different Jewish Voice, and the Netherlands-based ICCO (an interchurch organization for development cooperation), alongside lawyers and Palestinian and Israeli organisations, convinced the bank to divest from Veolia. In clear terms, ASN Bank notified Veolia of its decision: 'We believe that

Veolia's involvement in the JLR project is not in line with the UN demand to stop all support for Israel's settlement activities, and is therefore not in line with ASN Bank's social criteria.' ASN Bank's decision sent a clear message: BDS activism can be successful.[4]

More activists soon began to raise their voice against Veolia's involvement in the JLR. At the end of October 2008, Palestinian, progressive Israeli and international organisations and social movements adopted a plan to improve international coordination at a gathering in Bilbao, in the Basque Country, Spain.[5] They noted the failure of States to end Israel's impunity for its ongoing violations of international law and human rights. Therefore, they concluded that civil society must use its collective power to hold Israel and companies involved in these violations to account. In Bilbao, the participants selected Veolia and Alstom as a target for the BDS movement; the Derail Veolia and Alstom Campaign was born.

SOLID INFORMATION AS THE BASIS FOR ACTION

The BDS call by Palestinian Civil Society offers the framework for the Derail Veolia and Alstom Campaign. The campaign operates as a network in which information and ideas are shared, and any campaign needs to be based on solid, up-to-date information. The international cooperation of activists, researchers, photographers and concerned professionals made it possible to collect 'hard' evidence on Veolia's activities in the oPt. Moreover, the cooperation resulted in the disclosure of Veolia's involvement in more projects in the oPt.

Tovlan Landfill

In 2008, the campaign received photos of Tovlan landfill in the occupied Jordan Valley, showing a Veolia flag waving at the entrance. Following this lead, civil-society group Who Profits? (<www.whoprofits.org>) uncovered that Onyx, a subsidiary of Veolia Waste Management, holds a contract to operate the landfill site that was established in 1999.[6] Claims that Tovlan also serves the Palestinian town of Nablus are not realistic. The use of the site is highly restricted for Palestinian towns due to the numerous Israeli checkpoints which need to be crossed to arrive at the site, and the high fees charged to dump waste in Tovlan. The British watchdog CorporateWatch executed research on the ground in 2010, and found the Onyx sign still up at the site.[7] Around 600–700 tonnes of waste was being dumped per day at that time, including waste from the Israeli cities of Afula and Petah Tivka. CorporateWatch also observed that Veolia trucks were picking up waste from the Israeli settlements of Tomer and Massua in the Jordan Valley.[8]

Bus Services to Settlements

Veolia's involvement in bus services to Israeli settlements in the oPt was first spotted by a member of the network in 2009. Subsequent research by Who Profits? revealed that Connex, a subsidiary of Veolia Transport, operates bus lines 109 and 110 that connect communities in Israel to Israeli settlements in the West Bank, including Beit Horon and Givat Ze'ev. The bus lines reinforce the process of incorporation of the settlements in the same way as the JLR.

In a letter of 16 June 2011, Veolia Water North America asserted that the company is not involved in other bus services in the West Bank besides bus lines 109 and 110. Two months later, Who Profits? presented evidence that Veolia operates two other bus services to settlements in the West Bank. Bus line 7 runs from Modi'in in Israel to the settlements of Hashmonaim and Kfar Ha'oranim. The company also operates bus line 19 which runs between Modi'in and the settlement of Mevo Horon.[9] In practice, these four bus lines are not designed to be used by 'West Bank Palestinians' despite travelling through the West Bank, as the buses use only settler roads and do not stop in Palestinian population centres.

DIVERSITY AND CREATIVITY IN ACTION

A major strength of the Derail Veolia and Alstom Campaign is the freedom to organise tailor-made activities that fit the local situation. It is tempting to list all the different forms of actions, but I will limit this chapter to examples that might be useful for the planning of further activities.

Targeting Local Authorities

In several countries, activists have called on local authorities to do no business with Veolia. At the initiative of BDS activists, city councils have debated motions that proposed to deny contracts to Veolia for the delivery of local public services. Particularly in Ireland, this approach has been successful.

In several countries, activists have campaigned around procurement procedures for public contracts, calling for the exclusion of Veolia. The company lost contracts in Australia, France, Sweden and the United Kingdom; however, city councils have not yet officially stated publicly that their decision was related to Veolia's activities in the oPt. BDS activists and researchers Maren Mantovani and Michael Deas have calculated that Veolia lost contracts worth more than €10 billion in the cities where BDS activists have campaigned intensively against their activities.[10]

In several countries, lawyers are actively supporting the BDS movement and providing activists with their expertise on international and national law. Such legal support has proved invaluable in many cases.

Divestment

Calls for divestment directed at responsible investors and pension funds have also been used as a method to hold Veolia to account. Dutch banks ASN Bank and Triodos Bank made clear that they have excluded Veolia from their investment universe because of its involvement in Israel's occupation of Palestinian land. Pension funds in the Netherlands, Scandinavian countries, the UK, and the US continue to be pressured to divest from Veolia. In Sweden and the Netherlands, pension funds have engaged with Veolia in an attempt to convince the company to end their activities in the oPt. If, as seems probable, Veolia refuses to comply with their requests, this engagement may well result in divestment.

The Swedish national pension fund AP7 excluded Alstom from its portfolio because of the company's involvement in the JLR.[11] In addition, the monitoring network Banktrack added to the growing unease when it noted that financial investment in Veolia is 'dodgy'.[12]

Legal Action

Legal action requires experienced lawyers, time and substantial financial resources. This can in some cases limit the use or the method of legal action in BDS activism. However, the French *Association France Palestine Solidarité* (AFPS) and the PLO took Veolia and Alstom to court in October 2007. Almost four years later, the court in Nanterre found that under French law the international law provisions, as listed in the AFPS and PLO's petition, have no direct effect on private individuals and companies who are not a party to the conflict. Under French law, only States which signed the Geneva Conventions of 1949 and the Hague Regulations of 1907 can be regarded as being bound by the specific treaty provisions. Subsequently, the court did not look into the question of Veolia's involvement in breaches of international law in relation to the JLR. The AFPS and the PLO will appeal against the ruling.[13] Moreover, the AFPS undertook legal action against the French state for not respecting its obligations under international law in relation to Veolia and Alstom's involvement in the JLR, in 2010. This case is still pending, and at the time of writing it is not clear when to expect a ruling.

LESSONS TO BE LEARNED

The power of social justice movements has been shown by the Anti-Slavery Movement, the African-American Civil Rights Movement, and the Anti-Apartheid Movement led by African liberation movements, amongst many others. These examples illustrate the power of citizens and their organisations when they persistently work together towards clear goals, and the work of Ghandi is an inspiration for us here. In 1938, he observed 'a small body of determined spirits fired by an unquenchable faith in their mission can alter the course of history.'[14] Indeed, a movement can be sparked off by a *small body* of persons when they are *determined* and have an *unquenchable* faith in the mission of their social justice movement. That is exactly what I experienced through my involvement with the Holland Committee on Southern Africa that, for decades, supported the resistance against South African apartheid. The anti-apartheid struggle demonstrated that international civil society can be a significant factor in bringing about social change. After several hundred years of colonialism and more than forty years of formal apartheid, President De Klerk and other white leaders had to face the reality that fundamental change was inevitable in South Africa. Demographic pressures, the deplorable state of the economy, the international isolation of 'white South Africa', the increasing anti-apartheid protests both inside and outside South Africa and the outreach policy and multifaceted resistance of the ANC were all important factors in bringing about this fundamental change.[15]

Right from the start, I was convinced that the BDS movement in solidarity with, and called for by, Palestinians could be successful. Within the movement, I could apply many of the lessons that I learned in campaigns to pressurise the Dutch-British oil company Shell to pull out of apartheid South Africa. Shell's stubborn resistance to withdraw from supporting the Apartheid regime provided an excellent opportunity for anti-apartheid publicity for many years. My subsequent involvement and contribution to the Derail Veolia and Alstom Campaign is based on similar principles. The campaign represents an excellent and highly visible target for the BDS movement, and it has developed at a surprisingly high speed with some notable successes already achieved.

One lesson that the wider BDS movement can learn from the Derail Veolia and Alstom campaign is that international cooperation around a specific target can clearly be effective. The consistent efforts to hold Veolia to account by the Palestinian BDS National Committee, Palestinian, Israeli and international organisations, principled citizens and professionals, churches, trade unions, social movements, researchers, photographers, and lawyers, has paid off. As a result, a wide audience has been educated about Israel's violations of international law and the basic human rights of the Palestinian people. The trickle-down effect will be that more politicians start to realise that part of their constituency wants, and will be active in its demands for, a change in national policies. Although there is still a long way to go and much work to be done, we must take hope and learn from the progression of this campaign and its achievements to date. The challenge ahead is to pursue the rights-based goals of the BDS movement and develop our campaigns until States finally address their responsibilities in ending Israel's impunity.

NOTES

1. Adri Nieuwhof and Maria Lherm, 'Legal action in France against Veolia and Alstom', *Electronic Intifada*, 14 March 2007 <http://electronicintifada.net/content/legal-action-france-against-veolia-and-alstom/6810> (accessed 8 September 2011).
2. The Grassroots Palestinian Anti-Apartheid Wall Campaign, 'Challenging Tramways of Apartheid – Swiss activists block Connex shuttle run', *Stop the Wall*, 20 March 2006 <http://stopthewall.org/worldwideactivism/1120.shtml> (accessed 8 September 2011).
3. The Grassroots Palestinian Anti-Apartheid Wall Campaign, 'Connex Ireland forces to cancel contract with Occupation', *Stop the Wall*, 19 August 2006 <http://stopthewall.org/worldwideactivism/1277.shtml> (accessed 8 September 2011).
4. Adri Nieuwhof, 'Principled Dutch ASN Bank ends relations with Veolia', *Electronic Intifada* 26 November 2006 <http://electronicintifada.net/content/principled-dutch-asn-bank-ends-relations-veolia/6547> (accessed 8 September 2011).
5. 'Bilbao initiative: declaration and action plan', *Electronic Intifada*, 4 November 2008 <http://electronicintifada.net/content/bilbao-initiative-declaration-and-action-plan/865> (accessed 8 September 2011).
6. Adri Nieuwhof, 'Veolia involved in Israel's waste dumping in West Bank', *Electronic Intifada*, 16 December 2008 <http://electronicintifada.net/content/veolia-involved-israels-waste-dumping-west-bank/7858> (accessed 9 September 2011).

7. Corporate Watch, 'Still doing Israel's Dirty Work: Veolia's Tovlan landfill in the Jordan Valley', *Corporate Watch*, 12 July 2010 <http://corporateoccupation.wordpress.com/2010/07/12/still-doing-israels-dirtywork-veolias-tovlan-landfill-in-the-jordan-valley/> (accessed 8 September 2011).

8. CorporateWatch, 'Veolia – Taking out Israel's Trash', *CorporateWatch*, 31 March 2010 <http://corporateoccupation.wordpress.com/2010/03/31/veolia-taking-out-israels-trash/> (accessed 9 September 2011).

9. Adri Nieuwhof, 'Veolia keeps silent about two bus services to illegal settlements', *Electronic Intifada*, 24 August 2011 <http://electronicintifada.net/blog/adri-nieuwhof/veolia-keeps-silent-about-two-bus-services-illegal-settlements> (accessed 9 September 2011).

10. Maren Mantovani and Michael Deas, 'French giant Veolia cut down to size for abusing Palestinian rights', *Electronic Intifada*, 26 August 2011 <http://electronicintifada.net/content/french-giant-veolia-cut-down-size-abusing-palestinian-rights/10316> (accessed 9 September 2011).

11. Adri Nieuwhof, 'Divestment campaign gains momentum in Europe', *Electronic Intifada*, 24 March 2009 <http://electronicintifada.net/content/divestment-campaign-gains-momentum-europe/8151> (accessed 11 September 2011).

12. Veolia Environnement company profile, *Banktrack*, 8 March 2011 <http://www.banktrack.org/show/companyprofiles/veolia_environment> (accessed 9 September 2011).

13. Daniel Machover and Adri Nieuwhof, 'French court decision on Jerusalem light rail must be challenged', *Electronic Intifada*, 27 June 2011 <http://electronicintifada.net/content/french-court-decision-jerusalem-light-rail-must-be-challenged/10115> (accessed 11 September 2011).

14. A. Dutt Misra and R. Gupta (2008), *Insipiring Thoughts Of Mahatma Gandhi: Gandhi in daily life*. New Delhi: Concept Publishing Company.

15. Adri Nieuwhof, Bangani Ngeleza and Jeff Handmaker, 'Lessons from South Africa for the peace process', *Electronic Intifada*, 1 Fenruary 2005 <http://electronicintifada.net/v2/article3587.shtml> (accessed 31 January 2011).

17
The Case of the Edinburgh 5

Mick Napier

On a sunny August morning during the 2008 Edinburgh International Festival, a solid security cordon stood between thirty protesters and the Queens Hall in Edinburgh. Due to perform was the provocatively named Jerusalem Quartet, about whom the World Zionist Press Service had proudly stated 'carrying a rifle in one hand and a violin in the other', they make 'the ultimate Zionist statement'.[1] This 'praise' stood alongside their role as 'Cultural Ambassadors'[2] of the state of Israel and 'Distinguished IDF Musicians'.[3] Scottish supporters of freedom and human rights could not see why the Jerusalem Quartet should be able to work with Israeli Army human rights violators and then play unopposed in Edinburgh.

Immediately following the launch of the Palestinian campaign for Boycott, Divestment and Sanctions (BDS), the Scottish Palestine Solidarity Campaign (SPSC) had declared its support and, given the complicity of the British government in Israeli crimes, had recognised BDS as the most effective strategy through which civil society could contribute to the struggle for Palestinian freedom. Israeli state-backed cultural initiatives had been included in the BDS appeal and we confirmed with the Palestinian Boycott National Committee that the Jerusalem Quartet fell squarely within the boycott criteria.

In the weeks preceding the scheduled performance, a campaign of letters to the Director of the Edinburgh International Festival (EIF) went officially unanswered although generated local press coverage. SPSC President Marion Woolfson was among many calling for the invitation to the Jerusalem Quartet to be rescinded and demanding that the prestigious EIF must not host a cultural propaganda arm of the Israeli regime. The Festival's management responded in bad faith, remaining silent for weeks before replying to the SPSC's letter the day before the recital. Their claims that the Jerusalem Quartet had no connections with the Israeli Army would easily have been publicly refuted in the media had their response come sooner.

On the day of the performance, our protests alerted attendees to the nature of the Jerusalem Quartet's links to the Israeli Army; not killers themselves, they soothe the brows of other soldiers potentially disturbed by their brutalisation of Palestinians under their military power. A few ticket holders heeded our protests, and a handful joined us in our leafleting work outside the Queens Hall.

All Israeli performers supported by the State of Israel must sign a contract in which they agree 'to promote the policy interests of the State of Israel via culture and art, including contributing to creating a positive image for Israel'.[4] This declaration is tantamount to defending Israeli violations of human rights.

We organised to peacefully disrupt the performance and draw attention to the siege of Gaza and the performers' militarised status in Israel. Five of us took our seats inside for the live recording by BBC Radio 3 (the same BBC that later refused to broadcast even a humanitarian appeal for Gaza) and, at regular intervals, stood up and made the points we were there to make by shouting, 'These men are Israeli military musicians' and 'End the siege of Gaza.' We were roughly ejected, handcuffed, arrested, taken to police cells, and charged with 'breach of the peace', before being released eight hours later. Unlike Palestinians, however, we were not shot or tear-gassed during our protest, and we did not suffer torture during our short incarceration.

The aim of the protest was the same as for all our BDS activities; to send a message to Palestinians that they enjoy growing support worldwide and to the Israeli regime and its advocates that they will pay an increasing price as long as they continue with their crimes. We also hoped to draw the members of the Jerusalem Quartet into open court where we could cross-examine them on their contract with the Israeli government, and the exact nature of their relationship to the Israeli occupation forces. Furthermore, we aimed to seek explanations as to the level of knowledge of those who invited the Jerusalem Quartet to Edinburgh regarding the musicians' role as official entertainers for a military force guilty of heinous human rights violations.

Although some ticket-holders supported the protest, our intended audience was not the genteel folk who turned up to hear music they naively considered to be 'above politics'. Most of them were indeed angry at the mention of human rights whilst the violins of the 'Distinguished IDF Musicians' entertained them. One prominent left-wing politician, ex-MEP Hugh Kerr, publicly attacked the protestors for 'harming the Palestinian cause', although he later gracefully conceded he had been wrong and endorsed the Palestinian call for BDS. In a bygone era, irate Scottish rugby fans had similarly objected to our banners against South African apartheid at their rugby games and our subsequent pitch invasions. As time passed, more and more people began to support that principled stance, and the same will be true one day of today's BDS actions. We didn't seek those earlier confrontations with Scottish rugby fans, nor with Edinburgh music lovers, but conflict is unavoidable sometimes between those who prioritise human rights issues over personal, sporting, or cultural pleasure and those who believe that their right to undisturbed entertainment is paramount.

In the aftermath of our arrest, we prepared for a trial in which we would plead 'not guilty', argue justification for our actions, and work to put the Jerusalem Quartet and the Israeli occupation under the spotlight inside the court, and on trial in the court of public opinion. Between August 2008 and our scheduled trial came Operation Cast Lead. Some thought that the public revulsion that followed the mass killings in Gaza would lead to the charges being quietly dropped; they were wrong.

The trial date was set for 9 March 2010, but in the preceding week a senior Procurator Fiscal – the Scottish legal term for a prosecutor – announced that she would replace the 'breach of the peace' charge with a very different one of 'racially aggravated conduct'. At the time, she claimed that 'new evidence had come to light'; none ever has. Very possibly, the Procurator Fiscal was responding to the London Declaration on Combating Anti-Semitism of February 2010. With grief and trauma still blanketing Gaza, the British Foreign Office had hosted the inaugural conference of the Inter-parliamentary Coalition for Combating Antisemitism (ICCA) to 'create an action plan to tackle ... the escalating global threat of anti-Semitism'. The conference was attended by ministers from a dozen governments and members of the US Congress.

The London Declaration on Combating Anti-Semitism was an unoriginal effort to conflate anti-Semitism with opposition to the policies, practices, or apartheid structure of the State of Israel. It classified defence of the idea that the State of Israel is structurally racist as a criminal act. Significantly, the Declaration went on to include BDS campaigning in its definition of the behaviours that ought also to become criminal offences: 'Education Authorities should ... protect students and staff from illegal antisemitic discourse and a hostile environment in whatever form it takes including calls for boycotts.'[5] The clear implication was that a call to support the Palestinian call for BDS should be treated as 'illegal anti-Semitic discourse'.

A few days later, on 25 February, Gordon Brown signed the London Declaration on Combating Anti-Semitism on behalf of the British Government and announced that a conference would be called within a month by the Department of Communities and Local Government 'to look in detail at how the Government can implement the London Declaration'.[6] At the signing, John Mann MP, founder of the ICCA, commended 'the British Government [for] taking the London Declaration so seriously ... Following this, I know meetings are taking place to implement the recommendations in the declaration.'

We don't know exactly what decisions were taken at the meetings, but the timing was curious to say the least: Prime Minister Gordon Brown signed the Declaration at the end of February which specifically highlighted BDS campaigning, a follow-up conference was arranged for March to discuss implementation, 'meetings' were announced to 'implement the recommendations', and racism charges were levelled against us a few days later.

Strategically, we were delighted. The new charges moved the focus from our actions during the protest to the question of our motivation. This allowed us to shift some of the legal discussion to the issue of what is actually happening in Palestine, together with the complicity of the British government in Israeli actions. The incessant Zionist claims that supporters of Palestinian freedom are driven by anti-Semitic tendencies would now be debated in open court. This presented us with an opportunity to demolish that falsified accusation and thus strengthen the BDS movement by weakening a core element of the Zionist smear campaign against the struggle for Palestinian freedom.

It was not a question of whether we would win, but when. Even if lower courts convicted us, we prepared ourselves to appeal any conviction through progressively higher courts and use the process to flag up the issues of Israeli human rights violations. We had a pre-planned strategy, and the longer the legal battle turned out to be, the greater would be the opportunities to publicise the reality of Israeli ethnic cleansing.

Unfazed by the charges, we had total confidence in our morals and actions, and knew that the law could also be made to work for us in this instance. We knew we would be forced to the front line of defending the burgeoning BDS campaign in Scotland. The SPSC also had substantial previous experience of successful legal battles with pro-Israeli organisations in Scotland, despite their deployment of top London legal firms against us. In one case, a legal victory against opponents whose literature labelled us as anti-Semitic led to the pulping of 6,000 copies of their defamatory book;[7] in other cases, we saw off high-powered legal threats to BDS campaigning by inviting our accusers, whether the Jewish National Fund (JNF) or lawyers representing an Israeli-owned Edinburgh hotel, to meet us in court. We wanted to debate their lawyers over issues of Israeli ethnic cleansing, dispossession, bulldozing, murder and apartheid and their clients' complicity in these activities. Despite hair-raising threats, their supposedly supercharged lawyers declined to face poorly financed opponents in court. This reluctance to face cross-examination in open court is far from unusual for defenders of Zionism, who clearly lack confidence in their legal standing in such a challenge as much as they are aware of the political damage that legal defeats would cause them.

Although confident, we organised carefully for the legal battle. We knew that popular opinion would support us much more than the Zionists, provided we campaigned for it. We worked on a twin-track of tight, legal defence alongside, more importantly, appeals for support to the arena that is ultimately decisive: the court of public opinion. Every court appearance was preceded by a rally outside the court building, with BDS placards, banners and loudhailers denouncing the Procurator Fiscal's politically motivated charges. Supporters also packed the courtroom for the more significant court sessions. It was important that the case became a vehicle for discussion around BDS and its rationale, that is, Israel's crimes in Palestine, and did not fall to the Zionist tactic of trying to shift the focus away from what they know well to be indefensible Israeli practices.

Our 'not guilty' plea was based on the argument that anti-Semitism, like all forms of racism, is repugnant to us, but that active opposition to crimes of the Israeli state is a duty, just as opposition to aggressive wars or South African apartheid is and was a moral and political imperative for many. We derided the charges from the start as a politically motivated attempt by a government that was complicit in Israeli crimes, aiming to intimidate, to silence criticism and to impede democratic, legal, non-violent boycott campaigning against a military and political ally of the UK government. We insisted that this was a free speech issue, that the legal authorities were working to implement the oppressive recommendations of the London Declaration and Gordon Brown, and that this constituted a threat to civil liberties and free speech for all.

Strategically, the most difficult decision we faced was whether to contest the validity of the 'racially aggravated conduct' charges in a pre-trial, or to proceed directly to potentially more fruitful courtroom exchanges involving witnesses. To protect our right to appeal later to higher courts we agreed, not without some reluctance, to follow the pre-trial process after which the Sheriff (the Scottish equivalent of a court judge) would rule on whether the charges were valid or should be dismissed. In the event that the Sheriff dismissed the charges at the pre-trial stage, the BDS campaign would lose the opportunity for further publicity and awareness that would come from producing a string of persuasive witnesses in open court.

Each of us was assigned a personal lawyer, as well as a higher-level Advocate (Barrister in England) for detailed legal argumentation; there were some difficult discussions and political disagreements between these legal personnel and the accused. We did not, for example, want to win on a technicality that avoided the political issues at stake. Clients are formally held to 'instruct' their lawyers, but the instructions for most lawyers flow in the opposite direction, from lawyer to client. We had to make very clear to our lawyers that we had a considered, collective, politico-legal strategy which would drive our position in the courtroom. Lawyers sometimes had different expectations from the defendants, such that one lawyer initially dismissed the very idea that we could bring Palestinian farmers and musicians into the courtroom at all. At several key stages in the legal process, an awareness of political forces at work in this issue proved invaluable.

After many months of effort, BBC Radio 3 finally responded to a court order and released a recording of the events in the Queens Hall. The transcript finally disproved the Procurator Fiscal's claim that one of us had made protestations against 'Jews' during our action inside the hall. This debacle for the Procurator Fiscal led some of our legal team to conclude, somewhat naively, that the case would fall on that score alone. They underwent something of a personal voyage of discovery once they appreciated that the charge of 'racially aggravated conduct' that the Procurator Fiscal was actually alleging was something quite different to what they had imagined, and what most sane people would imagine. The Procurator Fiscal next asked the Sheriff to change the basis of the charge of 'racism' to include the idea that we had discriminated against the IDF Distinguished Musicians on the basis of their 'nationality'. In doing so, he evidenced his deep ignorance of Israel's apartheid legal system that privileges an officially recognised 'Jewish' nationality over 'Arab' or other 'nationalities' within the same body of formally equal citizens. Our lawyers initially asked to challenge this request by the Procurator, failing to appreciate the opportunities it provided to publicly debate the structures of Israeli apartheid in court. With his misunderstanding of the nature of Israeli apartheid, the Procurator was actually making his case unwinnable.

Our strategy during the pre-trial process was to challenge and ridicule the notion that anti-Semitism was the root of BDS campaigning. We would show that our motivation was opposition to Israel's crimes and the UK government's complicity in those crimes, from the 1917 Balfour Declaration to the present. To that end, we secured an extensive list of expert witnesses, including Palestinians who could testify to Israeli ethnic cleansing, murder, kidnapping, political imprisonment, the crime of apartheid, and Israeli manipulation of the concept of anti-Semitism to silence critics. Among Palestinians who agreed to attend the trial as witnesses were Dr Ghada Karmi and Leila Khalid. We also planned to call South African Ronnie Kasrils, Auschwitz survivor Hajo Meyer, international law experts, authorities on apartheid, and veterans of the UK struggles against South African apartheid and the war in Vietnam. MP Peter Hain, a veteran of the British anti-apartheid campaigns in the 1970s, insisted he would not appear. A ministerial post in the New Labour government had clearly led him to view the world differently.

As the two-year legal battle began to draw to a close, a replacement Procurator Fiscal told a packed court, to gasps from the public benches, that it was racist to say the words 'End the siege of Gaza', anywhere, even on a public highway during a demonstration. It was criminal, he asserted, to utter the words 'Genocide in Gaza', and the crime would be compounded if the words were repeated several times. Amazed, laughing at this bizarre turn of events, we left the court after being summoned to return a week later to hear the Sheriff's ruling.

We duly took our places in the dock for the final session, awaiting the legal judgment on the charges against us. Would they be thrown out, finally, after seemingly interminable court sessions? Sheriff Scott had run a tight court throughout the proceedings: he had, for example, quickly insisted on silence when many had gasped audibly the previous week. This time, however, he evidently enjoyed the opportunity for satire that the

Procurator Fiscal had presented. He came firmly down on the side of free speech and against the repressive London Declaration on Combating Anti-Semitism, Gordon Brown and the British government:

> If persons on a public march designed to protest against and publicise alleged crimes committed by a state and its army are afraid to name that state for fear of being charged with racially aggravated behaviour, it would render worthless their Article 10(1) rights. Presumably their placards would have to read, 'Genocide in an unspecified state in the Middle East'; 'Boycott an unspecified state in the Middle East', etc.

He dismissed the allegations of racism against BDS activists: 'The procurator fiscal's attempts to squeeze malice and ill will out of the agreed facts were rather strained', 'rather strained' being an understated way of saying utterly without foundation, since our comments in the Queens Hall 'were clearly directed at the State of Israel, the Israeli Army, and Israeli Army musicians', and not targeted at 'citizens of Israel' per se.[8]

It was noteworthy that the Sheriff didn't hide behind generalities on the bench, but dealt explicitly with the case of Israel. Lawyers representing others facing charges designed to criminalise BDS activities as racist will have this precedent to refer to: a ruling given with considerable care by a Sheriff in a Scottish court. Since much of UK and Scottish law is case law, our success has left a roadblock for those who seek to de-legitimise and demonise the BDS campaign.

Our success, when it came, was swift and complete. The London *Times* reported that the charges were 'thrown out of court' in a 'landmark case'.[9] As BDS activists, we have no choice but to face such challenges, for our victory in them strengthens our hand, defends Palestinian rights as well as our own, and can shorten the road ahead of Palestinians that leads to freedom and justice. The BDS campaign has already, in the words of an Israeli government think tank, the influential Reut Institute, produced 'a significant setback in [Israel's] international standing', and has the potential to 'constrain future Israeli military planning and operations as effectively as any Arab army could'.[10]

The stakes, therefore, could not be higher and we must expect attacks when we stand up for Palestinian human and national rights, which has meant, above all, developing the BDS campaign. Our own case pitted supporters of human rights against prosecutors who strove to put Israel beyond criticism. They failed and were humiliated on this occasion, but they will try again elsewhere. Supporters of Israel – Gordon Brown and David Cameron, for example – need to limit our democratic rights in order to defend the indefensible against a rising tide of popular anger at Israel's crimes.

Charges such as those we faced are primarily aimed at suppressing resistance, and they can succeed if we are not organised, strategic and fully prepared. We have to be sure of the principled political ground that we occupy, as well as the reasons why Israel enjoys unstinting support from western governments, yet minimal popular support across Europe. Tragically but inevitably, the BDS campaign will be largely fuelled by Israel repeatedly crossing 'red lines', and committing continuous and even greater crimes against the Palestinian people. Our job is to organise the BDS campaign to reduce the price that the Palestinian people are paying and will pay for their freedom; the level of this reduction is incalculable, but we can be sure that it will be proportionate to our effort.

NOTES

1. S. Kleiman (1998), 'Israeli Musicians also have Military Strings Attached' <http://www.jewishaz.com/jewishnews/980619/musician.shtml> (accessed 13 June 2011).
2. Jerusalem Foundation (2007), 'Jerusalem Quartet' <http://www.jerusalemfoundation.org/project_overview.aspx?TAB=0&MID=550&CID=578&PID=654> (accessed 13 June 2011).
3. Jerusalem Foundation (2006), 'The Jerusalem Quartet' <http://www.jerusalemfoundation.org/uploads//Culture/Innovation%20and%20Expansion/Jerusalem%20Quartet/Jerusalem%20Quartet%20Report%202006.pdf> (accessed 13 June 2011).

4. Y. Laor (2008), *Ha'aretz*, 25 July <http://www.haaretz. com/misc/article-print-page/putting-out-a-contract-on-art-1.250388?trailingPath=2.169%2C> (accessed 25 September 2011).

5. Department for Communities and Local Government (2009), The London Declaration on Combating Anti-Semitism <http:// www.communities.gov.uk/documents/corporate/pdf/1151284.pdf> (accessed 13 June 2011).

6. British Embassy in Israel (2009), 'British Prime Minister Signs London Declaration on Combating Anti-Semitism' <http:// ukinisrael.fco.gov.uk/en/news/?view=News&id=14159560> (accessed 13 June 2011).

7. M. Napier (2010), 'Zionist "leaders" of Scottish Jewish community under attack for fabricating anti-Semitism wave' <http://www. scottishpsc.org.uk/index.php?option=com_content&view=articl e&id=3353:zionist-leaders-of-scottish-jewish-community-under-attack-for-fabricating-anti-semitism-wave&catid=552:spsc-sees-off-legal-attacks&Itemid=200522> (accessed 13 June 2011).

8. Journal Online, 'Sheriff dismisses racism charges against anti-Israel protesters', 9 April 2010 <http://www.journalonline.co.uk/ News/1007901.aspx> (accessed 13 June 2011).

9. L. McIntosh, 'Racism case over Edinburgh Festival anti-Israel protest thrown out', 9 April 2010 <http://www.timesonline.co.uk/ tol/news/uk/scotland/article7092668.ece> (accessed 13 June 2011).

10. G. Grinstein (2010) 'Israel delegitimizers threaten its existence' <http://www.reut-institute.org/en/Publication.aspx? PublicationId=3763> (accessed 13 June 2011).

18
Worker-to-Worker Solidarity:
BDS in the Trade Union Movement

Rafeef Ziadah

Boycotts played a vital role in the overthrow of apartheid in South Africa. We wholeheartedly share the sentiment of our comrades in Palestine that boycotts, divestment and sanctions (BDS) is the kernel to overthrowing Israeli apartheid.

Congress of South African Trade Unions Statement, 2011.

In July 2005, over 170 Palestinian organisations urged the world to adopt a campaign of Boycott, Divestment and Sanctions (BDS) against Israel in the manner of the campaign against South African apartheid. This call was signed by all the main Palestinian trade union federations, along with women's, student and refugee groups. The BDS call represented the broadest political statement to come out of Palestine since the beginning of the second Palestinian uprising in September 2000, and it precipitated a powerful global solidarity campaign that has grown dramatically since its establishment.

Many trade unions have heeded the BDS call, either by passing BDS resolutions at their conventions, initiating rank-and-file education campaigns and sending delegations to Palestine, or through taking direct action by refusing to handle Israeli goods. Just as was the case with the South African Anti-Apartheid Movement, trade unions have a key role to play in highlighting the plight of Palestinian workers and organising principled solidarity campaigns that go beyond sloganeering to concrete actions. Activists remember fondly when postal workers refused to handle mail from apartheid South Africa and dockworkers refused to offload South African produce; these moments will stay forever etched in the memories of trade unionists who understand that workers' actions do indeed effect change. The case for BDS against apartheid Israel is reinvigorating the trade union movement, and rank-and-file activists are once again building alliances, doing the long-term educational work and strategising to respond to the call for solidarity from the Palestinian people.

One of the main reasons the BDS call has gained significant support among trade unions internationally is the clarity of its demands. The Israeli state must be isolated in the same manner as apartheid-era South Africa was, until three conditions are satisfied: the Israeli occupation of all Arab lands is ended, there is full equality for Palestinian citizens of Israel, and Palestinian refugees are allowed to return home. These three demands encapsulate the Palestinian experience since 1948: a people who have been uprooted from their land and prevented from returning home, while those who remained are treated as second-class citizens inside Israel or living under a brutal military occupation in the 1967 territories. The demands of the BDS campaign are all rooted in international law.

The Palestinian trade union movement, stemming from its deep belief in worker-to-worker solidarity, appealed to the international trade union movement to support, endorse and, most importantly, act upon the BDS campaign. In essence, Palestinian workers have taken the same actions any principled trade unionist undertakes: after years of failed negotiations with the Israeli state that resulted only in greater Israeli colonisation and the infliction of even more daily hardships on the Palestinian people, the Palestinian trade union movement set up a picket line and asked for solidarity from ordinary people around the world, basing this call on the tried and true union slogan: 'an injury to one is an injury to all.'

BDS SUCCESSES IN THE TRADE UNION MOVEMENT

Despite the fact that when the BDS call was first initiated some suggested that such a campaign was too ambitious, the campaign quickly gained ground. The year 2011 saw an intensification in the BDS campaign within the trade union movement. The South African Congress of Trade Unions, one of the earliest supporters of the Palestinian BDS campaign, issued a statement fully endorsing the Palestinian Boycott, Divestment and Sanctions National Committee's (BNC) call for a mandatory comprehensive arms embargo against Israel similar to that imposed against apartheid South Africa. In a unique campaign, which is quickly spreading as a model for other unions to undertake, the South African Municipal Workers Union (SAMWU) promoted 'Israeli Apartheid Free Zones' to ensure their municipalities have no links with the Israeli regime.

In light of the 'Arab Spring', it was heartening for the Palestinian BDS campaign to receive the full endorsement of the Egyptian Independent Union Federation (EIUF), which was formed in Tahrir Square during the revolution. In a statement on the topic of BDS, Kamal Abu Aita, a representative of the EIUF, confirmed that it rejects any attempt to 'normalise' relations with Israel. He explained:

> From the beginning, the revolution has worked in the interests of the Palestinians, by stopping the export of Egyptian gas to the Zionists, and opening the border crossings. Egyptian youth besieged the embassy of our enemy and demanded the expulsion of the ambassador. We reject any relationship with the Histadrut [the Israeli labour federation] because it is part of this racist regime. We call on all friendly unions to boycott the Histadrut as part of the campaign to get rid of racist regimes all over the world.[1]

This position clearly signals that support for BDS in Eygpt at the union level will go beyond pre-revolution sloganeering from official unions, to serious targeted action to sever relationships with Israeli institutions. There is much to be done in this direction especially as most free-trade agreements over the past decade between the US and Arab states have included provisions that relationships with Israel must be normalised. In the Qualified Industrial Zones (QIZs) which have resulted from such free-trade agreements, Israeli money is invested – and as with all free-trade zones – workers' conditions are abysmal. These types of zones exist in Egypt and Jordan, thus there is much organising still to be done in order to uncover the reality of how these zones function and to launch a concrete BDS campaign.[2]

In Europe, the Irish Congress of Trade Unions, representing the entirety of the trade union movement across the island, passed resolutions in support of BDS in 2007, and, at their Biennial Delegates Conference in 2011, they reiterated their commitment to BDS and moved motions to begin researching and implementing divestment through their pension funds. The Norwegian EL & IT union, which represents over 30,000 energy and telecommunications workers, adopted BDS and called for a boycott of the Histadrut, the Israeli labour federation. In a statement, the union announced that it would take steps in support of a consumer boycott of Israeli produce, a two-way arms embargo on Israel and the imposition of sanctions on Israel by the UN. The statement also calls on LO, the Norwegian trade union federation, to cut ties with the Histadrut.

The decision of the Trades Union Congress (TUC) in Britain, representing almost 7 million workers, to launch a campaign to boycott settlement goods was a step forward for the BDS campaign, and organisers have vowed to work to further the policy along the lines that many individual unions in Britain have done by supporting the BDS call in its entirety. The Scottish Trade Union Congress has taken steps in support of BDS and again towards severing ties with the Histadrut. The University and College Union (UCU) in Britain was among the first to take up the question of the institutional academic boycott and has implemented a full boycott. UNISON, the largest public-sector union in Europe voted, in the wake of the attack on the Freedom Flotilla, to suspend ties with the Histadrut; a motion to revisit the severing of the ties for a position of 'constructive engagement' was defeated on the conference floor in 2011.

In yet another significant development in 2011, Brazil's largest Trade Union Confederation (CUT), voiced its support of the BDS call and called for the suspension of Israeli-Brazilian economic agreements and military ties on 28 January. In its statement,

CUT singled out the growing military trade and economic links being built between Brazil and Israel:

> We regret that Brazil is the third largest consumer of arms from Israel through the Plan of National Defense Strategy of the Ministry of Defense of Brazil, and that arms agreements contribute indirectly to the occupation of Palestinian territory. It is therefore necessary that the Brazilian government suspend current agreements and bilateral economic/military negotiations between Brazil and Israel. It is unacceptable that the Free Trade Agreement between MERCOSUR and Israel becomes a reality.[3]

One of the most inspiring trade union direct actions in the BDS campaign thus far has come from dockworkers' unions. In the wake of the Israeli attack on the Freedom Flotilla in the summer of 2010 and after an appeal was issued by the Palestinian unions, the Swedish Dockworkers Union blocked more than 500 containers weighing approximately 500 tons during a week-long blockade of exports to Israel. Dockworkers in Oakland, California respected a labour and community picket by refusing to unload an Israeli cargo ship for 24 hours. These actions followed those of the South African Transport and Allied Workers' Union which pioneered the boycott against Israeli maritime trade in February 2009, by refusing to offload a ship in Durban in protest of Israel's war of aggression on the Gaza Strip.

The BDS campaign is growing in geographical scope as well. The New Zealand Council of Trade Unions Te Kauae Kaimahi, which brings together over 350,000 New Zealand union members in 40 affiliated unions, called in 2009 upon the New Zealand government to take a number of BDS actions. Across Australia, more than 15 unions or state branches of unions adopted some form of BDS and rank-and-file activists have begun to seriously coordinate their actions across sectors to put pressure on the main national labour bodies to endorse and support BDS.

Very significantly, on the Palestinian side, 2011 also ushered in the new Palestinian Trade Union Coalition for BDS (PTUC-BDS). In commemoration of May Day, a Palestinian trade union conference for BDS was held in Ramallah, organised by almost the entirety of the Palestinian trade union movement, including federations, professional unions, and trade union blocks representing the entire spectrum of Palestinian political parties. The conference established PTUC-BDS as the largest coalition of the Palestinian trade union movement to provide the most representative Palestinian reference for international trade unions involved or wanting to be involved in the BDS campaign. PTUC-BDS representatives have already spoken on trade union speaking tours in several countries, explaining the conditions of Palestinian workers and arguing for BDS as the most important form of solidarity that can be given to the Palestinian people, because it focuses explicitly on ending complicity with Israel's Apartheid regime.

The establishment of PTUC-BDS will hinder those organisations that continue to misrepresent the Palestinian trade union movement and shed doubts on the BDS call – the reality is that the Palestinian trade union movement has historically been at the core of anti-normalisation initiatives with the Israeli regime and, during the First Intifada, Palestinian strike action had a significant impact on Israel. The fact that Israel responded to Palestinian workers' action by replacing their labour with migrant labour speaks volumes about the Israeli state's view on the dispensability of workers. PTUC-BDS is in line with the long history of the Palestinian trade union movement's role at the forefront of the Palestinian struggle for self-determination, and from its inception, the PTUC-BDS's crucial role in internationally advancing the BDS campaign was already evident.

BDS: THE MOST EFFECTIVE FORM OF
TRADE UNION SOLIDARITY WITH PALESTINE

For decades, Israel has enjoyed impunity and the so-called international community has done more in the way of protecting Israel than stopping its crimes against the Palestinian people. Due to its treatment as a state above the law, Israel continues its gradual and deliberate ethnic cleansing of Palestinians, particularly in occupied East Jerusalem, the Jordan Valley and the Naqab (Negev) desert. The decades-long military occupation continues with its theft of land and natural resources, the construction of illegal colonial settlements and the Apartheid Wall, and the inhuman siege of Gaza. Israel's systematic destruction of the Palestinian economy, expropriation of the most fertile agricultural land, as well as humiliation and racist discrimination against Palestinian workers have all become part of the apartheid reality that the BDS campaign aims to highlight and works to end. Given the complete failure of nation states to hold Israel accountable to international law, the appeal is to international civil society, and from the Palestinian labour movement, the appeal is specifically to the international trade union movement, to take concrete action to at least end their own organisation's complicity with Israeli apartheid and its institutions.

When over 1.5 million people in the Gaza Strip have literally been imprisoned behind a military siege in one of the cruellest examples of collective punishment in recent times, and the international community aids Israel in upholding its siege (as was the case with the Greek government not allowing the Gaza Freedom Flotilla to leave its shores), it is then incumbent on people of conscience to act. It is also no coincidence that the same governments supporting Israel are the ones who passed austerity measures aimed at making workers pay for a financial crisis they did not create.

The situation in Gaza reveals what Israel hopes to create in the West Bank. Only 45 km long and about 10–12 km wide, Gaza is one of the most densely populated places on earth. Over 70 per cent of Gaza's population are refugees denied their right of return to their homes. Gaza has become a heavily guarded mass open-air prison. Israel has continued to prevent movement in and out of the area while subjecting its residents to repeated military incursions, shelling and house demolitions. This same story is being duplicated in the West Bank, where the situation will be most difficult for Palestinian workers – forced into further open-air prisons with only the ability to work within the 'industrial zones' run by corporations with Israeli state investment. There is very little information on the proposed industrial zones, but it is becoming clear that unionisation will not be allowed. Similar projects (called Qualified Industrial Zones) exist already in Jordan and Egypt. Unionisation is barred and human rights organisations have documented serious abuse of workers. Aside from the long, humiliating waits at checkpoints and the total control of everyday life by the Israeli military, Palestinian workers are being stranded in a dependent economy, where Israel has destroyed the agricultural sector. Palestinian workers are essentially a captive workforce.

Already the abuse of workers in the Occupied Territory has been well documented, especially among workers on settlements in the agricultural sector. They receive well below the minimum wage, they work long shifts and child labour is common. The produce that Palestinian workers are involved in cultivating is later exported, mainly to Europe, and given tax exemption because of the EU's free-trade agreement with Israel. Carmel Agrexco, until recently Israel's leading produce exporter, has routinely mislabelled produce from settlements and submitted documentation claiming that it originates inside the Green Line in an attempt to have it qualify for preferential customs treatment under the EU-Israel Association Agreement. The EU Court of Justice has ruled that settlement produce should not qualify for such preferential treatment.

When these connections are made between the actual physical labour of Palestinian workers and the products that end up with consumers, it becomes obvious that trade unions have a key role to play in standing in solidarity with Palestinian workers. Trade unions have a rich history of international solidarity and – much as with the South African example – have a responsibility to stand firmly with the oppressed.

SEVERING TIES WITH THE HISTADRUT

The Palestinian trade union movement has also called for the severing of ties with the Histadrut, the Israeli trade union federation. Many individual unions and national trade union congresses have heeded this call or have started a process to do so. However, this remains an obstacle for the BDS campaign because of the long history some trade unions have with the Histadrut, and its well-crafted image as a progressive force in Israeli politics – nothing could be further from the truth.

From its inception, the Histadrut played a key role in perpetuating Israel's occupation, colonisation and system of racial discrimination. It was founded as an exclusively Jewish organisation to facilitate the colonisation of Palestine, and it worked hand-in-hand with the Jewish Agency to promote the exclusion of Palestinian labour and produce. Histadrut leader David Hachoen captures the founding ideology of the Histadrut succinctly, when speaking about the railway workers' union, which was fighting to include workers of all religions; he said, 'the railway workers forget that the mission of the Hebrew workers who are part of the movement for settling Palestine, is not to be bothered with mutual assistance to Arab workers, but to assist in the fortification of the Zionist project on the land.'[4] It is clear that the Histadrut was never founded on the basis of class solidarity, but rather as an instrument to strengthen the colonial project.

More recently, the Histadrut has openly supported Israel's violations of the Fourth Geneva Convention and other tenets of international law. It continues to maintain active commercial interests in Israel's illegal settlement enterprise,[5] and allows Jewish settlers in the occupied West Bank to join the organisation.[6] In a manner absolutely not befitting a labour union federation, it supported Israel's war of aggression on besieged Gaza in 2008–09 and later justified Israel's massacre of humanitarian relief workers and activists aboard the Freedom Flotilla on 31 May 2010.[7]

The Histadrut is also illegally withholding over NIS 8.3 billion (approximately $2.43 billion) of Palestinian workers' dues. This was money deducted from Palestinian workers' wages for social and other trade union benefits that they never received. Palestinian workers from the Occupied Territories pay for but do not receive the vast majority of social rights for which they are legally mandated to pay. Even though there was a signed agreement for this money to be paid back to the Palestinian Trade Union Federation this payment never materialised.

Inside Israel, the Histadrut refuses to assist Palestinian citizens of Israel in their fight against racial discrimination in the workplace. In one notorious example, the Histadrut did nothing when, in 2004, Palestinian workers' hardhats at a building site in the Knesset grounds were marked with a red X, to facilitate assassination in case of emergency.[8]

Some have called for 'critical engagement' with the Histadrut. The problem with this approach is that it misunderstands the nature of the organisation. The Histadrut is not a trade union in the normal sense of the word. For over sixty years it has been an integral part of Israel's colonial project. It is closely tied to the Israeli state and is thus directly party – in fact, a leading force – in the construction of Israeli apartheid. As with any other institution of Israeli state policy, normalisation with the Histadrut must thus be rejected.

WORKING FOR BDS INSIDE LABOUR UNIONS

Building solidarity for Palestine within the trade union movement is not a quick process. One important lesson of trade union organising is the ability to build structures patiently, even during emergency situations when one is responding to atrocities and war crimes. Thinking strategically about building alliances and doing rank-and-file education is key to the success of BDS in unions. It is good to pass resolutions at times of emergencies, but the real work happens between conferences.

For example, the experience of the Canadian Union of Public Employees (CUPE) Ontario in passing Resolution 50 in support of the BDS campaign not only highlights the importance of BDS, but also how much BDS actually benefits the unions that undertake it themselves. By opening up democratic spaces for discussion and focusing on rank-and-file education, it teaches a new kind of social unionism. While opponents of BDS claim that it closes down discussion, in reality passing the BDS motion in CUPE Ontario meant that members were now able to hold workshops, ask questions and engage critically with a topic that had often been presented as 'too complicated' by the mainstream media.

Activists in CUPE Ontario followed the resolution with an education campaign within the union locals and committees that has been widely praised as the most effective grass-roots campaign in the union's history. Literally thousands of rank-and-file members received materials on BDS or participated in workshops about Palestinian workers' rights. This work itself revitalised the CUPE Ontario international solidarity committee, building a large, open and active member-led campaign.

This campaign demonstrated the main strategic significance of BDS union resolutions – as a tool to educate and mobilise rank-and-file members and build an appreciation for international solidarity as an integral part of a principled labour movement. In April 2008, the BDS movement in Canada received another historic boost when the national convention of the Canadian Union of Postal Workers (CUPW) passed a resolution modelled on CUPE Ontario's Resolution 50. The CUPW resolution was doubly significant: it represented the first motion by a national union in support of BDS, and also supported the CUPW's historic principles, having been the first Canadian union to pass a boycott resolution against South African apartheid.

While for decades international solidarity organising had become a form of 'charity' work that unions undertake, the BDS movement is bringing back memories of the fight against South African apartheid and activating those members who had been involved in that campaign but had become disillusioned with the new forms of organising. BDS motions don't simply help Palestinian workers, but also have an important effect on the unions that pass them as well. Translating BDS motions from ink on paper to active campaigns is the urgent work of solidarity activists within unions today.

The work around the CUPE Ontario motion was modelled on the work of the South African Coalition of Trade Unions (SACTU) Solidarity Committee in Canada during South African apartheid. That committee contacted 10,000 Canadian trade unionists per year at the peak of its work. This was done at union conferences, union schools and local union meetings. Taking the message to the local level is one of the goals of the BDS campaign. There is no short-cut to this longer-term planning and the BDS movement is strongest when there is an informed rank-and-file membership. When the Palestinian narrative continues to be purposely obfuscated in the mainstream media, the ability to speak directly to workers in labour unions is critical.

MOVING FORWARD

Ken Luckhardt, the official representative of the SACTU Solidarity Committee in Canada, summed up the reasoning and urgency for mobilisation within labour unions in support of the Palestinian BDS campaign:

> The commitment to systematic political work to defeat Israeli apartheid needs to be taken on with the same determination that defined the global anti-apartheid movement in the struggle for a non-racial democracy in South Africa. Freedom for the Palestinian people combined with the social justice and peace in the region is the only real option. This is the key struggle for international solidarity activists in the trade union movement today.[9]

As BDS activists in the labour movement, we understand that the trade union movement internationally is operating in a harsh environment where attacks are made on basic workers' rights, and in which austerity measures that cut back public spending come along with a severe push for privatisation across nation states. Sometimes people tend to see international solidarity issues and local workers' struggles as unrelated issues, yet through the rhetoric of 'lets focus only on bread-and-butter issues' and 'only saving our jobs', we all lose. If we are to wage an effective fight back against neo-liberal policies such as privatisation, lay-offs and union busting, then all unions must also stand with workers struggling against oppression internationally.

The increasing number of BDS resolutions and effective labour movement actions in solidarity with the Palestinian people indicate that a deep recognition that Israel must be isolated in the manner of apartheid-era South Africa, is becoming an established principle of progressive and principled trade union politics. There is much work ahead – but at least the BDS campaign gives the workers' movement a clear direction and it has a proven record, as most remember from the South African Anti-Apartheid Movement and various other international solidarity campaigns in which trade unions played a key role. The reality is that despite the ongoing brutality of the Israeli regime, Palestinians remain as determined as ever to resist and achieve their full rights, and BDS actions in the international trade union movement demonstrate unequivocally that international solidarity makes a significant and powerful difference to this just struggle for freedom.

NOTES

1. 'Egypt independent trade unions endorse BDS': press release 2 July 2011 <http://www.bdsmovement.net/2011/egypt-independent-trade-unions-endorse-bds-7491>.
2. For more information on industrial zones, see Adam Hanieh, 'Palestine in the Middle East: Opposing Neoliberalism and US Power', *MRzine*, 19 July 2008 <http://mrzine.monthlyreview.org/2008/hanieh190708b.html>.
3. 'Largest Brazilian Trade Union backs Boycott', statement, 7 February 2011 <http://www.bdsmovement.net/2011/cut-backs-boycott-5455>.
4. Ilan Pappe, *A History of Modern Palestine: One Land, Two Peoples*, Cambridge: Cambridge University Press, 2006, p. 111.
5. The Histadrut own 25 per cent of the shares of Yahav Bank for Government Employees. This bank has a branch in occupied East Jerusalem and offers services to the settlements <http://www.whoprofits.org/Company%20Info.php?id=889>.
6. For a detailed history of the Histadrut, see Tony Greenstein, 'Histadrut: Israel's Racist "Trade Union"', *Electronic Intifada*, 9 March 2009 <http://electronicintifada.net/content/histadrut-israels-racist-trade-union/8121>.
7. The justification can be found in 'Histadrut Statement on Southern Israel and Gaza', 13 January 2008 <http://www.labourstart.org/israel/Histadrut_on_Gaza.pdf>. The Histadrut press release

justifiying Israel's attack against the Freedom Flotilla going to Gaza can be found at <http://www.histadrut.org.il/index.php?page_id=1801>.

8. See Greenstein, 'Histadrut: Israel's Racist "Trade Union"'.

9. Ken Luckhardt, 'Unionists and the Anti-Apartheid Struggle: Lessons from the South African Experience', *Relay*, November–December 2006 <http://www.socialistproject.ca/relay>.

19

The Derry versus Raytheon Struggle

Eamonn McCann

At the June 2011 Paris Air Show, the Israeli state arms manufacturer Rafael and its US partner Raytheon unveiled their latest joint venture; the 'David's Sling' air defence missile system. The Israeli Air Force hopes to take delivery of the first elements of the system in 2012 and to begin phased deployment the following year. David's Sling will replace the Raytheon MIM-23 Hawk missile system.

The joint venture consolidates an unusual and already close relationship between Israel and Raytheon. It was this relationship which, in 2006 and again in 2009, prompted activists to occupy and disrupt production at Raytheon's plant in Derry, Northern Ireland. As a result, Raytheon pulled out of Derry in March 2010. This represented a significant success for a campaign which had faced opposition from all the mainstream parties in the area, which were either equivocal about Raytheon (the SDLP – Social Democratic and Labour Party – and Sinn Fein) or outright supportive (the Democratic Unionist Party and the Ulster Unionists).

Raytheon produces missiles for more than forty US-allied countries,[1] and employs 71,000 workers.[2] Sales in 2011 reached \$25 billion.[3] Over the last decade, the company has delivered high-tech weaponry to countries with toxic human rights records, including Egypt, Saudi Arabia, Turkey, Indonesia, Malaysia, Oman, Singapore, Taiwan and South Korea.[4] But perhaps the company's strongest relationship (other than with the US, its biggest customer) is with Israel.

Raytheon has an ideological as well as a commercial relationship with Israel. Company spokesman Adam Cherrill suggested in 2002 that 'To qualify for self-determination, a people must show some kind of national identity ... What political organizations, social institutions, literature, art, religion, or private correspondence express any ties between the Palestinian people to the Land of Israel?'[5] Joshua Reubner, co-founder of Jews for Peace in Palestine and Israel, commented:

> Adam Cherrill is not a member of a shadowy, millennial cult busily preparing for the building of the Third Temple in Jerusalem. If he were, then it would be easy enough to dismiss what he had to say. But he is a person of considerable clout – the program manager for Raytheon's joint marketing of the Black Sparrow ballistic target missile with the Israeli weapons manufacturer Rafael.[6]

The arms company's arrival in Derry in August 1999 was presented as the first instalment of a 'peace dividend' arising from the 'Good Friday Agreement' that had been signed in April the previous year. The announcement took place amid jubilant scenes on the steps of Derry Guildhall. Local MP John Hume and Northern Ireland's First Minister David Trimble were among dignitaries present. The pair were much lauded in the course of the event, this being their first engagement together since being jointly presented with the Nobel Peace Prize in Oslo eight months earlier. There was a blindingly obvious irony in all of this.

Anti-Raytheon agitation was under way within days, led by the Derry Anti War Coalition (DAWC) and the Foyle Ethical Investment Campaign (FEIC). There was a substantial overlap in the membership of these two groups. The FEIC was founded as an anti-arms trade lobby specifically targeting Raytheon, while DAWC had had a wider remit since its formation in 1991 at the time of the first Iraq War. DAWC's focus was on the wars in Iraq and Afghanistan and on Israeli aggression against Palestine and other neighbouring countries.

The Raytheon campaign organised 'die-ins' in city-centre shopping areas, public rallies, regular protests outside council meetings, a 'Passion for Raytheon' Good Friday walk from the plant to the city centre, 'People's Juries', hedge schools, trade union resolutions, petitions and lobbying of political parties. No conventional stone was left unturned.

The plant at the Springtown Industrial Estate about two miles from Derry city centre was occupied by DAWC and FEIC members during the first month of the Iraq War in March 2003, the day after a Raytheon bomb killed 62 people in the Shu'ale marketplace in Baghdad.[7] The protesters left quietly after a few hours. No damage was done by protesters at the plant, and the action received little media coverage and no discernible ripple on the surface of politics. These facts provided valuable lessons which would go on to affect the strategies of resistance that were used in the struggle against Raytheon.

For the next two years, campaigners continued to lobby, issue statements and leaflets, write letters to the local and national press (few of which were published), display anti-Raytheon placards at demonstrations in Belfast, Dublin and London, and hold regular demonstrations of one kind or another in Derry. The FEIC also held monthly vigils at the company premises.

One of the most bizarre aspects of the campaign was the adamant refusal of some mainstream parties to accept that Raytheon was engaged in arms-related work in Derry, despite a mass of evidence that was sufficient to prove the proposition ten times over. This made it difficult to sustain a clear-cut debate. Local journalists produced documents obtained under the Freedom of Information Act recording explicit discussions about arms-related work in Derry between Raytheon, the Invest Northern Ireland agency, council officials and others. DAWC made and distributed hundreds of copies of an article in an internal Raytheon magazine featuring photographs of Derry workers meeting British military personnel, with captions explaining, even boasting, that they were sharing information on hi-tech missile guidance systems. The official record of NI Office Minister Angela Smith telling a Commons committee about the significant military work being done by Raytheon in Derry was also reproduced.[8]

Two former Raytheon workers who had approached the FEIC gave an extensive interview to *Derry News* confirming that they'd worked on military software at the Springtown factory.[9] But local politicians, including some who occasionally presented themselves as radicals, continued to scratch their heads

over the baffling business of whether Raytheon in Derry was
or was not engaged in arms-related activity. This stance was
sternly maintained through two council meetings in 2004 called
at the urging of DAWC and the FEIC specifically to discuss the
Raytheon issue. On both occasions, the moderate Nationalists
of the SDLP and the more militant Sinn Fein – who held 24
of the 30 council seats between them – denounced the arms
trade in ringing terms and declared that if it were ever proven
that Raytheon was dabbling in arms-related work in Derry, the
council would take a very dim view.

A joint SDLP/Sinn Fein motion to one of the meetings
following publication of unanswerable evidence of Raytheon's
arms-related activities gives a flavour of the subtle elusiveness
of the Nationalist parties:

> Council had received assurances that the Raytheon facility here in Derry
> would only be engaged in activities that had civilian applications ...
> Council acknowledges that Raytheon's core global business is the arms
> trade ... Council wants no part of that trade in this city ... If it is shown
> that Raytheon have broken their understanding to engage in only civilian
> work in Derry, then Council's position will change.[10]

The main reason for the resort to this dodge-and-weave strategy
was that the prospect of jobs in work-starved Derry had put local
politicians under pressure to play dumb about the arrival of an
arms factory in our midst. The need to protect these same jobs
then constrained politicians from withdrawing support, even
when proof of the company's line of work had become clear.
More fundamentally, the main Northern Irish political parties
are all neo-liberal now. The model of economic development
which they see as the only way forward depends on the areas
they represent being able to compete with other areas – including
other areas of Northern Ireland – for available investment. 'If
we don't accept these jobs, somebody else will,' runs the refrain.
The argument is commonly applied also to questions of wage
levels, work patterns, union rights and the protection of the
environment. Multinational companies, and not just arms
companies, demand the abandonment of decency as the price

of their dubious beneficence. (It should be acknowledged that members of the Nationalist parties, including councillors, did, nevertheless, turn out on particular anti-war demonstrations, and were always made welcome. Contradictions abound in politics everywhere, and not least in post-ceasefire Northern Ireland. It should be reiterated, too, that the reason the Unionist parties are not singled out for analyses of their positions is that they reckoned the manufacture of arms an admirable activity altogether and the presence of Raytheon a delightful feather in Derry's cap.)

The launch of the Israeli assault on Lebanon on 12 July 2006 triggered an escalation of anti-war activity in Derry, as elsewhere. By this time, direct Boycott, Divestment and Sanctions (BDS) work was figuring more prominently as a strategy within the campaign. In the first days of the assault, every supermarket in the city was flooded with leaflets listing Israeli goods and urging shoppers to boycott them and look for alternatives. Activists blocked checkouts by filling trolleys with Israeli goods, queueing up in checkout lines and then refusing to pay and demanding the removal of the produce from the shelves. Thousands of leaflets were distributed in the city centre detailing events in Lebanon and spotlighting the Raytheon connection.

A DAWC public meeting had been scheduled in Sandino's pub on 2 August to hear former US Army Abu Ghraib interrogator Joshua Casteel and Iraqi lawyer Hani Lazim argue the case for withdrawal of US and British troops from Iraq. In the event, inevitably, the discussion turned quickly to Lebanon. The now-infamous bombing that had taken place three days earlier of a residential building in Qana had a particularly significant effect on the meeting. A large number of people had been crushed to death, all of them civilians, many of them children, when the building where they were sheltering in the basement was crumpled by a 'bunker-buster' bomb. We knew that Israel's supplier-of-choice of these bunker-busters was Raytheon.

Local trade unionist Eileen Webster, chairing the meeting, declared, 'We have tried everything to force the main parties and the local papers to take a stand against Raytheon. We cannot go on like this, holding vigils and collecting petitions. We have to take action.' Reference was also made to the acquittal in Dublin the previous month of five members of the Pitstop Ploughshares group who had damaged US warplanes at Shannon Airport shortly after the launch of the second Iraq War in 2003, and to anti-war activists who, just days earlier, had invaded Prestwick Airport in Scotland to draw attention to the transport through the airport of Raytheon bunker-busters en route to Israel. By the end of the meeting at Sandino's, the occupation of Raytheon had been decided.

Around thirty activists turned up outside the Raytheon building before 8 a.m. on 9 August. The date was significant as it marked the anniversary of the atom-bombing of Nagasaki. A worker arrived, the front door opened to admit him. We rushed the building. Nine of us made it past security guards, broke open an internal door and were into the plant. The two or three Raytheon workers present immediately rose and left. We piled desks and chairs against the doors to provide a barricade. Documents were tossed from the windows, and computers were also hurled down and smashed. The mainframe was decommissioned by bashing it repeatedly with one end of a fire extinguisher, then filling it with foam from the other. These actions may sound destructive, and they were, both intentionally and strategically. In the absence of any action by political parties to truly defend human rights and prevent Raytheon's continued role in inhuman Israeli attacks against civilians, we had to act ourselves.

After eight hours, about forty police officers in riot gear smashed through the doors and stood in a semi-circle around us, many holding Perspex shields, some pointing plastic-bullet guns. Holding formation, they inched forward. The officer in command shouted orders to 'surrender'. By this time, we were sat playing cards at a desk in the centre of the room. We were seized, handcuffed and dragged along a corridor, down a flight of stairs and out through a back entrance, where land-rovers were waiting to take us away either to Coleraine or the Strand Road (Derry) police stations, where we were formally arrested and held in cells overnight.

In the morning, we were re-handcuffed and driven in police vans to the courthouse in Bishop Street. A large, lively crowd of supporters greeted us with jaunty chants, which boosted morale tremendously. We were remanded in custody, and charged with aggravated burglary and unlawful assembly.

After two days, we appeared by video-link at the High Court and were given bail. Judge Declan Morgan remonstrated with our barrister, Joe Brolly, when he mused that 'The last thing we want here are sound-bites. We are, after all, dealing with merchants of death, your honour.' (The original charges were 'scheduled', which meant under emergency law that we would not have been entitled to a jury trial. The charges were later changed to burglary and criminal damage, restoring our right to trial by jury.)

When the case came to court almost two years later, we pleaded not guilty on the ground that we had not committed a crime but had in fact been trying to prevent one. We likened ourselves to a person who, when walking along a street, hears a child being brutalised inside a house and so proceeds to kick in the door and thumps and drags the assailant away. Would this person be guilty of breaking and entering, or of assault, or of any crime at all?

The judge directed that to establish this defence we would have to demonstrate that at the time of occupation we had had a genuine belief based on reasonable evidence that (a) crimes against humanity were being committed by Israel in Lebanon; (b) the Raytheon company was aiding and abetting these crimes by knowingly supplying the weapons being used to commit them; (c) the company's Derry plant was complicit with the Raytheon company as a whole in aiding and abetting the crimes, and (d) putting the Derry plant out of operation would prevent or further delay such crimes. After a trial which ran into three weeks, the jury accepted our argument and acquitted us.

The key finding was the first one – that there was good evidence that Israel was committing war crimes in Lebanon. We established this with the help of dozens of news reports, clips from television coverage, the findings of Amnesty International and Human Rights Watch, medical reports, statements from UN personnel on the spot – and through cross-examination of Raytheon executives by our barristers. One executive did the company no favours at all by claiming that he didn't know there had been a war in Lebanon in 2006, much less whether his company had supplied any side involved in it with arms.

The news of our acquittal was greeted by messages of congratulations and solidarity from campaigners around the world – among them were demonstrators at Raytheon plants in the US, Mexico and Australia, and UK groups in Bristol, Glenrothes, Brighton and others who were fighting their own direct-action battles against the death machines. We felt part of a global movement which we had only half-known about, which somehow seemed wonderful. However, hopes that our acquittal might shame Raytheon out of town proved unfounded. The company professed itself 'disappointed', but claimed to have been heartened by the continued support of government agencies and others.

Five months after our acquittal came news of the Israeli attack on Gaza in December 2008. Again, we watched coverage of the slaughter of civilians, the use of phosphorus, the targeting of UN installations, the pitiless bombing. News reports told of the use of 'Guided Bomb Units' – bunker-busters – against tunnels linking Gaza to Egypt and other targets. The action at Raytheon might have been a success in that we'd been acquitted and the company's role in supplying weapons to a regime that was using them against civilian populations had been publicly highlighted, but in much more important respects it appeared to have made little difference.

In the first week of January, there was a flurry of controversy in Scotland when anti-war activists objected to US transport planes being allowed to land at Prestwick with cargos of GBUs en route to replenishing Israel's stockpile. Raytheon was continuing to supply weapons to the Israeli war machine, even more blatantly than in relation to Lebanon. Another meeting in Sandino's produced another decision to occupy. This time, on 12 January, nine women undertook the action.

'Our intention was to bring down the mainframe as the men had done', Goretti Horgan, one of the nine women involved told Indymedia. 'We knew from the men's trial that when the Derry mainframe went down, all of Raytheon's UK plants were knocked-out. In other words, it wasn't a moral gesture but a practical way of stopping or at least disrupting the war machine.'

Newly enhanced security at the plant managed to seal off the premises. The women weren't able to reach the inner area where the mainframe was located. They chained themselves together and barricaded themselves into an outer area. After four hours, the local police chief pledged that if they left, an investigation would be launched into whether Raytheon had been complicit in war crimes. On this basis, the occupation ended. (The police, it hardly needs saying, later reneged on this agreement.)

The women came to trial in Belfast in May 2010 charged with trespass and criminal damage. They offered the same defence as we had done before the same judge with the same result. During the trial, Israeli commandos attacked the Freedom Flotilla making its way to Gaza to break the blockade and bring relief supplies, killing nine unarmed civilians. In the week afterwards, six activists went on trial in Bristol for non-violent disarmament actions at another of Israel's main arms suppliers, EDO/ITT, in January 2009. They, too, were to be declared innocent. By this stage, Raytheon had already announced that it was closing its Derry plant and leaving town. The company complained that it no longer felt safe in Derry, and was to express disappointment at the outcome of the trials. Internal documents obtained by the *Londonderry Sentinel* revealed that InvestNI had been pleading with Raytheon not to be hasty and strongly hinting that if the company stayed its hand it wouldn't have to pay back all of the money it owed to the state.[11] Raytheon refused to reconsider.

While it would be nonsensical to suggest that anything positive came from Raytheon's decade-long presence, the fact that the anti-war movement in Derry had a very public and controversial target available locally gave the FEIC and DAWC a function and presence which equally committed activists elsewhere might have found difficult to match. Issues to do with Israel, Palestine and the Middle East generally were constantly arising in the local media, the local council, and local trade unions. One indirect result was that the Irish Congress of Trades Unions became the first national union federation anywhere to formally consider a policy towards Israel of Boycott, Divestment and Sanctions.

The motion to the 2007 ICTU biennial conference in Bundoran, Donegal, came from Derry Trades Council, where it had been proposed by supporters of DAWC/FEIC. The motion committed the congress:

> ... to support and promote a boycott campaign of Israeli goods and services similar to the boycott of South African goods during the Apartheid regime ... to support and promote a policy of divestment from Israeli companies as a means of encouraging the Israeli Government to comply with international law and to end the human rights violations of the Palestinian people ... to campaign for a policy of ethical investment against Israeli companies and other companies who directly support the Israeli Government's occupation and destruction of Palestinian land and infrastructure.

The resolution was passed by a large majority and remains the official policy of the Irish trade union movement.

In so far as the movement against imperialist war and Israeli aggression has had some success in Derry, it has been on account of a combination of tactics. In this light, BDS activism must be wide-ranging and incorporate a range of strategies. The campaign must also be inclusive, it must look for, and build on links between different social and rights-based movements, many of whom have common links. In our case, direct action has been combined with political lobbying, street mobilisation and trade union activity. This doesn't amount to a strategic breakthrough. But it does, perhaps, provide an experience to ponder from which lessons can be learned, or at the very least, further ideas may be generated.

NOTES

1. 'Q&A with Raytheon Missile Systems', interview with Raytheon Missile Systems President Taylor Lawrence <http://www.treoaz.org/Business-Success-Stories-Raytheon.aspx#>.
2. <http://www.raytheon.com/ourcompany/>.
3. Ibid.

4. William Hartung, 'Raytheon', *Press for Conversion!*, 55 (December 2004): 4 <http://coat.ncf.ca/our_magazine/links/55/Articles/55_34. pdf>; individual contracts with these states are also described on Raytheon's official website <www.raytheon.com>.

5. Joshua Ruebner, 'An Iron Triangle', *Counterpunch*, 11 February 2003 <http://www.counterpunch.org/2003/02/11/an-iron-triangle/>.

6. Ibid.

7. Cahal Milmo, 'Serial Numbers Prove US Missile Killed 62 In Iraqi Market', *The Independent*, 2 April 2003 <http://rense.com/general36/kske.htm>.

8. In a Memorandum to the Select Committee on Defence dated 27 February 2006, Angela Smith MP, Department for Enterprise, Trade and Investment (NI), wrote about Raytheon, '... the Northern Ireland operation is involved in leading-edge work in phased array radar systems and the development of leading-edge software for civil and military air traffic control systems. The company has participated in major MoD contracts, including the ASTOR and JETTS programmes' <http://www.publications.parliament.uk/pa/cm200506/cmselect/cmdfence/824/824we27.htm>.

9. Paddy McGuffin, *Derry News*, 22 April 22 2004 – quoted in 'FEIC vindicated over Raytheon' <http://www.innatenonviolence.org/news/119nn.shtml>.

10. SDLP/Sinn Fein motion to a special council meeting on 7 January 2004.

11. 'Raytheon pursued for cash payback', *Londonderry Sentinel*, 22 May 2010 <http://www.londonderrysentinel.co.uk/news/local/raytheon-pursued-for-cash-payback-1-2101936>.

20
Israeli Apartheid Week:
A Gauge of the Global BDS Campaign

Hazem Jamjoum

In 2005, a small group of university students in Toronto organised a series of events under the title 'Israeli Apartheid Week' (IAW). By 2011, IAW had been organised in almost a hundred cities across the globe. Despite the participation of people from different age groups both on and off university campuses, IAW is sometimes described as the 'youth wing' of the BDS campaign,[1] and has become a highlight of the BDS campaign calendar, offering a space to BDS activists in which to share and disseminate ideas, network with other groups and other cities, and raise the profile of their local BDS campaigns. In this article, I sketch the beginnings of Israeli Apartheid Week, describe its spread and examine some of the key issues that have faced its organisers over the past six years.

BEGINNINGS

The first Israeli Apartheid Week took place at the University of Toronto in February 2005. Zionist organisations saw the event's titular connection between the state of Israel and the crime of apartheid as provocative. Led by B'nai Brith, these organisations launched a public campaign demanding the university's cancellation of the event and called upon the Toronto police to attend the events prepared to arrest people for committing hate crimes.[2] The result was a massive media storm of coverage for the event. Almost all the corporate, campus and independent media in Canada carried stories about the event, or at least about the controversy surrounding it, and many international media outlets spread the news of this humble lecture series. Most of the media frenzy took place before the week even started, resulting in packed halls on each night of the week. Normally, this amount of Zionist and media pressure on the university to cancel such events and censure their organisers would have met with success, but previous experiences at the University of Toronto led to a different response by the university administration.

The organisers of the first Israeli Apartheid Week were the Arab Students' Collective (ASC), a group of about thirty students from different parts of the world. One of the ASC's first events was the Toronto Palestine Solidarity Conference, co-organised with Al-Awda (the Palestine Right to Return Coalition) and scheduled for 22–23 November 2003. To ensure a safe space for Palestinian and Palestine-solidarity activists to speak freely, the organisers decided to include a six-point 'basis of unity' that participants had to sign in order to register; this tactic is used frequently in anti-racism events to protect participants from being identified and targeted by racists. Soon after the conference was announced, off-campus anti-Palestinian organisations began exerting pressure on the administration to cancel the event. Indeed, less than 24 hours before the event was supposed to begin, the university administration informed the organisers that the room-booking had been cancelled, and that the official reason for the cancellation was that the 'basis of unity' violated students' right to attend the conference. Signs were posted on the doors of the building and rooms where the conference was supposed to take place stating that the event had been cancelled.

The ASC was quick to respond. Letters were sent across the globe asking for support in the form of a letter-writing campaign, and indeed hundreds of letters poured into the university's mailboxes denouncing the cancellation of the conference as a violation of students' right to organise, as well as a violation of freedom of expression. Within a few days, over sixty students and several community members marched into and effectively occupied the administrative office responsible for the cancellation, taking turns laying out arguments explaining their rage at the administration's cancellation of the conference, and demanding that the university immediately compensate by covering all expenses related to hosting the conference the following weekend. These actions effectively embarrassed the university as it claimed commitment to freedom of expression. On the following day, and after some interesting negotiations, the university gave in to the students' demands.

Learning from its previous error, and recognising the no-longer-latent force of the ASC and the Palestinian Anti-Apartheid Movement, the university administration was hesitant to cancel the inaugural IAW in 2005, instead spinning its inability to bow to Zionist pressure as evidence of a new-found respect for freedom of speech. The administration did attempt to stop the organisers from setting up a mock Palestinian refugee tent from which thousands of leaflets were distributed but, following a new round of student action and negotiation, finally ended up providing the tent that the organisers would use.

Despite an attempt at disruption on the very first night and the strong presence of apartheid supporters who asked questions that clearly betrayed the racism inherent to a consistent Zionist position; the week-long event went smoothly and attracted hundreds of people. One of the major successes of IAW was that the concept 'Israeli apartheid' began to circulate as a subject worthy of discussion and debate, particularly through the media coverage of the event that extended to corporate media beyond the confines of Canada. The concept of Israeli apartheid was put forward not as a catchy slogan, but as a description that reflected Israel's very real institutionalised racist policies and practices in Palestine; spurring a debate on and off campus about whether Israel is an apartheid state. This discussion even induced some faculty members to devote time in their classes to this discussion.

While the first IAW took place before the official July 2005 Palestinian Civil Society Call for BDS was issued, the seeds of the BDS movement had already been sown. Those seeds, including the 2001 Durban Conference, the grass-roots refugee boycotts of USAID handouts in Palestine, campus divestment campaigns in the US and calls for academic boycott in Palestine and the UK were becoming more widespread. The keynote address for the first IAW in Toronto followed suit when Professor Ilan Pappe delivered his presentation under the heading 'Resisting Apartheid: Divestment and the Palestinian Intifada'.

INTERNATIONALISING ISRAELI APARTHEID WEEK

The year 2006 marked the thirtieth anniversary of the Convention for the Suppression and Punishment of the Crime of Apartheid, a fact highlighted by the second annual IAW in an attempt to bring out a clearer understanding of apartheid as not only a crime committed in the context of southern Africa in the twentieth century, but as one with a clear legal definition and universal scope.[3] This commemoration became the first line on all of the Israeli Apartheid Week outreach material in Toronto, as well as in three cities in which anti-apartheid activists had adopted the idea of organising the week simultaneously: Montreal and Kitchener-Waterloo in Canada, and Oxford in the UK. It was also a useful coincidence that year that the week before IAW in 2006, Chris McGreal published a two-part article covering the similarities between Israeli and South African apartheid and the history of the alliance between the two apartheid states.[4] The ASC, a signatory to the 2005 Palestinian Civil Society Call for BDS, and the IAW organisers in the other cities also used the 2006 events to publicly highlight their full support for the BDS movement. IAW was becoming a tangible and growing platform for building the global BDS movement. Clear evidence of this was that many of the labour activists who were involved in drafting and arguing for the adoption of a BDS resolution in the Ontario branch of the Canadian Union of Public Employees were among the organisers, speakers and those in attendance at IAW. The week was thus part of the broader process of building networks and alliances, raising awareness and mobilisation that were necessary building-blocks for the emergence and growth of a BDS movement.

Although a highlight of the Palestine solidarity calendar, IAW was by no means the only – or even the most important – Palestine solidarity event to take place in the countries where it was held. By 2007, the only difference was that it had become institutionalised as part of the calendar and so audiences were anticipating it when it happened. IAW also began to receive increased support from South Africa. Ronnie Kasrils, the Jewish anti-apartheid leader and then South African Information Minister, wrote a powerful statement endorsing IAW activities. The number of IAW events almost doubled in 2007; as the Universities of London (SOAS) and Cambridge joined Oxford in the UK; Ottawa and Hamilton joined Toronto and Montreal in Canada; and, perhaps most significantly, New York also launched the first IAW in the United States.

As 2007 progressed, it had no longer become simply a radical statement to describe Israel as an apartheid state. Later that year, former US president Jimmy Carter published a book describing Israeli policies as apartheid policies, albeit limiting his analysis to the West Bank and the Gaza Strip and largely forgetting the rights of the refugees and the fact that violating the right of return is an apartheid practice.[5] UN Special Rapporteur John Dugard, a South African anti-apartheid activist himself, reported to the UN General Assembly that Israel was guilty of three regimes inimical to human rights: colonialism, apartheid and protracted occupation.[6] Through statements by prominent South African anti-apartheid figures such as Archbishop Desmond Tutu and former President Nelson Mandela which described the similarities between Israeli policies and those of South Africa under apartheid, the interconnection between the two anti-apartheid struggles had become popularised. Since the global BDS movement against the Apartheid regime in South Africa was in many ways an inspiration for Palestine's BDS movement, the support of South Africans to IAW and the burgeoning BDS movement – as solidified in 2008 when South African activists organised the first IAW in their country – was hugely significant.

Alongside the general BDS platform of IAW, the central demand of IAW was the implementation of possibly the least understood of the BDS movement's founding demands: the Palestinian refugees' right to return. In fact, the first ever IAW event held on 31 January 2005 was titled 'Al-Nakba and the

Palestinian Refugees', featuring presentations on the Nakba, the Right of Return, the conditions of Palestinians in the refugee camps of Lebanon, and the racism and deportations suffered by Palestinian refugees in the Canadian immigration and refugee determination process. The Fourth Annual Israeli Apartheid Week took place under the banner: '60 years of ethnic cleansing and dispossession, Palestinian refugees will return.' As such, IAW was part of 2008's global 'Nakba-60' campaign events, perhaps the largest ever global mobilisation in support of Palestinian rights.[7]

Taking place in 28 cities across the globe over a span of two weeks, IAW 2008 included hundreds of important and notable events. Most significant was the fact that cities in Palestine and South Africa began to hold IAW, and the global launch of the week was a talk given by the exiled Dr Azmi Bishara in Soweto, the site of the infamous 1976 student uprising against the South African Apartheid regime. His lecture was taped and broadcast to the Arab world through Al-Jazeera's live channel, and screened at the opening events of IAW in most of the other cities holding the event.[8]

Since 2008, IAW has gone from strength to strength, growing hugely in terms of participating cities and involved activists. Similarly, the greater public clarity regarding Israeli apartheid and the wider support for BDS principles have grown tremendously. The 2011 campaign featured events in 97 cities around the world. Events in Canada, the UK and the US have grown measurably in number and scope, and the same can be said with regards to Europe, Australia, South Africa, Latin American and the Arab world. Significantly, growing every year now are wide-ranging events held in universities, refugee camps and cities throughout Palestine on both sides of the 'Green Line'. A demonstration of the increasingly prominent involvement from within Palestine shone when an open BDS letter was written and published by Palestinian university students in October 2011, in which they recognised the significant achievements of global student activism and appealed for students around the world to 'put BDS at the forefront of your campaigns and join together for the [2012] Israeli Apartheid Week, the pinnacle of action across universities worldwide'.[9] In response, organisers across the globe began gearing up for the Eighth Annual Israeli Apartheid Week in support of Palestinian Civil Society's call for Boycotts, Divestment and Sanctions (BDS). Also significant is the growth and spread of IAW in Lebanon and Jordan, where discussion of matters relating to Palestine and Palestinians remains to some extent taboo and even dangerous for those publicly involved in organising around such issues. The 2012 IAW was held in more than a hundred cities around the world.

While the entire repertoire of past events are far too many to list in this chapter, experiences from previous years support some general statements about how the week has evolved since its establishment. One clear aspect is that IAW has become a global event that provides a space for activists to present and discuss issues of local concern; whether connections with local movements for justice, or highlighting local campaigns (such as the Leviev campaign in New York or the Chapters-Indigo campaign across Canada). Another aspect is the wide diversity in the types of events that local organisers utilise to forward the message of the BDS and Palestinian Anti-Apartheid Movement, such as hip-hop concerts, spoken word poetry competitions, demonstrations, art and photography exhibitions, street theatre and even puppet shows and public 'flash-mob' actions. Also noticeable is the diversity of angles from which the topic of Israeli apartheid is analysed, whether through direct comparisons with South Africa, connections between movements for social and global justice, theoretical analysis of the architecture of apartheid, or analysis of apartheid through various arts and media-based creations. The Toronto IAW has featured continuous 6-hour live radio broadcasts from York University community radio station CHRY105.5fm entitled 'Anti-Apartheid Frequencies' and a conference for high school students organised by their peers who wanted to bring young people together to discuss how they could support and be a part of the global BDS campaign. Other aspects of IAW are that different places organise events according to their capacities. As such, some cities organise one or two events as their contribution to the week, while others have one or more events on every day of the week. Also noticeable is the increasing coordination with regards to multiple speakers essentially performing speaking tours from one city to another as part of IAW, and even more clearly with the sharing of the IAW Azmi Bishara lecture in several international cities in 2008.

While beginning as no more than a humble lecture series, IAW has helped clarify the analysis of Israel as an apartheid state, both directly to those who have attended the various events, and through the media coverage which, despite its often negative perspective, certainly opens up spaces for discussion and debate. More recent space given to the event has in fact served to highlight the contradictions inherent in trying to oppose the event, whether by exposing the fact that cries of hate speech do not apply since IAW's criticism and opposition is directed at a state and not a people; or by engaging journalists and commentators on the reality of Israeli apartheid. Ironically, attempts by some university administrations (such as McMaster, Ottawa and Carlton universities in Canada) or other spaces such the LGBT Centre in New York to ban IAW events,[10] have spawned controversies that have broadened the discussion on Israeli apartheid. Those concerned about freedom of expression learn about the realities of Israeli apartheid, who may not have otherwise been engaged on this issue. In this way connections with other struggles have been identified, as activists have learned about each others' struggles, alliances have thus been built, and discussion about Israeli apartheid and BDS has spread into new spaces, while BDS activists have extended their solidarity to other struggles for justice and dignity.

LESSONS LEARNED IN ORGANISING

The process of organising IAW has been at least as significant, and from this progression several valuable lessons can be learned. Within cities and towns where IAW is organised, activists have had to develop their capacities to put together a series of events in a coordinated fashion with other places around the world, while struggling against some of the obstacles discussed above. In many cases, this process has led groups to work collectively that may not have done so otherwise. Also significant is the fact that the international nature of the event has necessitated increasing levels of international coordination, allowing active organisations and individuals to develop links with one another based on common purpose, and analysis based on the understanding that Israel is guilty of committing the crime of apartheid; that this crime has and continues to be committed against Palestinians in the 1967 Occupied Territory as well as Palestinian citizens of Israel and Palestinian refugees; that this crime does a great disservice to Jewish people around the world since it is done in their name and, in the case of Jewish Israelis, forces them to be actively or passively complicit in a heinous atrocity, and that the way forward is through support for the Palestinian popular resistance by isolating the Apartheid regime through BDS until the crime is put to an end and its consequences reversed to the greatest extent possible.

One of the most important aspects of IAW has been the way it has been used to cement ties between the global BDS movement and other struggles. Toronto's 2008 IAW featured a highly significant closing-night event in which Mohawk activist Kahentinehta Horn awed the audience of 500 people with an exposition of Canada's ongoing genocide against its indigenous population, and the policies and practices of the Canadian settler state which had a great deal in common with Israeli policies and practices. Perhaps without realising it, Horn's explanation of Canada's process of co-opting and creating native leaders as part of controlling the indigenous population (in what are called 'Band Councils') provided deep insight into Israel's approach toward the Palestinian Authority. The entire crowd stood as she raised her fist at the end of the talk in a call for unity between the peoples of the world fighting against colonialism, occupation and apartheid. The next day was the coldest day of two years, and yet eighty people gathered in Toronto's central square for the first ever demonstration to direct a call for BDS at the Canadian government and society. While those who attended may still remember the numbness in their fingers that day, they will also remember the euphoria of shutting down Toronto's two busiest streets as they marched chanting 'Fight the power, turn the tide – end Israeli apartheid!'

Highlighted was the fact that it was Canada's 'reservation' and Indian status system forced upon indigenous peoples as part of a process of genocide that was used as the model for the South African Apartheid regime, which in turn provided an example for Israeli apartheid to emulate. The same connections were made in Montreal and New York. Throughout the world, IAW has become an important space in which BDS activists provide a platform for and share ideas with activists in connected struggles. These have ranged from anti-homophobia and anti-poverty struggles to movements for migrant and refugee and landless peoples' rights. In this sense, IAW is not only a gauge of the growing BDS movement, but a gauge for a resurgence of internationalism: the globalisation of peoples' intifadas.

Despite the successes, there is still much room for improvement. Through the years of IAW, hundreds of events have included important information and analysis that has only been accessed by those who happened to attend. Making these presentations, performances and exhibits accessible to the broadest audience possible, whether through video, audio, or written transcription would be a valuable asset to the Palestinian Anti-Apartheid Movement as a whole, as well as to other movements with whom alliances have been formed. Furthermore, while the organisers have in a sense formed a network of anti-apartheid activists, further effort is needed to bring all of these people together to meet one another and discuss the possibility of moving the campaign forward, and it is likely that contact between all the different locations is limited to a handful of liaisons. Finding creative ways to increase the chances of people working within the IAW framework, which for all intents and purposes is the same framework as the BDS movement, to meet and communicate could go a long way in strengthening the movement overall. This is especially the case given the increasing alarm, apprehension and opposition that Zionist organisations seek to mobilise against the event and its organisers.[11]

In opening his 2008 IAW lecture in Soweto, Dr Azmi Bishara stated that he was taken to visit the Apartheid Museum before coming to give his lecture. Agreeing with the speakers before him, he stated that whilst there continued to be many social grievances in South Africa, 'at least one thing [has been] gained … Apartheid is in a Museum.' There is no doubt that IAW has already begun to achieve its goal of contributing to the movement that aims to send Israeli apartheid to a museum.

NOTES

1. 'Global actions, backlash during Israeli Apartheid Week', *Electronic Intifada*, 11 March 2011 <http://electronicintifada.net/content/global-actions-backlash-during-israeli-apartheid-week/9264#. TqaPL94Uqso>.
2. B'Nai Brith, 'Jewish community disappointed by U of T' <http://www.bnaibrith.ca/article.php?id=869>.
3. For an elaboration of this argument, see Hazem Jamjoum, 'Not an Analogy: Israel and the Crime of Apartheid', *Electronic Intifada*, 3 April 2009 <http://electronicintifada.net/content/not-analogy-israel-and-crime-apartheid/8164#.TqaOo94Uqso>.
4. Chris McGreal, 'Worlds Apart', *Guardian*, 6 February 2006 <http://www.guardian.co.uk/world/2006/feb/06/southafrica.israel>.
5. Jimmy Carter, *Palestine: Peace not Apartheid*, New York: Simon and Schuster, 2006.
6. John Dugard, 'Report of the Special Rapporteur on the situation of human rights in the Palestinian territories occupied since 1967', 21 January 2008, UN Doc. A/HRC/7/1.
7. 'Editorial: Overcoming the Nakba', *al-Majdal* ('Overcoming the Nakba: BDS and the Global Anti-Apartheid Movement' special issue), 38 (Summer 2008): 2.
8. The video of Dr Bishara's lecture is available online in four parts <http://www.youtube.com/watch?v=d6_Aw812feQ>.
9. 'An open letter from Palestinian students to their peers in Europe', *USACBI*, 21 October 2011 <http://www.usacbi.org/2011/10/an-open-letter-from-palestinian-students-to-their-peers-in-europe/>.
10. In 2008, McMaster University banned the use of the phrase 'Israeli apartheid'. Subsequent student action resulted in the university retreating from this position and pretended it had all been the result of a misunderstanding (see Karen Ho, 'McMaster ban on

phrase "Israeli Apartheid" stirs protest', *The Varsity*, 28 February 2008). In 2009, Carleton and Ottawa universities, whose presidents had recently returned from visits to Israel partly funded by the Canadian Council for Israel, banned the poster used to advertise Israeli Apartheid Week (see 'U of O bans pro-Palestinian poster', *CBC News*, 24 February 2009 <http://www.cbc.ca/news/canada/ottawa/story/2009/02/24/palestinian-poster.html>). In 2011, pressure from Zionist pornographer Michael Lucas (known for his 'Men of Israel' films and 'rabidly right wing' views) resulted in the cancellation of IAW's 'Party to End Apartheid', set to be held at New York's LGBT Center (see Steve Thrasher, 'Gay Center Axes Israeli Apartheid Week Event After Boycott Threat by Porn Activist', *Village Voice*, 23 February 2011 <http://blogs.villagevoice.com/runninscared/2011/02/apartheid_week.php>).

11. For examples of Zionist research and policy recommendations regarding IAW, see Avi Weinryb, 'The University of Toronto – The Institution where Israel Apartheid Week was Born', *Jewish Political Studies Review* (Fall 2008); see also the Ontario legislature's discussion on condemning IAW: 'Private Members Public Business: Israel Apartheid Week', *Hansard*, 25 February 2010 <http://www.scribd.com/doc/27478484/Israel-Apartheid-Week-Instant-Hansard>.

21
Palestine's South Africa Moment has Finally Arrived

Omar Barghouti

First they ignore you, then they laugh at you, then they fight you, then you win.

Mahatma Gandhi

After years of ignoring the challenge of the global, Palestinian-led Boycott, Divestment and Sanctions (BDS) campaign,[1] Israel and the Zionist movement have woken up, rattled and quite startled, to the bellowing sound of an alarm and have started shouting 'Existential threat!' This panic culminated in the adoption by the Israeli Parliament (Knesset) of an exceptionally draconian anti-boycott law, dropping the mask of democracy that has been used for decades by Israel in an attempt to cover its regime of oppression against the Palestinians.[2] This time around, though, hardly anyone is impressed by Israel's crying wolf. Its systematic violations of international law and the basic rights of the Palestinian people have helped create a fertile ground for the spectacular growth of BDS as a civil society campaign that has dragged Israel into a new, global, battlefield, so to speak, where Palestinian moral strength largely neutralises Israel's massive weaponry, including hundreds of nuclear warheads, and even more massive lobby influence in the US and other western states.

Given the centrality of the question of Palestine in the Arab region, the 'Arab Spring' of democracy, social justice and freedom (or what I call the prelude to an *Arab Renaissance*), that is sweeping this region today and that is at least partially inspired by the decades-old Palestinian popular struggle for freedom and self-determination, promises to provide a fertile environment for the advancement of the latter struggle. It has undoubtedly added further weight to the global BDS movement which has finally begun to take root, in an institutional way, in the Arab world.

Already, the Arab Spring has triggered new forms of Palestinian resistance hitherto believed to be improbable. The 2011 Nakba commemoration protests[3] looked more like a Palestinian refugees' Intifada, inspired by the Arab Spring as well as years of Palestinian popular and civic resistance. Whether in the occupied Gaza Strip or West Bank, among Palestinian citizens of Israel, or at the borders of historic Palestine, the majority of the heroic peaceful protesters were refugees yearning to return to their homes of origin as stipulated under international law. The successes of their brethren in Tunisia and Egypt to overthrow their respective dictators and embark on a path of freedom and social justice formed a crucial and inspiring background to the first phase of the refugees' Intifada which may well be a turning-point in the Palestinian struggle for freedom, justice and self-determination.

Many of the leaders of the still evolving Arab revolutions admit that the Palestinian liberation struggle was their main inspiration. However, due to more than 18 years – since the 1993 Oslo Accords – of systematic American, European and Israeli corruption and co-optation of a whole class of Palestinian politicians, businessmen and intellectuals, the Palestinian culture of resistance and heritage of struggle has been distorted and undermined for the new generation of young people. The first chapters of the unfolding Arab Renaissance came as a rude awakening to Palestinians, shattering a sense of hopelessness and powerlessness that had been engrained in many for so long, and giving young people renewed hope and confidence that they can indeed make a difference and even change the world.

The main lesson learned from the Arab peoples' revolutions so far is that when a critical mass of the oppressed transcend their long-entrenched fear and decide to fight for their rights, for justice and dignity, their collective power is immeasurable and can be unstoppable. Palestinians had reached that conclusion well before most Arabs, in fact.

Years before the Arab Spring, on 9 July 2005, Palestinian civil society launched what is now widely recognised as a qualitatively different phase in the global struggle for Palestinian freedom, justice and self-determination against a powerful, ruthless system of oppression that enjoys impunity and that is intent on making a self-fulfilling prophecy of the utterly racist, myth-laden, foundational Zionist dictum of 'a land without a people for a people without a land'. In an historic moment of collective consciousness, informed by almost a century of struggle against Zionist settler colonialism, the overwhelming majority in Palestinian civil society issued the BDS Call against Israel until it fully complies with its obligations under international law. Since 2008, the BDS movement has been led by the largest coalition of Palestinian civil-society organisations inside historic Palestine and in exile: the BDS National Committee (BNC).[4]

The so-called international community, under the hegemonic influence of the United States, has not only failed to stop Israel's construction of its expansionist Wall and settler colonies, both declared illegal by the International Court of Justice in 2004,[5] but has colluded in undermining hitherto UN-sanctioned Palestinian rights. This has prompted Palestinian society to reassert its basic rights, paramount among which is the right to self determination. The BDS Call, with unprecedented near-consensus support among Palestinians inside historic Palestine as well as in exile, reminded the world that the indigenous Palestinian people include the refugees forcibly displaced from their homeland – by Zionist militias and later the state of Israel – during the 1948 Nakba[6] and ever since, along with their descendants who were born in exile, as well as the Palestinian citizens of Israel who remained steadfast on their land and now live under a regime of state-sanctioned racial discrimination.[7]

Figures as diverse as Desmond Tutu, Jimmy Carter, and former Israeli attorney general Michael Ben-Yair Israel have described Israel as practising apartheid against the indigenous Palestinians.[8] Characterising Israel's legalised and institution-alised racial discrimination as such does not attempt to equate Israel with South Africa under apartheid; despite the many similarities, no two oppressive regimes are identical. Rather, it stems from the argument that Israel's system of bestowing rights and privileges according to ethnic and religious identity fits the UN definition of the term as enshrined in the 1973 International Convention on the Suppression and Punishment of the Crime of Apartheid and in the 2002 Rome Statute of the International Criminal Court. One disingenuous or manifestly misinformed argument that rejects the apartheid charge on the basis that Jewish Israelis form a majority, unlike the whites in South Africa who were in the minority, ignores the fact that the universally accepted definition of apartheid has nothing to do with majorities and minorities.

Coming on the heels of its devastating war of aggression on Lebanon (2006), Israel's latest bloodbath in Gaza (2008–09) and its multi-year illegal and immoral siege of the still-occupied Strip have stimulated a real transformation in world public opinion against Israeli policies and system of oppression. The United Nations and leading human rights organisations have amply documented the devastating consequences of the siege on the health of the Palestinian population, especially children, among whom stunted growth and anaemia have become widespread. A May 2010 report by the BBC revealed, for example, how Israel, through its siege, was allowing only the 'minimum calorie intake needed by Gaza's million and a half inhabitants, according to their age and sex', as a form of severe collective punishment.[9]

When the heart-wrenching images of Israeli phosphorus bombs showering down upon densely populated Palestinian neighbourhoods and UN shelters in Gaza were beamed across the world during Israel's Operation Cast Lead in 2008–09, they triggered worldwide outrage which translated into sustainable, organised, and very promising boycotts and divestment initiatives in economic, academic, athletic and cultural fields. Former president of the UN General Assembly Father Miguel D'Escoto Brockman, Archbishop Desmond Tutu, distinguished artists, writers, academics and filmmakers, progressive Jewish groups, major trade unions and labour federations, church-affiliated organisations, and many student groups have all endorsed, to varying degrees, the logic of boycott, convincing many that our 'South Africa moment' has finally arrived.

THE 'SOUTH AFRICA MOMENT'

BDS has seen unprecedented growth after the war of aggression on Gaza and the May 2010 attack on the Gaza-bound humanitarian flotilla. People of conscience around the world seem to have crossed a threshold, resorting to pressure, not appeasement or 'constructive engagement', to end Israel's impunity and western collusion in maintaining its status as a state above the law.

'Besiege your siege' – the everlasting cry of the Palestinian poet Mahmoud Darwish – acquires a new meaning in this context. Since convincing a colonial power to heed moral pleas for justice is, at best, delusional, many now understand the need to 'besiege' Israel though boycotts, raising the price of its oppression and thus *compelling* it to comply with international law.

Israeli supporters of BDS formed the group 'Boycott: Supporting the Palestinian Call from Within' (or 'Boycott from Within', for short),[10] and the Israeli Coalition of Women for Peace launched a database of companies implicated in Israel's occupation, providing BDS campaigns the world over with an invaluable resource.[11]

BDS campaigners have successfully lobbied financial institutions in Scandinavia, Germany and elsewhere to divest from companies that are complicit in Israel's violations of international law. Several international trade unions,[12] from South Africa to Brazil to the UK to Ireland and Canada, among many other countries, have endorsed the boycott. Following the attack on the flotilla, dockworkers' unions in Sweden, India, Turkey and the US heeded an appeal by Palestinian unions to block offloading Israeli ships.

Endorsements of BDS by authors and cultural figures[13] such as John Berger, Naomi Klein, Iain Banks, Judith Butler, Roger Waters, Ken Loach, Alice Walker and Sarah Schulman, and the spate of cancellations of events in Israel by artists including Meg Ryan, Elvis Costello, Gil Scott-Heron and the Pixies have raised the movement's international profile, bringing it closer to the western mainstream. Scepticism about its potential has been largely put to rest.

ECONOMIC IMPACT

Dismissing all the spectacular and concrete achievements of the still very young BDS movement as 'largely symbolic', opponents of BDS, including some who are widely seen in the West as supporters of – at least some – Palestinian rights, have argued that the boycott of Israel, unlike that waged against apartheid South Africa, is unrealistic and impractical, as it cannot possibly hurt Israel's formidable economic interests, which are protected by western powers. Established analysts and leaders of the struggle against apartheid rule in South Africa who now support the Palestinian BDS movement against Israel recall how this same flawed and often disingenuous argument of economic unfeasibility was used in an attempt to demoralise, thwart, or take the wind out of the sails of their struggle as well, often by liberals who ostensibly opposed apartheid but preferred 'softer' tactics than boycott and divestment.[14]

Durban-based economist Patrick Bond, in a lecture in Ramallah on 26 September 2010, cautioned his Palestinian audience not to fall for the insincere argument that the economic 'invincibility' of Israel translates into the ultimate futility of BDS tactics. Seemingly unconquerable economic powers, he argued, have fallen much faster than many had thought possible. South Africa was no exception.[15]

While it is still too early to definitively expect BDS to have a considerable economic impact on Israel, in actual fact the movement has started to bite and, crucially, to empower activists worldwide, illuminating to them a path with great potential for raising the price of Israel's intransigence and disregard of international law.

As early as April 2009, in the aftermath of the Israeli bloodbath in Gaza in the winter of 2008–09, the Israel Manufacturers Association reported that '21% of 90 local exporters who were questioned had felt a drop in demand due to boycotts, mostly from the UK and Scandinavian countries.'[16] While we have no up-to-date data, there are compelling indicators that this trend is growing. Israeli President Shimon Peres has recently sounded the alarm about the deepening impact of economic boycotts and sanctions: 'There's no need for boycotts. It would suffice for ports in Europe or Canada to stop unloading Israeli merchandise. It's already beginning.'[17]

In the same vein, Israel's defence minister and most decorated general, Ehud Barak, stated:

> There are some pretty powerful elements in the world that are active in the matter – within countries, including friendly countries, in various organisations of workers, academics, consumers, green parties ... And this drive boils down to a large movement called BDS, which is what they did with South Africa. It won't happen at once. It will begin, like an iceberg, to advance on us from all corners.[18]

A CONSEQUENTIAL ACHIEVEMENT

The most consequential achievement of the first five years of the BDS movement was to expose the 'essential nature' of Israel's regime over the Palestinian people as one that combines military occupation, colonisation, ethnic cleansing and apartheid.[19] Israel's mythical and carefully cultivated, decades-old image as a 'democratic' state seeking 'peace' may, as a result, have suffered irreparable damage.

The 13 September 2010 *Time* magazine cover story, 'Why Israel Doesn't Care about Peace',[20] may be one of the most prominent indicators yet of the growing feeling among many in the western mainstream that Israel is a belligerent outlaw that has no interest in peace, particularly given that it has not yet been compelled to pay a serious price for its crimes and persistent violations of international law.

The by-now customary calls by Israeli Foreign Minister Avigdor Lieberman, even from the podium of the UN General Assembly,[21] for ethnically cleansing Palestinian citizens of Israel and rejecting any peaceful settlement demanding a significant withdrawal of Israel from the Occupied Palestinian Territory have only accelerated the spread of the view of Israel as a world pariah.

A prominent Israeli academic commented thus on the far-right politics of Israeli cabinet ministers:

Israel is currently the only Western country whose cabinet includes the likes of Foreign Minister Avigdor Lieberman, Justice Minister Yaakov Neeman and Interior Minister Eli Yishai. The last time politicians holding views similar to theirs were in power in post-World War II Western Europe was in Franco's Spain.[22]

THE WAY FORWARD

Compared to the global boycott against South African apartheid, the Palestinian-led BDS movement has achieved much more in its inaugural years, despite the fact that Israel, unlike the South African Apartheid regime, has decisive influence in Congress and, by extension, the White House and, therefore, the world. Aside from adopting strategies that take into consideration the lessons learned from the South African experience and from decades of Palestinian resistance, the BDS movement owes part of its spectacular growth to information and communication technologies that have magnificently amplified its reach and effectiveness.

Still, much remains to be done to reach a tipping-point whereby complicity by world governments, led by the US, in maintaining and protecting Israel's three-tiered system of colonial oppression is more than outweighed by effective, broad grass-roots movements that turn Israel into a shunned and economically haemorrhaging pariah, as apartheid South Africa was. For this to happen, the movement needs to win wider segments of the mainstream and to persist in nuancing and evolving its strategies to respond to the volatile and dynamic nature of this struggle.

The most crucial component in this strategy is adhering to the movement's characterising rights-based approach and deepening even further its commitment to international law and universal human rights. BDS is far more about achieving the three basic rights of the Palestinian people than about the diverse acts of boycotting and divesting. The former are non-negotiable, inalienable rights, best embodied in the BDS movement's slogan, 'Freedom, Justice, Equality', while the latter, the tactics, are flexible, relative, context-sensitive, gradual and subject to ongoing effectiveness evaluation and, accordingly, adjustment. BDS must be associated with FJE – Freedom, Justice, Equality – in the public mind everywhere. Those who adopt the three rights listed in the BDS Call are not expected to adopt immediately sweeping boycotts or divestments. In fact, targeted boycotts that suit any particular setting usually work best to achieve cumulative and sustainable victories. BDS, after all, is not about feeling good and giving it your best shot, only. It is about transforming the current balance of powers through sustained, wide and consequential achievements that undermine Israel's impunity and international complicity in maintaining it.

While many unions have adopted BDS, not enough has been done to develop strategies for implementing the boycott in a gradual and effective manner. This vertical entrenchment of the boycott is just as crucial as the need to horizontally grow the movement. The work that the Palestine Solidarity Campaign (PSC) is doing in the UK in supporting the development of concrete boycott campaigns within the Trades Union Congress (TUC), which represents over 6 million workers, is a good example of this entrenchment.

The movement's intolerance to all forms of racism, including anti-Semitism, must also be maintained. With its liberal and universal message of rights, BDS is growing among Jewish communities in the West who can no longer accept Israel's speaking in their names while committing horrific crimes against the Palestinians. This crucial distinction between Israel and Jews worldwide, which rejects the racist claim that Israel or Zionism represents all Jews, is increasingly depriving Israel of the blind support it used to count on from these communities. The gradually spreading Jewish-Israeli support for BDS is playing a key role in this trend that has become alarming to Israel.

The following BDS campaign priorities[23] are in line with the above strategic directions of the movement and reflect the collective experiences in the BDS movement since its inception in 2005:

Promoting a general boycott of all products and services of Israeli companies as well as international companies implicated in profiting from or otherwise supporting Israel's violations of international law and Palestinian rights until Israel fully complies with its obligations under international law and ends its multi-tiered oppression of the Palestinian people;

Promoting a boycott of all Israeli academic,[24] cultural, athletic and tourist institutions that are complicit in maintaining the Israeli occupation and Apartheid regime;

Promoting ethical investment by trade unions, faith-based organisations,[25] local councils, private investment funds and national pension funds, among others, by divesting from Israel Bonds and from all companies, banks and other financial institutions that profit from or are otherwise complicit in maintaining Israel's occupation, denial of Palestinian refugee rights, or apartheid system of racial discrimination against the indigenous Palestinian citizens of Israel;

Promoting ethical corporate responsibility leading to divestment from and a boycott of products of companies – whether Israeli or international – that are implicated in Israel's violations of international law and human rights;

Working to expel Israel and its complicit institutions from international and inter-state academic, cultural, sporting (such as the Olympics and FIFA), environmental and other fora until it fully complies with its obligations under international law;

Promoting ethical pilgrimage to the Holy Land to directly benefit Palestinian hotels, restaurants, coach services, guides and other tourist infrastructure, thus denying Israel, its airlines, its travel agencies and its other apartheid institutions the lucrative revenues that accrue from such pilgrimage. Alternative Palestinian tourism should also be considered;[26]

Applying public pressure to ostracise the Jewish National Fund (JNF), and to deny it its current legal status in most western countries as a tax-exempt, 'charitable' organisation;[27]

Lobbying local councils and regional governments to strictly apply domestic and international laws which urge the preclusion from public contracts of companies involved in 'grave misconduct', as EU regulations stipulate, for instance, especially at the human rights level;

Pressuring parliaments and governments to apply an immediate military embargo against Israel,[28] as a crucial step towards ending Israel's unlawful and criminal use of force against the Palestinian people and other peoples and states in the region and as a non-violent measure to pressure Israel to comply with its obligations under international law;

Calling for an immediate suspension of all free trade[29] and other preferential trade agreements with Israel until it comprehensively and verifiably ends its violations of international law and Palestinian rights;

Holding Israel and complicit partner-states, as the case may be, legally accountable for fully compensating the Palestinian people for all the illegal, wanton destruction it has brought and continues to bring upon Palestinian society, economy, as well as private and public property in its sieges, attacks and wars of aggression against the Palestinian people, especially the recent war on Gaza and past invasions and military offensives in the occupied West Bank;

Applying pressure for the immediate and unconditional implementation of the recommendations included in the Goldstone Report, adopted by the UN Human Rights Council, the UN General Assembly and almost all the main international human rights organisations, to hold Israel and all colluding parties accountable for committing war crimes and crimes against humanity and to prosecute accused war criminals, among other legal actions.

In challenging Israel's oppression, the global BDS campaign does not call for Israel to be treated according to higher or lower standards than those that apply to any other state committing similar crimes and violations of international law. The crucial demand is for Israel to be taken off the lofty pedestal on which it has been placed by the same western powers that sponsored and justified its creation on the ruins of Palestinian society and that have largely sustained its three-tiered system of oppression against the Palestinian people.

Western civil society, in particular, carries a unique responsibility to hold Israel accountable to international law due to the exceptional level of complicity of western governments in buttressing Israel's system of colonial and racial oppression through vast diplomatic, economic, academic, cultural and political support – all in the name of western citizens whilst using their tax money without their consent. Deep complicity engenders profound *moral* responsibility. This complicity, though, should not be reduced to merely a function of Holocaust guilt; while the Holocaust is utilised to rationalise the indefensible and blatant western support for Israel's crimes and acts of genocide,[30] this support fundamentally stems from the western establishments' hegemonic economic interests, lingering colonial racism, and belligerent crusade to preserve a system of privilege and exploitation, based on might and a monopoly on the tools of mass devastation, coercion and intimidation.

Collusion and moral duty aside, the responsibility to promote and support the BDS campaign against Israel also derives from common interest. While the US and other western states fund Israel's endless atrocious wars and system of apartheid to the tune of billions of dollars every year, millions of children in parts of the West are still left behind in substandard housing, inadequate, or non-existent health care, pathetic education and an establishment that consciously and bureaucratically disen-franchises them when they grow up from effectively and actively participating in the democratic political process. At the same time as the oil, military, homeland security and banking industries are aggrandising their colossal wealth, constantly propping up and nourishing fear and xenophobia to maintain the 'health' of the market, most working people in the West are steadily seeing their civil rights and economic well-being erode before their very eyes. A progressive transformation in US and EU priorities from directing these nations' great human and material resources into wars and imperial hegemony on the international scene to investing in universal health care, dignified housing, a school system that is conducive to critical and contextual learning and development, decent jobs, and reversing the fatal damage to the environment, is not only good on its own merits for the peoples of the West; it is also great for the world – for Iraq,

Afghanistan, South Asia, Latin America, Africa, Lebanon, and, most certainly, Palestine.

Leading South African international law expert and former UN special rapporteur on human rights in the Occupied Palestinian Territory (oPt), Professor John Dugard, wrote in 2007:

> The West cannot expect the rest of the world to take issues it regards as important seriously if it persists in its present attitude to the [Israeli occupation]. For the rest of the world the issue of Palestine has become the litmus test for human rights. If the West fails to show concern for human rights in the OPT the rest of the world will conclude that human rights are a tool employed by the West against regimes it dislikes and not an objective and universal instrument for the measurement of the treatment of people throughout the world.[31]

The global BDS movement for Palestinian rights presents a progressive, anti-racist, sophisticated, sustainable, moral and effective form of civil, non-violent resistance. It has indeed become one of the key political catalysts and moral anchors for a strengthened, reinvigorated international social movement capable of ending the law of the jungle and upholding in its stead the rule of law, reaffirming the rights of *all* humans to freedom, equality and dignified living.

Our South Africa moment has finally arrived!

NOTES

1. See <www.BDSmovement.net>.
2. Omar Barghouti 'Dropping the Lat Mask of Democracy', *Al-Jazeera*, 3 August 2011 <http://english.aljazeera.net/indepth/opinion/2011/08/20118173637829317.html>.
3. 'Nakba Day, from Golan to New York to al-Walaja to Qalandia to Maroun Ar-Ras', *Mondoweiss*, 17 May 2011 <http://mondoweiss.net/2011/05/nakba-day-from-golan-to-new-york-to-al-walaja-to-qalandia-to-maroun-ar-ras.html>.
4. See <http://www.bdsmovement.net/BNC>.
5. See <http://www3.icj-cij.org/docket/files/131/1671.pdf>.

6. For more on the planned and systematically executed Zionist campaign to dispossess and uproot the Palestinian people, see Ilan Pappe, *The Ethnic Cleansing of Palestine* (Oxford: Oneworld, 2006).

7. There are at least twenty Israeli laws, including Basic Laws (equivalent to constitutional laws), that legalise and institutionalise the Israeli system of racial discrimination against Palestinian citizens of the state for being 'non-Jews'. See Adalah, 'Major Findings of Adalah's Report to the UN Committee on the Elimination of Racial Discrimination', presented in Geneva, March 1998 <http://www. adalah.org/eng/intladvocacy/cerd.htm#major>.

8. Michael Ben-Yair wrote: 'We enthusiastically chose to become a colonial society, ignoring international treaties, expropriating lands, transferring settlers from Israel to the occupied territories, engaging in theft and finding justification for all these activities ... In effect, we established an apartheid regime in the occupied territories', Ben-Yair, 'The War's Seventh Day', *Haaretz*, 3 March 2002 ,http:// www.haaretz.com/hasen/pages/ShArt.jhtml?itemNo=136433>.

9. Tim Franks, 'Details of Gaza blockade revealed in court case', 3 May 2010 <http://news.bbc.co.uk/2/hi/middle_east/8654337. stm>.

10. See <http://boycottisrael.info/>.

11. See <http://www.whoprofits.org/>.

12. 'Trade Unions', *BDS Movement* <http://www.bdsmovement.net/ activecamps/trade-unions>.

13. 'After the Flotilla Massacre: Cultural Boycott of Israel Takes Off', *PACBI* <http://www.pacbi.org/etemplate.php?id=1291>.

14. Ronnie Kasrils, 'South Africa's Israel Boycott', *Guardian*, 29 September 2010 <http://www.guardian.co.uk/commentisfree/ 2010/sep/29/south-africa-boycott-israel>.

15. From notes I took at this lecture.

16. Rachel Shabi, 'Israeli Exports Hit by European Boycotts after Attacks on Gaza', *Guardian*, 3 April 2009 <http://www.guardian. co.uk/world/2009/apr/03/israel-gaza-attacks-boycotts-food-industry>.

17. Yossi Verter, 'Peres Warns: Israel in Danger of Ceasing to Exist as Jewish state', *Haaretz*, 17 June 2011 <http://www.haaretz.com/ print-edition/news/peres-warns-israel-in-danger-of-ceasing-to-exist-as-jewish-state-1.368132>.

18. Gidi Weitz, 'Peace, Politics, and Patek Philippe: An Interview with Ehud Barak', *Haaretz*, 9 May 2011 <http://www.haaretz.

com/weekend/week-s-end/peace-politics-and-patek-philippe-an-interview-with-ehud-barak-1.360701>.

19. For a thorough study of Israel's three-tiered system of oppression, see Palestinian Civil Society, 'United against Apartheid, Colonialism and Occupation: Dignity and Justice for the Palestinian People': October 2008, position paper for Durban Review Conference, 20–24 April 2009 <http://bdsmovement.net/files/English-BNC_Position_Paper-Durban_Review.pdf>.

20. 'Why Israel Doesn't Care About Peace', *Time* magazine, 13 September 2010 <http://www.time.com/time/covers/0,16641,20100913,00.html>.

21. In his 28 September 2010, speech before the UN General Assembly, Lieberman stated, 'Thus, the guiding principle for a final status agreement must not be land-for-peace but rather, exchange of populated territory. Let me be very clear: I am not speaking about moving populations, but rather about moving borders to better reflect demographic realities' <http://www.mfa.gov.il/MFA/Government/Speeches+by+Israeli+leaders/2010/FM_Liberman_Addresses_UN_General_Assembly_28-Sep-2010.htm>.

22. Zeev Sternhell, 'The Obligation of a True Patriot', *Haaretz*, 19 February 2010 <http://www.haaretz.com/print-edition/opinion/the-obligation-of-a-true-patriot-1.263621>.

23. Several of these recommendations were adopted at a civil-society peace and justice forum held in Bilbao, the Basque Country (Spain), in November 2008, with the participation of tens of Palestinian, European and Israeli progressive organisations endorsing BDS <http://www.bdsmovement.net/?q=node/213>.

24. For more on the academic boycott, see <www.PACBI.org>. Also a recent study published by the Alternative Information Center documents many aspects of the complicity of the Israeli academy in Israel's oppression of the Palestinian people <http://alternativenews.org/publications/econoccupation/2223-the-economy-of-the-occupation-23-24-academic-boycott-of-israel.html>.

25. Major Christian Palestinian figures recently issued the Palestine Kairos Document calling on churches around the world 'to say a word of truth and to take a position of truth with regard to Israel's occupation of Palestinian land' and explicitly endorsing 'boycott and disinvestment as tools of justice, peace and security' <http://www.kairospalestine.ps/sites/default/Documents/French.pdf>.

26. See <http://www.atg.ps/>.

27. See <http://stopthejnf.bdsmovement.net/node/4>.

28. See <http://www.bdsmovement.net/activecamps/military-embargo>.

29. The EU-Israel Association Agreement and the MERCOSUR-Israel FTA are high priority targets, in this context.

30. Notable academics, including international law Professor Francis A. Boyle (University of Illinois) and Israeli historian and author Professor Ilan Pappe have described Israel's practices as amounting to the crime of genocide. Article 2 of the Convention on the Prevention and Punishment of the Crime of Genocide, which was adopted by the United Nations on 9 December 1948, defines genocide as 'acts committed with intent to destroy, in whole or in part, a national, ethnical, racial or religious group … .'

31. T. Skouteris and A. Vermeer-Kunzli (eds), *The Protection of the Individual in International Law. Essays in Honour of John Dugard.* Special Issue of the *Leiden Journal of International Law* (2007), p. 6.

Notes on Contributors

Kali Akuno is the national coordinator for the Malcolm X Grassroots Movement (MXGM) and the co-director of the US Human Rights Network (USHRN). Akuno is currently working on a book tentatively entitled *Confronting a Cleansing: Hurricane Katrina, the Battle for New Orleans, and the Future of the Black Working Class*.

Nidal al-Azza is a Palestinian refugee, an activist and a human rights lawyer. He is the Resource Coordinator at the BADIL Resource Center for Palestinian Residency and Refugee Rights and also the head of the Administrative Board of Lajee Center in Aida Refugee Camp.

Iain Banks is an internationally renowned Scottish author. He has published more than twenty novels of fiction and science-fiction, as well as a collection of short stories and a book about malt whisky. In 2010, Banks was listed by *The Times* as one of the '50 Greatest British Writers since 1945'.

Omar Barghouti is an independent Palestinian human rights activist and a co-founder of the Boycott, Divestment and Sanctions (BDS) movement. Barghouti is the author of *Boycott, Divestment, Sanctions: The Global Struggle for Palestinian Rights* (Haymarket, 2011).

Ramzy Baroud (<www.ramzybaroud.net>) is a US-based Palestinian author, internationally syndicated columnist and the editor of *PalestineChronicle.com*. His latest book is *My Father Was a Freedom Fighter: Gaza's Untold Story* (London: Pluto Press, 2010).

Professor Richard Falk is the United Nations Special Rapporteur on Human Rights in the Occupied Palestinian Territory, and a professor emeritus of international law at Princeton University. He is also the honorary vice-president of the American Society of International Law. In 2001, Falk served on the United Nations Human Rights Inquiry Commission for the Palestinian Territories, and from 1999–2000 on the Independent International Commission on Kosovo. He is the author or co-author of more than twenty books, and has worked in an editorial role on numerous others. He most recently authored *Achieving Human Rights* (Routledge, 2008).

Archbishop Atallah Hanna is the Archbishop of Sebastia from the Greek Orthodox Patriarchate of Jerusalem. Hanna was one of the founders of Kairos Palestine, and is a tireless and outspoken advocate for the rights of the Palestinian people.

Shir Hever is an Israeli economic researcher at the Alternative Information Center, a joint Palestinian-Israeli organisation working to promote the national and human rights of the Palestinian people. Hever's research focuses on economic aspects of the Israeli occupation, international aid and the BDS campaign. His first book, *Political Economy of Israel's Occupation: Repression Beyond Exploitation*, was published by Pluto Press in 2010.

Hazem Jamjoum is a Palestinian writer and one of the organisers of the first Israeli Apartheid Week. A former communications officer at the BADIL Resource Centre for Palestinian Residency and Refugee Rights in Bethlehem and editor of *Al-Majdal* magazine, Jamjoum is currently completing graduate studies in Arab and Middle East Studies at the American University of Beirut (AUB).

Ronnie Kasrils was an active member of the ANC in various capacities including intelligence chief in the military wing. After the fall of the apartheid regime, Kasrils served as a minister in the South African government from 1994–2008. He is the author of several books including *The Unlikely Secret Agent* (Jacana, 2010) and *Armed & Dangerous* (Jonathan Ball, 1993).

Rifat Odeh Kassis is the international president of Defence for Children International (DCI) and general director of its Palestinian section. A prominent Palestinian activist, he also worked in Central Asia in the 1990s before returning to his native Palestine. Kassis is a coordinator of Kairos Palestine, about which he published the book *Kairos for Palestine* (Badayl/Alternatives, 2011).

Ayesha Kidwai is associate professor of linguistics at Jawaharlal Nehru University, New Delhi. She is joint convenor of the Indian Campaign for the Academic and Cultural Boycott of Israel (ICACBI).

Paul Laverty is a former human rights lawyer who is now a screenwriter. He and Ken Loach are now working on their twelfth project together. He, Loach and Rebecca O'Brien have worked together for many years.

Ken Loach is one of the world's best known film directors. Amongst his many films, Loach directed one of the UK's most celebrated films, *Kes* (1969), along with *Land And Freedom* (1995 – award winner at the Cannes Film Festival), and the 2006 winner of the Palme D'Or at Cannes *The Wind That Shakes The Barley*.

Eamonn McCann is an Irish journalist, author and political activist. McCann won the Human Rights award at the 2011 Amnesty International Media awards for his work on Bloody Sunday and the Saville Inquiry. He is the author and editor of several books, most recently *The Bloody Sunday Inquiry: The Families Speak Out* (Pluto Press, 2005).

Mick Napier was active in the Vietnam Solidarity Campaign during the 1970s, and in 2001 he founded the Scottish Palestine Solidarity Campaign (SPSC) of which he is currently chair. The SPSC works in full support of all inalienable Palestinian rights, and has also campaigned vigorously against the Jewish National Fund (JNF) for many years. Napier now serves on the Coordinating Committee of the International Stop the JNF Campaign.

Adri Nieuwhof is a human rights advocate and consultant based in Switzerland, and a prominent figure in the Derail Veolia Campaign. In the 1980s, Nieuwhof was involved in numerous BDS projects for the Holland Committee on South Africa.

Rebecca O'Brien has been an independent film producer for twenty years. She has produced nine feature films, plus other shorts, with Ken Loach, including *Land And Freedom* (1995), *Sweet Sixteen* (2002), *My Name Is Joe* (1998), and *The Wind that Shakes the Barley* (2006).

Ilan Pappe is an Israeli historian, author and political activist. He is currently chair of the Department of History at Exeter University and the director of the university's European Centre for Palestine Studies. A leading figure amongst Israel's 'New Historians', Pappe is the author or co-author of many books including the acclaimed *The Ethnic Cleansing of Palestine* (Oneworld, 2006).

Prabir Purkayastha is the vice-president of the All India Peace and Solidarity Organisation (AIPSO), and a long-time activist for Palestinian rights. He is also a spokesman for the Delhi Science Forum.

David Randall is a musician and activist. He was the guitarist of iconic British dance music act Faithless and has released critically acclaimed albums with his own band Slovo. Randall has also toured internationally with 1 Giant Leap, Dido, Sinead O'Connor and others. In 2011, Randall wrote and produced the much talked-about OneWorld song, 'Freedom for Palestine'.

Raji Sourani is the director of the Palestinian Centre for Human Rights. He is a recipient of the Robert F. Kennedy Memorial Award for Human Rights, and was twice named as an Amnesty International Prisoner of Conscience. Mr Sourani is also president of the Arab Organisation for Human Rights, a vice-president of the International Federation of Human Rights, and a member of the Executive Committee of the International Commission of Jurists.

Archbishop Desmond Tutu is the Archbishop Emeritus of Cape Town and was awarded the 1984 Nobel Peace Prize for his leading role in the struggle against South African apartheid. He is the Chair of 'The Elders', and was Chair of the Truth and Reconciliation Commission in the post-apartheid period. Along with his Nobel Peace Prize, Tutu is the recipient of many other international awards including the Sydney Peace Prize (1999), and the Gandhi Peace Prize (2005).

Rafeef Ziadah is a third-generation Palestinian refugee born in Lebanon. Ziadah is a human rights activist and trade unionist, as well as a spoken word artist and an academic. She is currently a teaching fellow at the University of London School of Oriental and Asian Studies (SOAS) whilst completing her PhD thesis from York University (Toronto).

Index